Against Empiricism

Against Empiricism

On Education, Epistemology and Value

R. F. HOLLAND

Basil Blackwell · Oxford

© R. F. Holland 1980

First published 1980 by
Basil Blackwell Publisher
5 Alfred Street
Oxford OX1 4HB
England

British Library Cataloguing in Publication Data
Holland, R F
  Against empiricism. – (Values and philosophical
  inquiry).
  1. Knowledge, Theory of
  I. Title   II. Series
  121   BD161

ISBN 0-631-12311-3

Phototypeset in V.I.P. Bembo by
Western Printing Services Ltd, Bristol
Printed in Great Britain by
Billing and Sons Ltd,
London, Guildford and Worcester

Contents

Acknowledgements

Help has come to me over a long period of time from teachers, colleagues, pupils and friends. I am indebted particularly to Professor Sir Peter Strawson, the late Professor Gilbert Ryle, Mr Rush Rhees and Professor Peter Winch. I also thank Professor D. Z. Phillips for his patient editing.

I am obliged to the editors and publishers concerned for permission to use the material for the following chapters: 'Morality and the Two Worlds Concept', *The Proceedings of the Aristotelian Society* Vol. LVI, 1955–6; 'The Miraculous', *The American Philosophy Quarterly* Vol. 2, 1965; 'Suicide as a Social Problem', *Ratio* Vol. 2, 1970; 'Is Goodness a Mystery?', *The University of Leeds Review* Vol. XIII, 1970; 'For Ever?' *The Philosophical Quarterly* Vol. 24, 1974; 'Philosophers Discuss Education,' *Philosophy* Vol. 52, 1977. 'Suicide' and 'Absolute Ethics, Mathematics and the Impossibility of Politics' were lectures to the Royal Institute of Philosophy, subsequently published under the editorship of G. N. A. Vesey in *Talk of God*, Macmillan 1969, and *Human Values*, Harvester Press 1978.

1

Introduction

In the epistemology of the classical Empiricists a build-up of experience into something complex and unified was supposed to take place as the result of the mind's manipulation of fragmentary ingredients that had been delivered to it by the senses. Language, teaching and learning play no role in this process, or at least none that would permit them to stand in any fundamental relation with each other. So I hold that Empiricist epistemology, unlike Platonic epistemology, is unable to support a philosophy of education. However, a philosophy of education, whether or not it gets help from an epistemology, can hardly fail to be the expression of a philosophy of value.

If in approaching the question of the relation between education and value one takes education to signify in the first place systematic inculcation, that is, the processes of instructing and being instructed in particular subjects, the relation between education and value will then be considered in terms of the plurality of ways in which the distinctions between good and ill, right and wrong, better and worse, careful and slipshod and so on, enter into the disciplines. In other words the discussion will centre on standards. It will be possible to consider how the standards might grow up and what might be the best way of maintaining them. Also it will be noted that there is a carry-over from discipline to discipline and from disciplines to the rest of life. If that were all a philosophy of education could contain—as I think would be the case on one conception of the nature of value—the enterprise would be far from negligible:

any other kind of philosophy of education that were possible would have to include it and do it justice (which I hope it gets from my illustration in chapter 4 as well as from what I say in chapter 2). Whether a need is seen to attempt more will depend on one's conception of what is possible in the philosophy of value.

It seems to me that in the philosophy of value, anyone who looks at the history of the subject, and at what is going on at present, with a view to asking the question, 'What kind of discussion might be possible here?', is presented with a choice between two positions. Problems of linguistic machinery, that is to say consideration of types of significance or speculation about the manner in which uses of language can be extended, are not in the end decisive. A stance has to be taken, unless it goes by default, towards the difference between judgements that are of the highest significance for ethics and judgements that are not. In the former case I would say it is more a matter of registering an experience or marking an encounter than passing a judgement. I am thinking now of what can be seen in the unprofitable fineness of certain deeds or characters—and it is pointed to by the unprofitable vileness of others: the difference between the unqualified goodness attested or offended against there and the ordinary run of merits and demerits among people and their works, where the quality, although not so routine as in the case of meat pies and gardening gadgets, is still nevertheless limited and relative, only made more impressive by complications.

To speak in the way I was doing just then is of course to give expression to one of the two positions between which I said there was a choice. According to the other way of thinking, it is a matter of degree all along the line: from the lowest to the highest there is a continuous spectrum with no breaks. We have our criteria. They stand in some relationship to our needs and capacities. In principle if not in practice the criteria are specifiable and so are the relationships (at the point where we tail off, a lot of work is waiting to be done).

The view that there is a value which differs by a world of

difference from all other kinds of worth seeks expression in talk of absolute goodness. Adherents of the other view may say they are unable to understand what such talk means. But whatever the verdict on attempts to speak about it discursively, the idea of value as something absolute can show itself. For example it can make a difference to the theory and practice of education and I indicate the sort of influence it might have on proceedings there in chapter 5.

Chapters 6 to 9 are variations on the theme of the two ways of thinking about value, the two kinds of ethics. Absolute Ethics and Empiricist Ethics are the most appropriate labels I can think of for them and I want to offer a justification straight away for my claim that (to put it in Platonic fashion) Empiricist Ethics *is* something: Historically speaking it is possible to point to a pair of tendencies which, while they may enter into moral philosophy without being accompanied at the time by thoughts that the thinker would consciously recognize to belong to a particular theory of knowledge, are nevertheless generated by the epistemology that comes to us from the British Empiricists (although it was not exclusively theirs). One of these two tendencies in moral philosophy I would call Attitudinism: the other is Consequentialism. The two tendencies can be encountered separately, but they are readily welded together because they correspond to a pair of elements within Empiricist epistemology itself which tend naturally to capture each other and to form an amalgam.

The two elements of epistemology I have in mind are Phenomenalism and Predictivism. On the one hand there is the idea that material objects (statements about material objects) are analysable into sense impressions (statements about sense impressions) and on the other hand there is the idea that statements of fact are at bottom empirical hypotheses, that is, that they are statements involving predictions. The two ideas are brought succinctly together in Mill's dictum that matter is the permanent possibility of sensation. In other words there are sensations and there is the prediction of more. When the question arises as to where we should stand, or what our movements are to be, the point about sensations which assumes importance is that they can be divided into the pleasurable and the painful. Bearing that in mind, but putting the emphasis first upon the predictive element, let me now point out that Utilitarianism turns questions of the rightness and wrongness of actions into empirically determinable issues. For on the Utilitarian view when you see an action taking place and judge it to be right or wrong you are making a prediction—the proposition that expresses your judgement is theoretically verifiable or falsifiable by the balance between supposedly assessable degrees of happiness and misery in the resultant state of affairs. So one might say: The Ethics of Empiricism is Consequentialism. However, that is only part of the story and not perhaps the most important part.

One can equally say: The Ethics of Empiricism is Attitudinism. By Attitudinism I mean the idea that the source of the value is to be found in an attitude, for instance the attitude of approval. In the absence of the attitude, bearers of value would lack their worth. Until the badge of approval has been put on them they are neither good nor bad but simply thus or thus empirically, endowed with 'natural' properties only, and hence all on the same level. To formulate the point in another way, I mean by Attitudinism the idea that ethical judgements are, as regards any component of them which is not equally present in non-ethical judgements or which does not belong equally to the surroundings of non-ethical judgements, analysable into expressions of approval, commendatory performances, prescriptions and so on.

Attitudinism is to ethics what Phenomenalism is to the theory of knowledge. The classical exponent of both was Hume—of the two together I mean, for Berkeley was the classical exponent of Phenomenalism by itself. Hume was the less profound philosopher of the two although historically his has been the greater influence. Berkeley was guarded by his sense of the connection between perception and agency from supposing that the *esse* of a perceiver might be of the same inert constitution as that of the immediately perceived. Hume, however, applied his impressionism indiscriminately. And of the wholesale batch of deflationary idealizations that ensued, the one which, along with the reduction of goodness to approval had the capacity to mutate in such a way as to accommodate itself to more than one philosophical style, so that it has continued to flourish at a time when the sense-datum theory of vision is declining, is what I am inclined to call the sense-datum theory of causality—the idealization of causal transactions into relations of uninterrupted regularity between events. Somewhat as the latter idealization throws away all detail of the motions and strengths of the materials that crush, cut and bang into each other, and also into us as we labour in the physical world, so I want to say that the treatment of value as a logical construction out of the feelings that surround it makes the moving stuff of goodness disappear. Hume's contribution to the philosophy of causation is discussed in chapter 14. His moral attitudinism, together with its modern transformations, I consider in chapter 7, though without going into detail since what I am mainly concerned to speak about is the peculiar resistance to explanation which hinders attempts to account for the existence of goodness: unless attention is diverted to the onlookers, and it is this 'unless' that brings in Hume.

The two chapters on the subject of suicide take as their starting point remarks by Durkheim. In each case my discussion runs counter to Durkheim's scientism, that is, to the methodological standpoint that treats actions as ecological specimens. Durkheim turns deeds into social phenomena which are then looked at *botanically* (Durkheim is pleased by this analogy), so that a classification of them resting on external similarities, and believed to be systematic although really it is not, takes the place of a furtherance of the understanding that could only be achieved by arranging and connecting concepts.

The substitution of external relations for unrecognized internal relations is very much a feature of Hume's philosophy. His critique of belief in miracles affords an example and it seems to me that here as elsewhere he brilliantly muddied the ground. The aim of my discussion of the concept of the miraculous in chapter 12 is to free the topic from Hume's influence by considering afresh and on its merits the view that a miracle is, or would be if such a thing were possible, a violation of a law of nature. I reject the view for more than one reason. At the same time I dissent from the widely held opinion that there could never be sense in speaking of a violation of natural law. Perhaps I should add that the question whether it makes sense to speak of a violation of natural law is not in my opinion one that has much bearing on the issue between religious faith and scepticism. My purpose in discussing the question is simply to get the epistemology right.

I argue the case by describing, in terms that so far as I can see are perfectly consistent, circumstances in which an expression like 'occurrence of something that is conceptionally impossible' would have a use, circumstances in which we could speak of a contradiction in our experience. Dropping the meta-linguistic formulation so as not to be pussyfooted, I argue that we could meet with a contradiction in experience. Many people have an aversion to hearing this said, as though a blasphemy of some kind were being uttered; and indeed I could imagine a simple religious person's taking it to be that quite literally, on account of what might seem to be a slur on God's goodness. But those with the aversion I have come across take the offence to be against reason or against logic, having in mind no doubt the idea that a contradiction is incapable of describing anything—a proposition to which I do not respond with an 'On the contrary . . .': I say neither yes nor no to it. What the bringing about of a contradiction might amount to can be conceived in accordance with more than the model. However, when somebody tells me that my position 'obviously will not do' I have my suspicion as to what makes him think so: my diagnosis is that he subscribes to a 'mirroring' or 'map to terrain' view of language and its relation to reality.

Whereas my discussion of the miraculous contains an argument for the intelligibility of a notion—that of the breaking of a law of nature—which in philosophical circles is generally held to be incoherent, the chapter entitled 'For Ever?' questions the coherence of a notion invariably assumed to be satisfactory, namely the notion of Sempiternity or absolutely everlasting endurance. I say *absolutely* everlasting because in their ordinary employment expressions such as 'permanent', 'everlasting', 'unceasing', 'in perpetuity', 'always' and 'for ever' are used in a relative or indeterminate sense—'What is your permanent address?'. In the case of the example just mentioned of course it would never occur to anyone to try to construe the term 'permanent' in a sense other than the relative. If you are on your guard you might wonder whether the inclination to make the transition from 'permanent' to 'Permanent' or 'for ever' to 'For Ever' is, or should be, any greater in the case of something inordinately long lasting, like the nebula to which our solar system belongs.

The temptation is rather to be accommodating about the matter and to say that while you do not think this nebula will last absolutely for ever, nevertheless it is not inconceivable that it should. In other words, although you do not in fact suppose that any long lasting object you have ever heard of is going to last absolutely for ever, you believe that you could suppose this if you wanted to. And that is just what I hold to be a mistake: I do not believe you can suppose such a thing. 'The great big world keeps turning.' You may imagine it (picture it) keeping on for as long as you like. But my contention is that if you add 'and it might go on turning For Ever', no speculative meaning whatever can be attached to the addition.

'For Ever?' and 'The Link Between Cause and Effect' are companion pieces. The idealizations which they criticize are a contrasting pair: the idealization of 'for ever' into 'For Ever' works in the opposite direction from Hume's deflationary idealization of causal relations. But the similarity is much greater than the difference: in each case something palpable is subjected to an intellectual volatilization that makes nonsense of it.

Is my position then that idealization makes nonsense? Not at all, for in that case it would make no sense to do geometry. There is nothing chimaerical in Euclid: lines drawn in sand are read in a certain way which is not dictated but made possible by what has been given to us. Nor should it be thought that there need be anything chimaerical about a reading of something that finds in it a conformity with absolute goodness. But to idealize a physical object or material force and to suppose that in its idealized version the subject can maintain its material status—*that* I am saying is nonsense. In short, it is nonsense to assign an ideal status to a substance; and connectedly I reckon it makes nonsense to assign an ideal status to something belonging to a category internally related to the category of substance, for instance the category of cause. However, this does not imply that absolute predicates, for example 'good' when used in an absolute sense, cannot sensibly be predicated of subjects that dwell in the world. My proviso would be that the subjects concerned either should not fall within the categories of substance and cause or that they should possess, as non-accidental aspects of their natures, attributes which cannot be accounted for in terms of those categories. Human beings are examples of such subjects; so are their actions and their works of art.

The topic of my last chapter is the question whether the existence of all the evil in the world is compatible with the existence of an omnipotent, omniscient and perfectly good deity. In regard to this question there is something that can fairly be called an official doctrine. It does not determine whether the question be met with a 'yes', 'no', 'don't know' or with the contention that there is no way of showing a yes-answer to be erroneous. Rather the official doctrine consists in a view of what makes the co-existence of God and evil problematic. The reason why it is thought that one or the other must go, unless a reconciliation can be effected, is that their co-existence presents itself as a counter-example to a theoretical picture of the relation in which good and evil stand towards each other. An ideally good agent with unlimited power will, it is assumed, be a sight less tolerant than the Chief Constable of Manchester. He will eliminate evil completely so far as he can—unless the evil is going to make things better in the end, in which case he will have a reason for letting the evil be.

It seems to me a remarkable assumption; and more remarkable still that contemporary writers on the problem of evil should find the assumption so natural that they do not bother to examine it: as though they are prevented from seeing it properly owing to the nature of the background. The conceptual surroundings in which the problem of evil is customarily treated are provided by Empiricist ethics. The Supreme Consequentialist is brought up on a charge of having *prima facie* fallen short of what was expected of him. Any plea entered on his behalf has to appease a surrounding attitude consisting largely of a propensity to indignation.

Each of the chapters in this book can be read independently of the rest—an advantage deriving from the fact that they were originally presented as discussions on separate occasions (six are published for the first time; the others have appeared in journals). In most cases, but not in all, some knowledge of the history of philosophy by the audience is assumed. Those who have made no previous study of philosophy are recommended to begin with the two short chapters entitled 'Education and Values' and 'Education and the Spirit'. Both were delivered as talks to a society of teachers, and readers who begin with them may find it useful to continue with 'Is Goodness a Mystery?', 'Absolute Ethics, Mathematics and the Impossibility of Politics', 'Suicide' and 'Good and Evil in Action'. At whatever point readers may begin, it will be apparent to them that while the tenor of this book is against Empiricism, I am more concerned to speak for something than against anything. And I think that much of what I try to speak for can be found in Plato.

2

Epistemology and Education

Epistemology and the philosophy of education are closely connected. When the sense of this connection gets lost the result is a period of stunted epistemology and no philosophy of education worth mentioning. We are emerging from such a period. I am not alluding particularly to a defect in recently favoured styles of philosophy: the situation has persisted for a couple of hundred years at least. It is characteristic of the post-Cartesian tradition and of British Empiricism especially, which nowhere diverges more sharply from Platonism than in this respect.

The question whether something is knowledge and the question whether it is teachable were held by Plato to be mutually dependent questions. 'Among matters that have to do with the human spirit, what sort of thing would virtue be,' asks Socrates in the *Meno*, 'according as to whether it were teachable or not?'

If it is something unlike knowledge or something like it, is it or isn't it then something one can be taught—or be reminded of, as we were just now saying? But let us have no dispute about the word. Is it teachable? Or isn't it abundantly clear that the only thing men can be taught is knowledge?

(*Meno* 87 B)

Or take the reflections of Socrates in his argument with Protagoras, in the dialogue of that name:

The upshot of our discussion seems to me to accuse and taunt us like a human being. If it were given a voice it would say, 'What a queer pair you are, Socrates and Protagoras! You, Socrates, after saying first that virtue could not be taught, are now anxious to contradict yourself by trying to prove justice, temperance and courage—the whole lot—to be knowledge: which is the best way to make virtue appear teachable. . . . Protagoras, on the other hand, having supposed at first that it was teachable, now seems to support the opposite thesis, *i.e.* that it discloses itself to be anything but knowledge: which would not render it teachable in the least.

(*Protagoras* 316 A–C)

Recent epistemology has diverged more radically from Plato's than by the offering of a different type of answer to the questions he raised. It is rather that the central idea of his epistemology, namely the treatment of the problem of knowledge and the problem of education as two sides of the same penny, has been relegated to the periphery if not dismissed from consideration altogether. For instance there is a book called 'The Problem of Knowledge' in the *Pelican* series. You would be hard put to find in it any investigation of the concepts of education, teaching, learning and enquiry; and if you had been trained as a student of philosophy in the most famous of British universities, it might not have occurred to you to expect such a thing or deem its absence any loss. Looked at non-parochially this is a remarkable situation. To understand how it came about one must consider the nature of the philosophical tradition which, having established itself by means of a revolution in the seventeenth century, has continued amid all talk of another revolution in our time to be the most potent single influence upon English-speaking philosophy.

The conception which guided this tradition was the mechanistic view of the human mind as an instrument operating under more or less fixed conditions and perfect, or perfectable, within limits. This conception was shared by Rationalists and Empiricists alike. But whereas Descartes, Spinoza, Leibniz and Berkeley were preoccupied with the perfection, Locke,

Hume and Kant were more attentive to the limits. It is an obvious vulgarization of Locke's opinion to suppose that he held knowledge to consist in the *having* of ideas: they were rather the conditions of knowledge, or to speak more precisely there were two conditioning factors—the supply of ideas and the mind's ability to perceive agreements and disagreements among them. Anyhow Locke no less than Kant viewed human understanding essentially as something conditioned and, despite that modest pretention to underlabouring, his *Essay* was an attempt to establish the factors determining its operation.

That understanding has its conditions was, by itself, a splendid idea. But Locke's account of the conditions evokes a picture of industry under private enterprise. To set up in business an individual only has to be exposed to the elements with his senses unshuttered. Experience then will print its marks upon his mind as upon 'white paper', a share in this transaction being allotted to introspection on the ground that it is an 'internal sense'. The imprinted marks or ideas are simple and separate, but operations are performed on them to form complex and abstract ideas. Every mind is a complete and independent factory, where raw materials enter, are processed and emerge cut and dried. And when at the end each mind's eye surveys the products of its owner's efforts, perceiving an agreement here and a disagreement there, and so having knowledge, the results will be found to coincide with those of the rest, as though by pre-established harmony.

If any foothold for education is afforded by this account it must be either at the beginning when the individual is exposed to the elements, which would confine education at once to a matter of sensory experience, or else at the stage where he is held to perceive agreements and disagreements between his ideas. Locke distinguished four modes of agreement or disagreement, and in connection with one of them alludes to 'advances' in knowledge that depend 'on our sagacity in finding intermediate ideas'. He mentions algebra as an illustration (IV, III, 18).

Since an advance in algebra or anything else is open only to someone educated in the subject, and since the advance would have to be continuous with that education, it might seem as if Locke here were equating education in algebra with coming to perceive up to a certain norm or quota of ideal connections and making an advance with going beyond the quota. But an obstacle stands in the way of attaching sense to the implied conception of a norm. For the perceiving of agreements and the finding of intermediates is represented by Locke to be a process which presupposes no interaction between persons, rests on nothing in the way of established tradition and requires no conformity with public standards. It is thus made a matter of indifference to the algebraic understanding whether algebra should exist as an institution or not. Whereas in truth it is the institution that confers upon that understanding its identity: if the institution were lacking there would be nothing to determine it as either algebraic or understanding. The objection is not that Locke compels all algebraists to be autodidacts. An autodidact is one who initiates himself into a subject. What Locke destroys is the subject. And where there are no subjects there can be no teaching of any description, self-teaching included, owing to the absence of anything to be taught; no understanding, not even a God-given kind, owing to the absence of anything to be understood.

Furthermore, the existence of subjects or fields of knowledge—branches of learning where there are methods of working which can be understood or misunderstood, taught and improved upon—all this presupposes meaning. It presupposes the distinction between what makes sense within a particular framework and what does not. It necessitates that the algebraic signs, for instance, should form part of a language.

Neither Locke nor Plato could give a satisfactory account of the nature of language. But Plato's epistemology is compatible in all essentials with the giving of such an account: there is room for language to manoeuvre although the actual movements must remain obscure. Even the theory of Forms—which is not by itself the major part, though it is possibly the

most mistaken part, of Plato's epistemology—while implying
a false view of the behaviour of language in particular respects,
by no means makes nonsense of its working as a whole. On the
contrary, positive assistance towards a sound conception of
meaning can be derived from the objective and mind-
independent character of the Forms. To an older generation of
philosophical analysts, Plato's *Ideas* had an odour of metaphysics about them which Locke's *ideas* had not. But that was due
to a poorly developed sense of metaphysical smell. The
metaphysics of Locke's *ideas* is much the more noxious
because it pushes out language and thereby leaves us with an
epistemology which knowledge cannot enter except by being
smuggled in.

I say that language is pushed out by Locke's epistemology
despite the fact that in his *Essay* a whole book is officially
devoted to language. The position in that third book is characterized by the following features. First, meaning is taken to be
the correlate of word and identified with the object for which
the word stands. This is the Augustinian account of language
cited by Wittgenstein in his *Investigations*; it is a commonplace
of ancient and more recent philosophy alike and I pin nothing
on it here. Secondly, Locke holds the object and hence the
meaning to be something private. This, unlike the other, kills
language at the roots by removing all possibility of agreement
or disagreement about its use, and it would be fatal no matter
what were to be offered as an account of meaning in other
respects. The privacy doctrine is not dictated by the nature of
Locke's linguistic elements in themselves, but by the requirement that these should be related to his epistemological units
(the *ideas*). This would be ground enough already for saying
that Locke's epistemology excludes language. But thirdly,
language is in any case represented by Locke to be a gift from
God to men already endowed with understanding. The gift is
intended to make them, not rational, but sociable (III, I, 1):
thoughts that have been formulated in the seclusion of a man's
own breast can henceforward become a source of profit and
delight to others as well as to himself (III, II, 1).

Since thoughts cannot be formulated whether inwardly or outwardly unless there are ways of formulating them, that is, unless a language is already presupposed, it follows that Locke's epistemological units must already be functioning as crypto-linguistic units before he comes formally to consider language at all. His official account of language is thus in a way redundant. But on the other hand, the *ideas* which have usurped language's position are not equipped to do the job. They lack the institutional character which language requires. For this or for any linguistic attribute whatever to be theirs would be inconsistent with their origins as sensorily derived.

It is not to be supposed that Locke was guilty of an oversight merely, which he could have rectified by including language among the raw materials of sense. Not even in the smallest bits could language be given that way. For language is not characterized as what it is by any sensory quality. From the sensory point of view spoken words are no more than buzzes in the air and written words no more than smudges, and no amount of compounding, abstracting or other manipulation could turn them into anything else. They are indeed not so much as this, because buzzes and smudges belong to the common world and a compilation of sensory ingredients does not amount to the creation of a common world. Thought as a mutation of sense and the world of things as a construction out of sense-data are consanguinous misconceptions. To be sure, a being without senses would not acquire the use of language and would belong to no world. All the same, a language-using being does not sense the rudiments of his language, he learns them. Nor does he get to know the features of his world by sensing them or by building (logically constructing) them out of what he senses; but rather in learning the language he learns what these are and learns to carry on his life among them, learns to participate in the conversation and activities wherein human understanding displays itself.

One could say that language and the senses have different modes of being. If the world of experience be conceived metaphysically as something which we encounter through the senses then it immediately becomes necessary to postulate a second and higher world, a world of thought and knowledge, which will be distinct from the world of experience. This, the affirmation of a discontinuity which is at bottom the discontinuity between the senses and language, was perceived uncomprehendingly by Aristotle to be the hallmark of Platonism.

What Plato had separated, Aristotle and later the British Empiricists tried to weld together, turning epistemology into the familiar goose chase of tracking knowledge back to the senses. Such a programme either makes the connection between knowledge and language and hence between knowledge and learning, knowledge and education, appear entirely accidental, or else it compels language and learning to be construed themselves as species of sensory action-at-a-distance. Impressions have to be the touchstones of meaning and custom, association, instinct, or in other words some form of conditioning, is set up as 'the very guide of life'. This is the position of Hume when he proposed to smell out nonsense by asking the question, *from what impression is that supposed idea derived?* (Enquiries, I, II, 17).

However, a form of words or behaviour that would otherwise be senseless is not given meaning by the propinquity of an impression, nor can the difference between one impression and another account for the difference between one human activity and another. This is why for example the task which was one of Bertrand Russell's two great preoccupations is labour in vain: I mean the task of 'justifying' science by relating it to sense-data. A correlation between scientific activities and sense-data could only be established at the cost of leaving out everything capable of characterizing those activities as scientific. The notion of a form of understanding or field of learning, such as you get in science, is excluded from Empiricist theory of knowledge; and to say that understanding is excluded in any particular form is to say that it is excluded altogether. Empiricist epistemology is thus a pseudo-

epistemology and the only movements it is capable of supporting in the philosophy of education are those which would
disconnect the idea of education from the idea of understanding and connect it instead with other ideas, such as habituation,
adjustment or developing approved dispositions, growing up
to be a responsible citizen, serving society or serving the needs
of the child. Below the surface differences between such ideas,
and below the surface high-mindedness of some of them, lies
the conception of education as a species of causality—a device
for doing something to someone, in order usually that he or
she will then be of use to someone or something. Hume, with
characteristic directness, called education 'an artificial and not
a natural cause . . . built almost on the same foundation of
custom and repetition as our reasonings from causes and
effects' (*Treatise*, I, III, ix).

Can it be conceded that Empiricist epistemology will
accommodate an idea of education so long as by education is
meant lower education? This way of putting it makes Empiricism look a deal less confused than it is. For the distinction
between higher and lower education cannot be made in
Empiricist terms. Yet, as Plato intimates in the *Republic* where
this distinction is sharply drawn, it is only from the standpoint
of a higher education that lower educational procedures can be
directed and judged. That *lower* education must be founded on
(to use Hume's words) custom and repetition was actually
Plato's view, not Hume's; though it is thus far scarcely more
than common sense and leaves untouched the issue of what the
customs should be and what should be repeated. Plato settled
this by an appeal to philosophical considerations and to a
philosophical theory of art in particular, philosophy being for
him synonymous with higher education.

The distinction between higher and lower education which
we find in the *Republic* does not present itself to Plato as a
distinction between cognate species of the same genus: it
marks off a realm of teaching and learning, in which genuine
knowledge can be obtained, from something else which is not
in this sense a form of education at all. The early training of the

Guardians is not instruction or enlightenment but dispositional moulding which works:

> ... by the influence of habit, imparting no real knowledge, but only a
> kind of measure and harmony by means of melody and rhythm, and
> forming the character in similar ways through the content of the
> literature, fabulous or true.
>
> *Republic* 522 A4–9 (in Cornford's translation).

This is *paideia* in the literal sense of the term: Plato's view of what should be done with children. The Greeks did not accord to children the status of rational beings and the childhood training of the Guardians did not aim to turn them directly into such. But the *Republic* devotes a large amount of space to the details of this early training and only a relatively small amount of space to the education that comes afterwards, the only kind of education conceived by Plato to exist for souls capable of learning. If you assume, as the education departments of our colleges and universities do, that a balanced and comprehensive statement of Plato's educational philosophy is to be found in the *Republic*, then you come away knowing scarcely anything of what Plato thought about teaching and learning. For what these are and how they might be promoted is a question not explicitly considered in the *Republic*, although Plato specifies the context in which he believes they are at home, namely the mathematical disciplines (as preliminaries) and something called dialectic or discussion. And he gives strong hints about the nature of the discussion—for instance that it is a method (533 B2), that it requires us to give a rational account of our assertions or to make others give a rational account of theirs (531 E4–5), and that it questions assumptions but does not, in anything which it positively puts forward, employ them (533 C1–2, 533 C8). But what is likely to be made of this part of the *Republic* by the unphilosophical reader who is trying to find out what Plato thought about teaching method? He will suppose that a lot has been said about this already in Books II and III, although on Plato's view nothing was said there about it at all. And since he will assume the problem of the nature of education to be one thing and the problem of the nature of philosophy another, he will not realize that the Platonic equivalent of the English expression 'teaching method', is to be found precisely in the word *methodos* at 533 B2. He will not realize that *dialektikē*, besides signifying philosophy, signifies for Plato the one and only pure species of education, in which teaching, learning and discovery come together.

In order to be seen for what it is, this true form of education, which is philosophy, must be distinguished from its spurious counterpart, which is rhetoric—that faculty of persuasive speech-making on any subject which the sophist Gorgias represented to be an academic discipline and claimed particularly to teach. Plato judged the claim to be false, although he admitted that Gorgias was an exponent of something substantial. Rhetoric was not a form of education, but a fabricating of incentives (*peithous dēmiourgos pisteutikēs Gorgias* 455A): not a rational practice (*technikon*) but something you might pick up (*empeiria*), a 'gimmick' (*tribē*) cultivated by wide-boys and smooth operators (*psychēs de stochastikēs kai andreias . . . deinēs prosomilein tois anthrōpois*—463 A–B). The reason why rhetoric could not be a form of education was that it had nothing to do with knowledge, and the reason why it had nothing to do with knowledge was that it involved no criticism of received opinions, no putting of statements to the test, no insistence that an account be given of the nature of anything, no sifting the true from the false or distinguishing reality from appearance. Instead, success was its sole concern and efficacy its standard of excellence. People could certainly come to hold opinions as the result of listening to Gorgias, but to have been persuaded was not at all the same as to have learned (454D). Rhetoric was a way of dealing with folk, a kind of spiritual cookery (*antistrophon opsopoiias en psychē*—465D) which worked by flattery.

The *Georgias* aims to make clear what education is not, and Plato expects readers of the *Republic* to have read it. He also expects them to have read the *Meno*, in which a barely literate slave-boy is represented as having acquired the ability to construct a square twice the area of a given square by 'recollecting' the construction in question. The doctrine that learning is recollection is Plato's deliberately paradoxical epitome of all genuine education; and the surest way to make nonsense of it would be to imagine such an example as recollecting the good time we had last year in Brighton. He is using the word in a secondary or transferred sense obviously, and his own example is of something complex enough for the following six stages at least to be distinguishable within it:

1 The slave has to have it explained to him precisely what question he is being asked.

2 When this is clear he volunteers an answer without hesitation (*oktō*—82D7): he does not know the answer but he supposes he does (*oietai de ge*—82E10).

3 The implications of this first answer are elicited by Socrates' questioning, in response to which the slave realizes that his suggestion would result in a square four times the area of the original and twice as large as was wanted.

4 Acknowledging his mistake, the boy produces an alternative answer, again without hesitation and again mistakenly (*tripoda*—83E2). This likewise is criticized and the error exposed by Socrates.

5 The boy is now completely stuck and acknowledges his ignorance. But having received his shock from the stinging fish, he is in a position to embark on an enquiry (84C4), which is to be a joint enquiry with Socrates (*zētōn met'emou*—84C11).

6 As leader in the enterprise Socrates breaks though the *impasse*, sketching the figure, including the vital diagonal (84E4), and explaining the whole construction in such a way that it affords not only the solution to the problem but also an account of that solution's correctness.

Socrates pretends afterwards that the boy's recovery of knowledge was spontaneous (*to de analambanein auton en autō epistēmēn*—85D6), and this must be rejected; but his characterization of it as recollecting has plenty of point. In the first place it underlines the fact that advances in understanding do not come about by observation—opening one's eyes to let the data pour in. What is needed is reflection—the collection or recollection of thoughts. There has to be a re-minding. Meno's slave, though chosen for the experiment on account of his abysmal ignorance, does not start off with the *tabula rasa* postulated by Empiricist theory. His natural mental state is one of erroneous opinion, which has to be cleared away by criticism. The criticism takes in due course the constructive form of a prompting or jogging of the learner's mind into a re-cognization, establishing what fits together as consistent sense and distinguishing it from what does not.

All of this requires to be contrasted strongly with phantasy or arbitrary imagination, and here the notion of recollection enters in with particular effect, along with the theory of objective recollectable realities, namely the Forms (*Phaedo* 73B–75A); for it is in being a representation of independent reality that recollection distinguishes itself from imagination. The Forms on the one hand are standards—the standards which it is the business of the critical side of recollection to maintain. On the other hand they constitute principles of unity, patterns of connection, to which the dialectic of recollection ideally conforms and which its positive task is to reveal (*Phaedrus* 265D,E); they are the explanatory anchors (*Phaedo* 98A) by which true opinion is tethered to reality and so converted to knowledge.

The dialectic of recollection is its character as dialogue or discussion. This involves the raising of questions and the offering and testing of answers. Hence it is properly a matter for at least two people. The combining of both roles within a single personality—the soul's dialogue with itself—is a possible but inferior arrangement, conducive to fudging. Men are not equals in discussion any more than they are elsewhere, so one of the participants, Socrates in the Platonic dialogues, will naturally assume the lead.

Finally, the effect of the theory of Forms *qua* recollectable objects is to underline the point that recollecting, both in its character as criticism and as the endeavour to account for things, is a formal, that is to say theoretical, activity; not scientific necessarily, but theoretical as opposed to practical. Perhaps I can bring out the force of this by referring to one of the themes injected into recent epistemology by Gilbert Ryle.

In a paper called 'Knowing How and Knowing That' which he later used as a basis for one of his chapters in *The Concept of Mind*, Ryle wrote about the nature of intelligence as follows:

The intelligent application in practice of principles, reasons, standards, etc., is not a legatee of the consideration of them in theory. . . .
(*Proc. Arist. Soc.*, 1945, p. 11).

. . . mathematics, philosophy, tactics, scientific method and literary style . . . are not bodies of information but branches of knowledge-how (p. 15).

A scientist or an historian is primarily a man who knows how to decide certain sorts of questions (p. 16).

A scientist . . . is primarily a knower-how and only secondarily a knower-that (p. 16).

Having hinted at the beginning that he would like to turn the tables on Plato (p. 1) Ryle concluded the paper by saying:

The uneducated public erroneously equates education with the imparting of knowledge-that. . . . I hope I have provided part of the correction.

In *The Concept of Mind* he remarked that 'understanding is a part of knowing *how*' (p. 54).

Subsequently, P. H. Nowell-Smith in an inaugural lecture entitled 'Education in a University' (Leicester 1958), said:

. . . the word 'knowledge' is ambiguous. It may mean information and this is what it does mean to most undergraduates and, I am sorry to say, to many dons. But it may also mean skill, know-how, the ability to find out. And this, I suggest is what it should mean when we speak of a University as an institution for the advancement and dissemination of knowledge. It is an institution in which the dons apply to the advancement of knowledge the skills they have learnt and in which they transmit these skills to their students (p. 4).

Now the man in a university who struggles to advance his subject—a conception incidentally which Nowell-Smith undermines by urging us to 'rid ourselves of the fallacy that the aim of a scientific education is to teach a subject' (p. 5) —will often be in the position of not knowing how to proceed on account of some difficulty, and he may not even be clear about the precise nature of the difficulty he is in. 'What the man lacks is know-how' I can imagine being said facetiously, like *solvitur ambulando* when the problem is to get walking. Nowell-Smith would have liked it to have a serious meaning: the man lacks or is not applying the know-how which would solve his problem, the skill of (as it might be) relating the wave effects to the quantum effects and turning them into a single class of phenomena.

But what skill might this be supposed to be which physicists have thus far lacked? In wrestling with the problems that are important in a field of study, ideas not skills are what count; and the problems get solved, or transformed, or by-passed, by the man with the profounder conception. The very fact that problems exist—the fact that our fields of possible enquiry are indeed definable in terms of their problems, the fact that the histories of our arts and sciences are the histories of these problems and the achievements of those who made headway with them—shows up as superficial the notion that university education consists in the teaching and practice of skills. If there were a know-how of it all, there wouldn't be the problems, and so long as there are the problems there can't be (save in respects that are trivial and subordinate) a know-how.

I do not of course question, and neither would Plato have questioned, the fact that there can be practices without theories or that there were reasoners before Aristotle or that 'Some intelligent performances are not controlled by any anterior acknowledgements of the principles applied in them' (*Concept of Mind*, p. 30). If this were all that were involved in the thesis about the logical priority of knowledge-how, I should be one of its supporters. What I hold to be disastrous is the treatment of the knowing-that/knowing-how contrast as an exhaustive epistemological dichotomy and its inflation by Nowell-Smith into a philosophy of education. Seeds of this inflation were present in *The Concept of Mind*:

Intelligent practice is not a step-child of theory (p. 26).

Efficient practice precedes the theory of it (p. 30).

Such remarks would have been judged by Plato to be not general truths but general falsehoods, but not because he was prone to confuse and advance in understanding with a proliferation of knowings-that—like Heracleitus he believed that much information does not teach sense; nor because he was in some way impractical—a charge fabricated by Aristotle and still tending to stick although it flies in the face of the evidence. Plato's preoccupation with concepts, his recourse to dialectical methods, his conviction that education must be theoretical in character, are considerations which arise in connection with a concern for practice and are the measure of the intensity of that concern. Not that strictly speaking there can exist such a thing as concern for practice *simpliciter*: this is part of the trouble with an educational philosophy that highlights the idea of knowing-how. Readiness to enter into any old practice, so long as it be a practice, argues indifference. Those for example who profess enthusiasm for 'everything in music from Bach to boogie' must actually be indifferent to music or interested in it solely as a diversion, otherwise it would matter to them what kind of music they heard. Plato would have branded their 'broadmindedness' as dabbling (*polypragmosynē*). Here indeed is the source of the objection to stocking one's mind indiscriminately with information, not 'the uselessness of mere information'—an idea I should scarcely know what to make of. For some information is worth having and other information is not, so to be on the look-out for information about all and sundry is the mark of a busybody.

How much a person cares about a pursuit, whether it means much or little to him, is attested by the liveliness of his appreciation of the distinction between the superior and the inferior in that *genre*, between the genuine and the faked, the impeccable and the slipshod. These and similar distinctions are intelligible only in the light of standards. And the maintenance, let alone the raising, of standards involves criticism. But criticism is a 'recollective', not a practical matter; nor is somebody exercising know-how when he speculates upon and eventually establishes the principles according to which an advanced practice may proceed and without which it could not have come into being. Concern for advancement in regard to a practice, if it is to be more than a matter of smoothing out the wrinkles, must take the form of attention to theory, that is, to something other than the developing of skill, or else be absent. Even where it be not a question of advancement, indifference to theoretical considerations encourages crudeness and the cultivation of *ad hoc* efficacy—cracking nuts with sledgehammers: the mentor of that is Heath Robinson.

3

Philosophers Discuss Education

It has come to be expected that collections issued by the Royal
Institute of Philosophy will contain work that has quality or is
otherwise interesting. *Philosophers Discuss Education*, S. C.
Brown (ed.) (London: Macmillan, 1975), runs true to form
and presents both. It gives the proceedings of the conference
arranged by the Institute at Exeter in 1973, consisting of five
symposia together with Chairman's remarks of about eight
pages for each symposium and in three cases postscripts by
the first speaker. The contributors and topics are: R. F.
Dearden and Elizabeth Telfer on 'Autonomy as an Educational Ideal' with R. M. Hare as Chairman; R. K. Elliott and
Glenn Langford on 'Education and the Development of the
Understanding' with Paul Hirst as Chairman; David Cooper
and Timothy O'Hagan on 'Quality and Equality in Education' with R. F. Atkinson as Chairman; Mary Warnock and
Richard Norman on 'The Neutral Teacher' with Alan Monte-
fiore as Chairman; Stuart Brown and A. Phillips Griffiths on
'Academic Freedom' with R. S. Peters as Chairman.

Autonomy as an Educational Ideal

Beginning with a reminder about the need to hold the *autos*
aspect (self-originated activity) together with the *nomos* aspect
(rational or rule-guided activity) when considering the idea of
autonomy, Dearden asks us to think of a child's being made

autonomous by an educational policy much as we might think of a subject-state's being made autonomous by a colonial power that had 'carefully prepared the way by educational programmes and institutional reforms', the attainment of the colony's autonomy being marked by 'a symbolic act comparable to an individual's twenty-first birthday celebrations' (p. 6). A consideration arises out of this against the de-schoolers: while freedom is required for the exercise of autonomy it is not a necessary condition of its development. Dearden goes on to give a list of the activities he takes to be characteristic of a person who has grown up and been brought up 'to think of himself as autonomous' (p. 7). The list runs '(i) wondering and asking, with a sense of the right to ask, what the justification is for various things which it would be quite natural to take for granted; (ii) refusing agreement or compliance with what others put to him when this seems critically unacceptable; (iii) defining what he really wants, or what is really in his interests, as distinct from what may be conventionally so regarded' (he adds other items about conceiving goals, forming own opinions and governing actions accordingly). The paper concludes with a 'justification' of autonomy: it has a security value of which one important aspect is that it makes people less vulnerable to exploitation, it is fitting for a mode of social life in which there is both rapid change and scope for choice, and it is a source of intrinsic satisfaction and pride. However, the value of autonomy may be enhanced or diminished, he says, according to the different directions it can take; for example it might manifest itself in criminal planning—and so it could not constitute the whole of an educational ideal.

Miss Telfer concurs over the characteristics of 'the autonomous man': what they boil down to is that he has 'a mind of his own'. She stresses that while we can form our own opinions, that does not mean we can make them take what shape we like. Intellectual autonomy, that is, the aspect of autonomy falling within the scope of education, 'constitutes only a small part of educatedness' (p. 28). And we should in any case be cautious about intellectual autonomy as an educational ideal because the wish to form one's own judgements often betokens 'an arrogantly solipsistic approach' (p. 34). I am reminded of Mrs Shelley's rejoinder to a lady whom she had consulted about a suitable school for her son and who advised her to 'send him somewhere where they will teach him to think for himself'—'Teach him to think for himself? Oh my God, teach him rather to think like other people!' (the anecdote is in Matthew Arnold's *Essays in Criticism*).

Although Dearden's concluding *caveat* shows autonomy to be on his view a *dynamis enantiōn*, he evidently regards it in the way the *dynamis* of medical skill would generally be regarded—as a boon that an educational policy can and should produce; whereas Miss Telfer's account, which introduces a distinction between 'the autonomous man' and 'the educated man', makes autonomy look from the educator's standpoint like a wormed apple in a bowl of sound oranges. Not much enthusiasm for this educational ideal was generated in me I confess by Dearden's list of the activities characteristic of the autonomous man (what I found myself asking as I looked at the list was *When?*) and I wondered about the educational policies that might be supposed to produce them. If Dearden were right to associate autonomy, as he did at one point, with coming of age, then how far, I wondered, can these itemized characteristics, and any educational policies designed to produce them, have much to do with it? Educational policies aimed at making children 21? To the extent that being autonomous is a matter of coming of age then for good or ill it is going to come. To be sure, not all of those who are 21 can seriously be said to be grown up (the schools think they can help by teaching for instance 'civics'—I do not know what goes on and have my suspicions). There are different conceptions of what it is to be grown up or of what is most important in it and sayings that make different points: George Orwell for instance said somewhere that it is impossible to be a Catholic and grow up.

Dearden speaks of teaching 'the criteria which are to serve as the *nomoi* of thought and action' (p. 6). He seems to have in mind something general and I am not sure what, but one way of getting on to solid ground would be to think of the procedures of particular subjects. Hare in his Chairman's remarks does this and ends up with a disquisition on the autonomy of morals—'a subject . . . which, of conceptual necessity, impose[s] certain disciplines which the teacher can know just as he knows Latin or mathematics' (p. 40). So I suppose we may look forward to the time when some pupils will take their moral O levels and others their As, with the lucky few (those who show signs of α capability) proceeding on scholarships to Balliol for tuition in the highest aspects.

The extraordinary promise of Hare's conception of ethical autonomy ought not to distract us from the significance of the autonomy of subjects both for this symposium and elsewhere in the collection. When a topic is discussed in the vocabulary of a subject to which it does not belong, or is handled by methods alien to the material under consideration, or has a slant put on it that could not possibly be supported by the subject to which it does belong, or when the teaching is organized in a particular way not for academic reasons but to suit some conception of a social purpose, then that is servility, and the young who encounter it in the practice of their teachers are bound to be hampered in their development.

Academic servility has two major branches: one is *scientism* and the other, which is even more harmful, is *politicism*. The former can be found almost everywhere; the latter is endemic in the unfree countries of the modern world and the degree to which it has already had repercussions on the primary and secondary sectors of the British educational system is an index of the extent to which our country has become unfree. Such a growth of politicism would scarcely have been possible, or at least would have been slower and more fitful, without energetic pushing by the National Union of Teachers and assistance over a period of years from a fairly substantial though on the whole uncharacteristic (I mean uncharacteristic of universities) body of people within the university sector, located mainly in departments of education and social studies. And now we have Radical Philosophers, whose particular brand of servility will be found exemplified later in the proceedings.

Any teacher who in the face of such tendencies is able to communicate a sense of what educational servility is and foster a wary suspicion of both scientism and politicism (I think pupils can only catch this from individual teachers or writers; it could not be the outcome of any educational policy) will be contributing in the best possible way that he could to the development of the kind of intellectual autonomy or disciplined independence of mind that Dearden was meaning to talk about although he may not have succeeded in characterizing it very well.

Education and the Development of Human Understanding

Elliott's paper, which he calls 'Education and Human Being', is concerned with the problem of the relation between common understanding and understanding within the systematic disciplines. The topic is extremely important and proportionately difficult to handle. For in the first place it is not easy to say or even to make a start on saying what common understanding is, nor is there anything definite one can point to in order to characterize its development as there is in the case of advancement in, and the advancement of, academic studies. And this, together with the jingling of significance between common in the sense of non-special (which is what is intended here) and common in the senses of prevalent or vulgar, can lead to its being dismissed as a backwater of old wives' tales that only gets magnified into something substantial by nostalgic fancy. Thus Hirst in his Chairman's remarks speaks of 'understanding at the level of everyday concerns, at the level of common understanding in Professor Elliott's terms' (p. 93); and then, 'In particular [Professor Elliott] sees common understanding of nature, man and God as producing a sense of being within a whole. . . . To my mind this is nothing but a romantic vision that bears little relation to most people's

common understanding . . .' (pp. 94–5). Hirst's view of the
relationship Elliott finds troublesome is that 'The boundary
between the disciplines and common understanding seems to
me to be not one of any formal kind, but rather a socially
determined demarcation based on what as a matter of fact is at
any given time commonly understood' (p. 93). This does not
meet any problem for Hirst has seen none and what he says
settles nothing.

In speaking of common understanding Elliott has in mind
'the kind of understanding possessed in large measure by
Shakespeare' (p. 63). He also calls it 'unsystematic understanding', 'natural understanding' and plain capital U 'Understanding'—less happily 'pre-theoretical understanding' (what
theorizing is Shakespeare's understanding *pre*?) and least happily 'common knowledge'—but anyway he speaks of the rich-
ness of its content and the subtlety of its distinctions, of the
profound insight expressed by some of its not universally
accepted opinions and of its affording freedom and vitality but
limited scope for criticism (p. 64). And the reason why it is a
question how far education should be carried on through the
disciplines is that 'One could attain the level of understanding
achieved by many greater writers without undergoing an
education in the disciplines, for though it has a craft tradition,
Literature, so far as content is concerned, belongs entirely to
common understanding' (p. 66).

That is one reason at least and the difficulty would be serious
enough if it were the only one. But there is a further consideration that has to do with the problem of the relation between
the disciplines and their standards. Each of the relatively well-
established fields of enquiry has grown up in a certain way,
sometimes passing through doldrums and at other times
perhaps undergoing revolution. Its methodology will have
been refined by successive generations of practitioners and its
canons of excellence, its notions of what constitutes advancement and what at a given time is most worth investigation,
will have been shaped almost entirely by tendencies arising
from within the practice itself. Or so it may seem: I do not

think it is actually the case, but this is the view that Elliott finds in Peters and Hirst and he thinks himself that it is an accurate enough representation of what is generally the situation as regards the disciplines. But he does not think it *ought* to be so, because the kind of development that is involved here 'appeals to no value but the movement of the developmental change itself' (p. 47).

Elliott's objection then to Hirst's and Peters' approach to the philosophy of education is that when they relate education to knowledge and truth they 'locate the criteria of knowledge and truth within the disciplines' (p. 59) and hence, taking the view of the disciplines that they naturally enough do, they operate with a notion of development (*sc.* of the mind, or of knowledge and understanding as such) which employs only an internal norm—or rather, and worse still, an aggregate of internal norms, the subsumption of which into a unity is an unfulfillable task.

It seems to me that there is ambiguity in the notion that the disciplines are autonomous suppliers of their own standards. They have their different procedures. That is one point, and another is that the responsibility for maintaining standards lies with the practitioners—if *they* do not uphold whatever is best in the traditions of their subject no one else can. But if thirdly it is suggested that the disciplines are more or less immune against influences from outside then this is false, and not just on account of what may get carried over from adjacent disciplines. I am thinking rather of the effects that certain tendencies or changes in the life of a country at large—for example the growth of commerce and the movement towards large-scale units, the rise of bureaucracy and the increasing preoccupation with planning and utility—can have, and actually have had, on the manner and style of practices among the disciplines and on scientific practices especially. However, what I have just said adds grist to Elliott's mill, for the point he is most concerned to make is that a discipline can be applying its criteria effectively and all its practitioners be satisfied with it, yet without knowing where it is going and why, and with no guarantee of its 'rightness as a discipline'. He alludes to Husserl's thesis that, over a long period of time from Galileo to the present day, physics has been undergoing a gradual but massive change, with the result that (to quote Elliott's summary on p. 60) it 'no longer provides an understanding of the reality with which it was originally concerned; and that its own practitioners proceed for the most part technically and have only a technical understanding of what they are doing'. He adds remarks on aesthetics ('Criticism') and on systematic psychology and sociology, as disciplines prone to cultivate fashions that put them at variance with the sensitive insights of common understanding—insights which they often have pretentions to supersede.

Elliott holds that if there is a justification for education, that is to say for any type of formal education, it must be an account of two factors: that it should develop the life of the mind and that it should relate the person's understanding to things that matter. He adds that in some regions disciplines may be essential if depth of understanding is to be secured. He might I think have stressed the virtue of their *disciplinary* character, of the arduousness of their rigour, in connection with the problem of developing a capacity to go against the grain and to sustain attention in the face of what repels it. However before the question arises of giving a positive justification for formal education, there are two conditions which he says must first be met in the case of any particular discipline. One is that we must be reasonably sure the discipline is not likely to be detrimental to the life of the individuals who participate in it. And in this connection he stipulates that educators should have 'a clear understanding of the nature of each discipline, including the objects it studies, the motivations which contemporarily inspire it, and its relation to common understanding' (p. 69). It follows—although Elliott does not say this—that the educator must be a philosopher. There will then be the difficulty to be faced that philosophy itself is a discipline and one moreover that is particularly susceptible to debasement. In fact the issue which Plato made the topic of the *Gorgias*—the problem of spurious semblances, of the difference between worthwhile pursuits and their time-serving surrogates—runs through the whole of Elliott's discussion. And if we say along with him that the orientation of a discipline will be better or worse as it keeps or loses its connection with common understanding, we must be chary of the would-be developed and the would-be profound kind which manifests itself in for example the name-dropping knowingness that jumbles everything together as it tries to pot culture.

This brings me to the second of the two conditions Elliott believes must be satisfied if the teaching of a special discipline is to be justified. It is that 'we need to be able to teach or otherwise communicate some manner or method by which a person can recall himself from his discipline, once more adopt the relatively naive attitudes of common understanding even towards the objects of his discipline, and regain his capacity for the primitive synopsis' (p. 69). By the primitive synopsis he means the holding of three 'concepts' or dimensions of awareness together in a unity. These three dimensions correspond to the three most important things that there are for a human being to recognize and understand, namely Nature, Man and God (or the Transcendent). The sort of recognition that Elliott has in mind is, in the case of Nature the sense that the natural world is our dwelling place. In the case of Man it means having a sense of belonging along with others to the human race, and this involves a feeling for the past. In the case of the Transcendent he speaks of an enriching domain that is 'in a sense the furthest reach of the human environment' (p. 68); but this last does not strike me as illuminating—unlike what he managed to convey in the other two cases. He might perhaps have brought in here the wonder and beauty of creation, love of life and gratitude for it.

Hirst pooh-poohs Elliott's idea of a synopsis, but in the absence of something like it I doubt if it would be possible for a special discipline to be connected with anything that goes deep in common understanding. Of course what Elliott is urging that educators should try to do is entirely different from what customarily happens. Mathematics for example is introduced against a background of articles purchased and distributed or charged for at so much a square foot like window glass, thence on to the use of water-cylinders or sports cars accelerating to pass buses (all by the way matters of common understanding in the sense in which Hirst immediately started to think of it); and the teachers who condemn this as inadequate do so only because they want binary notation and group theory to be in from the start: so that either way it is a progression of technique and application from the more basic to the more sophisticated in which the sheer wonder of the history of mathematical invention from the Greeks, with its joyous perception of form and harmony and its sense of revelation at the unfolding of mediations between something given and something incommensurable, is scarcely communicated.

When Elliott speaks of developing the powers of the mind and when he offers sketches (pp. 48 and 49) of what understanding involves, he stresses the element of vitality and asserts that understanding cannot be achieved without the exercise of psychical powers that depend on intellectual *eros*—which he puts in the category of 'the natural'; so he is saying in effect that what is to be developed must be already there in embryo. Langford thinks this account 'goes wrong from the beginning' (p. 76) and objects that Elliott's introduction of the notion of development draws attention away from the fact that people have an open-ended capacity to learn. I do not see why it should. On the contrary, intellectual *eros* dies if it is not fed with suitable food—if we are not put in touch with aspects of reality that we can study and love.

A dozen pages of postscript on top of a lengthy and challenging paper make Elliott's contribution to this symposium one of heroic proportions. The other tilt against him or try to, but without showing much capacity to get to grips.

Quality and Equality in Education

Cooper's starting point is the question whether the relation between quality and equality is empirical or *a priori*. He argues that there is a conceptual incompatibility between them and that educational inequalities can be distinguished from social inequalities which happen to manifest themselves in educational systems. He also distinguishes between appropriate and inappropriate egalitarian demands (by inappropriate he means I think both senseless and morally repugnant), insisting that 'it is only appropriate to employ the principle of equality in criticism if those who are doing less well are doing so *because* others are doing better' (p. 120). And in order to investigate the qualitarian ideal, which he thinks can be defended against egalitarian objections, he considers its application to a simple model of an educational system where there are only two schools, the North School and the South, and educational resources can be redistributed but not increased. One school provides an education of better quality than the other, and we are asked to imagine that they could be replaced by two alternative schools, East and West, which would be of equal quality to each other.

O'Hagan disagrees with Cooper's contention about the incompatibility of quality and equality and suggests that the incompatibility only presents itself as an *a priori* one if you approach things according to 'the philosophy of the grocery store' (p. 131). The feature of Cooper's model that he is objecting to here is its staticness (see p. 133) or in other words its postulation of a scarcity of resources. 'Some such notion of "eternal scarcity" has been an implicit premise of elitist arguments from Plato to Hastings Rashdall but that is no reason to accept that it is correct' (pp. 138–9).

However, in objecting to this feature of Cooper's model, O'Hagan is not as he thinks objecting to its grocery store aspect, for his own approach to the problem of the relation between quality and equality needs a grocery store philosophy more than Cooper's does. What O'Hagan wants to do in fact is to insert into the model behind the grocer a wholesaler and to have him backed in turn by an infinitely expandable economy. In either version the model is revealing and calls for careful examination by anyone interested in the kind of assumption that has to be made if the discussion that is being engaged in by the two symposiasts is to be carried on at all.

The problem that the model in either form is supposed to pose is this: should the existing situation in which the North school is superior to the South be maintained (left uninterfered with) or should it be supplanted by (reorganized into) a new set-up in which there will be two different schools, East and West, of equal quality to each other? And I want to ask from what standpoint this question is being considered and why. Who is supposed to have this 'problem'?—I add the inverted commas because in the first place a school that is not as good as some other school can nevertheless be a worthy and satisfactory school, so on the information given there is no reason as yet to think that anyone has a problem. Maybe the citizens of the township of the South are proud of their school and have no wish to change it. On the other hand maybe they are dissatisfied with it, in which case they have a problem, in other words, how to make it better. North could have the same problem, but suppose that only South has it. Either way there is no call for the South people to construe their problem as the problem of making their school as good as North's. They may know nothing of North school or they may know of it and not care a fig—why bother about what happens on the other side of the Mendips? Or assuming that North is a good school, though that too was no part of the *data*, they may look at it with justified admiration and wish their own were like it. In which case maybe they would do well to study North's methods. But again that would be for the sake of improving their school (Gain parity with North? What would be the point? Besides, North might already be slipping).

If someone among the Southerners thought that they could do with having some of North's resources, what could he mean? Probably in these days that the buildings of South school were antiquated or there was a lack of tape-recorders—and a wiser member of the community would assure him that such things had little to do with the problem of quality. Possibly he might mean that, unlike North, South had few first-rate teachers, and the Southerners might or might not be able to put their finger on the reason for this. Could there be something in the atmosphere of their school that was not conducive to good teaching? Could they attract one or two of North's distinguished pedagogues?—Would any North-erner move south unless press-ganged?

Redistribution of resources means nothing in a discussion carried on by the people concerned under the assumption that the problem is *their* problem as free beings dealing with other free beings. Yet it is redistribution of resources that the prob-lem is presented as being about, and seemingly the people of the communities mentioned are not the raisers but rather the materials of it so to speak. So I asked whose problem it was, being aware that the reader was meant to take it in imagination to be his, though he was not encouraged to imagine the position he would have to occupy in order to handle it. For in so far as it poses a problem, Cooper's model has an ontological implication: somewhere there exist bureaucrats (they are not in the North nor South nor East nor West: they must be up in the sky). At this point let me emphasize that nothing I have said implies any criticism of *the model*, which seems to me to suit the theme of the symposium admirably.

The question now to be considered is what exactly the bureaucrats are meant to do in the context of Cooper's and O'Hagan's discussion—to do or not to do, because Cooper would like them to leave North and South alone, at least so long as certain conditions are satisfied. O'Hagan is the one for whom their activity is unconditionally indispensable. Indeed for him they have to be more eternal in their operations than 'eternal scarcity' itself, in order that eventually they should bring about the instantiation of the theoretical compatibility of quality and equality as 'ultimate states' (p. 134).

But what the bureaucrats are supposed to do is *redistribute quality*. That phrase is my own: the symposiasts use expressions some of which may seem less chimerical although they are not—expressions like 'educational resources' (Cooper p. 120, O'Hagan pp. 135, 140), 'educational goods' (O'Hagan pp. 131, 132, 134, 138), 'educational transformation' (Cooper pp. 115, 116), 'distributional rise in quality' (Cooper p. 124) and 'units of educational quality' (O'Hagan p. 134). O'Hagan puts this last one in quotes himself, asking us to note that he is deploying a purely abstract model, i.e. one that is not meant to do justice to the complexities of life; but when he gives a table of his units he envisages a 'type of reform bringing about the changes envisaged in the table'.

My contention is not that reforming—rearranging, redistributing, introducing new machinery or whatever else may be done by bureaucratic *fiat*—can have no effect on quality. The quickest way to destroy standards is to destroy the schools whose standards they are, and for bureaucrats with powers that nowadays are taken for granted in almost all countries there is nothing easier than to destroy schools: they are amalgamated with other schools, existing pupils are bussed out and new ones bussed in, the curriculum is modified for a special purpose and so are the teachers' duties, with administrative house-ships as prizes for the best. But the quality taken away from the place does not go somewhere else; there is redistribution but there is no redistribution of *that*.

Raising the quality or raising the standard (Cooper speaks of both, pp. 120, 121) can signify something certainly, and it is possible for an administrator to take some of the credit for doing this by removing an impediment which was stopping people from getting on their feet and which perhaps they could not see, although he happened to be in a position to see it and to do something about it as well; in which case he could thank the Lord for his good fortune in having got implicated in the highest form of activity open to administrators. But if raising the quality is to mean something positive in relation to a standard that might without foolishness be called 'high', then it cannot be done directly. High quality cannot be arranged and a *fortiori* not by any administrator. It is connected indissolubly with individuality and with spirit. It needs soil to grow on and roots with special connections. It has to belong to, or have taken up its home in, a place which it knows and which is different from other places. There has to be a tradition within which it can be passed on by those who have cherished it to others who will. There has to be a forebearance by any third party. High quality is never associated with a collectivity and belongs to no class. There are those who are gifted or are fortunate in their associations (some are both) and there are those who are not; institutions too may be fortunate or ill-starred in their development; and in the case of both individuals and institutions there is an inextricable interplay of non-material and material factors in the considerations that conspire to make the difference.

If someone were to tell me that the very idea of all this made him sick I could understand him, or understand him well enough, without supposing him to be thoughtless. But I would conclude that he had really given up thinking if, without the excuse of a mind untrained in philosophy, he ratiocinated that quality does not rest, or rests only temporarily, on standards and that standards do not rest, or rest only temporarily, on differences and that these connections can be disregarded on account of a putative counter-example in the shape of an 'ultimate' future state of affairs that would if it arrived have been brought about by politicians.

The Neutral Teacher

Tributes to teachers are often paid, if only on their retirement, but you never hear of a teacher's being praised for his or her neutrality. Can a neutral teacher do anything but pale into insignificance by comparison with a teacher of colour? On the other hand the neutral teacher will do no serious harm to his pupils, unlike a teacher who teaches in a spirit of loathing; so if this were the choice the neutral teacher would be infinitely preferable—'better dead than red'.

For my own part, as a university teacher I have to recognize that, in so far as I mark examinations and give assessments and compel students to study prescribed courses instead of exploring their own intellectual interest, I am helping to maintain a political system which I loathe.

This is not to deny that teachers can consciously attempt to counter these tendencies . . . (Norman p. 186).

I think one would have to conclude, apart from a qualification I shall mention, that Norman loathes most of what he is doing as a university teacher. For the bulk of the courses in a university degree scheme are prescribed and a university teacher's work mainly consists in teaching these courses—in so far as he is doing what his institution has appointed him to do (this is the qualification which in the present case has to be added).

The courses prescribed by our universities invariably cover, in the case of philosophy, central aspects of the subject and its history, so that students working for a degree in the subject are required to undertake some study of a representative selection of the great philosophers of past centuries (philosophers such as Plato, Aristotle, Descartes, Berkeley, Locke, Hume, Leibniz, Kant and Marx) and to acquaint themselves with some of the work of leading recent and contemporary writers as well as classical writers in such main sectors of the subject as logic, ethics, political philosophy, epistemology, philosophy of mind. Norman is not only objecting to these courses because they are prescribed; he is objecting to them for being constituted as they are. For he implies in the passage I have quoted that students of philosophy (who by the way are scarcely compelled to be that unless they have an interest in philosophy) are, when they pursue the prescribed central courses on philosophy to which I have alluded, doing something other than 'exploring their own intellectual interest', that is, that they are not doing what interests them as students of philosophy; and he wants them to do something else, to do something other than study the central aspects of philosophy—while yet remaining students of philosophy and with the encouragement of teachers who are supposed to be teachers of philosophy. Apparently there are people appointed to teach philosophy who would encourage this. No one after reading Norman's paper could say that he had not been warned.

Mrs Warnock says that in her experience those who advocate neutrality in teachers do so on one or other of two grounds and they do it with great passion. 'The first ground is the desire to avoid turning teaching into indoctrination. The second is the desire that pupils may learn whatever they do learn by discovering through experiment . . .' (p. 159). Another thing one finds is that advocates of a mode of teaching in which pupils should learn through experiment or 'engage in what interests [them]', 'explor[e] their own intellectual interest' (Norman pp. 180, 186), are often bent on ensuring that the pupils should of their own free will, though not without passionate encouragement, end up with certain attitudes rather than others.

Mrs Warnock would have liked to cut the issue of indoctrination down to size in order to create space for the kind of non-neutrality which is allied to decency and common understanding. She points out that for most of the time teachers are on well-trodden territory, inculcating skills, conveying information and presenting theory that is either established or questionable only at a more advanced level than the pupil has reached. But Norman has a dictum that 'questions about what to teach and how to teach it can only be answered in the context of some political perspective or other' (p. 187).

Mrs Warnock gives examples of questions about what to teach and how to teach it. One of them concerns the teaching of Latin and the question she raises is whether the syntax should be taught in the customary manner as so much fact, or whether—because there is a difficulty here concerning the relation between fact and theory, and alternative classifications are possible or perhaps desirable—the teaching should be hedged about with qualifications and provisos (p. 162). She argues that it should not and I agree, but that is by the way. The point I want to make is that this question, along with the many others that a teacher of Latin might have, about for instance the balance of vocabulary, whether a certain construction counts as good Latin or not, the virtues of various authors as models of style, the value of setting compositions in poetry as well as prose—these questions arise out of, and take the form they do within, the discipline of Latin; their *context* is this subject in its autonomous nature as a discipline. And what goes for Latin goes for other subjects too. If some other context is dragged in (which is what it would have to be) then this can only be done at the expense of the discipline that already furnishes the questions with their context, and any teacher by whom it is done will *pro tanto* be converting the period that was supposed to be spent on the subject into a period devoted to something else. Furthermore, if it is a political perspective that is going to be dragged in, as it would be by Norman, then the period that was meant to be spent on the study of Latin or whatever else will not be converted into a period devoted to some different form of study, because no other form of study has been mentioned—all that has been cited is a *political perspective*; so the time will be taken up by the 'teacher's' elaboration of and eulogy upon that. And Norman's dictum will now be put to the use which analysis has shown to be the only one left for it—of maintaining the pretence that a *bona fide* subject, that is to say the original subject whether Latin or some other, is still being taught, and that what is going on is something other than indoctrination into a political perspective.

Mrs Warnock argues that 'uncommitted neutrality in the teacher, in so far as it is possible, is not desirable' (p. 166). She distinguishes between displaying a prejudice and expressing a moral belief (p. 168) and says that a man both ought to have moral beliefs and to express them. 'There is nothing but benefit in the contemplation of a man of principle' (p. 170), whereas the spectacle of someone's remaining neutral in a highly charged dispute about a subject that affects everyone is like a nightmare: it is, she says, 'the nightmare of the knitters at the guillotine' (p. 168).

Norman hangs, or tries to hang, his position upon a view of the relation between facts and values, a question which he says Mrs Warnock leaves open, thereby 'obscur[ing] a crucial aspect of the question of neutrality' (p. 184). What, as the reader can verify, she brings out in connection with an example is that there are times when—places where, angles from which—we can distinguish between fact and evaluation (p. 166) and also times when this distinction cannot be made. 'Interpretation is going to enter into the presentation of the grounds right from the start' (p. 167). In the light of this discrimination it is Norman himself who imports the obscurity when without showing her distinction to be untenable he asserts that 'our factual knowledge is essentially value-laden' and that 'therefore we have to recognize the inevitable intrusion of values, and in particular political values, into the teaching and learning of facts' (p. 184). Here, since he rejects Mrs Warnock's distinction between contexts in which the issue of neutrality *versus* non-neutrality arises and contexts in which it does not, he is maintaining that values, and in particular political values, intrude inevitably into all topics at all levels and in every possible teaching situation; and he proceeds to extend his claim to cover the manner as well as the content of the teaching. But he does nothing—and I do not think there is anything he could have done—to show that this all-embracing claim is other than preposterous. Pointing to particular examples would be no use because if they were any good they could be cited in support of Mrs Warnock's position also; although to be sure her treatment of particular cases would hardly be likely to resemble his own. For into his thesis of the omnipresence of values Norman incorporates the further thesis that, whatever else might be said of them, the characteristic these values must have is that of being *political* values. I would like to consider one of the examples (it is his most extended and looks as if it ought to be his best) by which he thinks this position is supported.

Norman quotes a passage from David Thomson's *Europe Since Napoleon* on the affinity between Nazism in Germany, Fascism in Italy and Stalinism in Russia. Thomson classifies all three as totalitarianism. Norman says that in so doing Thomson, whose book is 'a standard work avowedly written for sober educational purposes, not for those of political partisanship' (p. 181), makes his political attitudes 'blatantly apparent' (p. 182). And Norman's ground for saying this is that Thomson's application of the single team 'totalitarianism' to all three regimes 'immediately commits him to a specific political stance'. I cannot see that this commits Thomson to a *specific* political stance since there are people of all sorts of political persuasions throughout the world who would also, and with good enough reason, categorize the three regimes as totalitarian. Nor can Norman's tone of disgust be justified by the fact if it is a fact that Thomson adopts a political stance, since it is Norman's own thesis that every historian has to adopt one anyway; so the disgust must be directed at the fact that Thomson says what he says, namely that Nazism in Germany, Fascism in Italy and Stalinism in Russia are all examples of totalitarianism. Norman goes on to assert that various political perspectives are possible; that each has its vocabulary; that the writer of history has to use one politically loaded vocabulary or another; that as a consequence the writer of history cannot escape being committed to a political perspective; and that to oscillate between one vocabulary and another 'would simply produce a bizarre history, not politically neutral but politically incoherent' (p. 183).

Norman is speaking of history *simpliciter* or 'general history' and in view of the thesis he maintains he could not possibly recognize any other. Not all history is general history: for example a historian is not writing general history if he writes the history of an art (say music) or a science (say biology) or a country's literature or a religion; or for that matter literature in general or the arts in general or the sciences in general or religion in general; or to mention yet another thing, the history of (or *a* history of) conceptions about the relation between the sexes. And I have now mentioned enough matters of importance to mankind for the question to arise of what is left.

I would say that there is not a great deal of run-of-the-mill general history that is politically neutral, both for the reason that it is customary for the general historian to take little else but politics as his subject matter and also for the reason that I am for the moment speaking only of the run-of-the-mill historian. Thus far then I am in qualified agreement with something that can be extracted from Norman. However, notwithstanding the tendency of general history to collapse into political history and for the run-of-the-mill historian to be politically committed, which mostly amounts to being a servile justifier of an establishment's misdeeds whether the establishment be that of his own country or some other, I am not in any agreement whatever with Norman; because the reduction of general history to political history and especially the collapse of the historian into political servility is exactly what he approves of, holds to be necessary, and would assist on its way to the extent that it had not occurred.

Norman shows no understanding of what can be achieved by a great historian and risen to often enough in patches by lesser men. In fact he says or implies that despite all the resources, many of them as old as Thucydides, that a historian has at his disposal, as indeed any other language-user has, such as mentioning and then commenting on the language that was used to make the mention, and the variety of other ways there are in which it is open to any author to put himself at a distance from the thoughts and actions he is representing, whether by the use of irony or not—notwithstanding all of this, Norman thinks that a historian can neither handle a political vocabulary without committing himself to a specific political stance nor move between vocabularies without getting himself into a pickle.

Norman would not have read the Melian dialogue. To be

sure, the power and human stature there has to be in a historian if he is to distance himself from his subject in a way that will enable him to speak across time as Thucydides does is rare. Thucydides speaks with an authentic voice that is detached and also committed—not neutral certainly. But non-neutral *alias* committed to a specific political stance *alias* whatever else would be said of it in terms of the intellectual currency Norman traffics in? Rubbish.

Academic Freedom

This becomes an issue when, as Brown puts it, 'some restriction is threatened or imposed on any of a wide range of privileges, rights and discretions enjoyed by academics, both individually and collectively' (p. 205). He does not believe there is any factor common to all such cases but proposes to confine himself to those in which the rights of certain people are involved.

Brown presents a 'theory' of academic freedom. Searle in his book *The Campus War* distinguished between two types of theory about academic freedom which he called special and general. Brown proposes a 'Special Theory' whereas Searle had advocated a 'General Theory'. A 'Special Theory' is one that attributes special rights to members of academic communities as academic persons, or in virtue of their *role* as academics, which they and other citizens cannot lay claim to as citizens. Brown's theory involves three assumptions, the first of which runs: 'Some value attaches to the advancement and dissemination of knowledge . . .' (p. 208). This is not going to be disputed since someone who is sceptical or treacherous will concur with a 'well *some* value obviously' and someone who is an enthusiast will say 'sure, now take antibiotics . . .'; while someone else might wonder whether the enthusiast's endorsement has anything to do with a feeling for the life of the mind or a sense of the difference that the spirit of enquiry can make to the culture of a people. And this third person will wonder also why Brown bothers to state what he states in this assumption and what purpose is being served by its being stated in the way that it is stated.

I do not think we are helped by any *theory* of academic freedom whatever. Brown admits that nothing specific follows from his, and in doing so goes on to make a valuable point: 'It seems that the rights of academic freedom cannot be derived from the assumptions I have stated alone. Indeed I think it is not possible to identify an issue of academic freedom as an issue about rights by means of a wholly unhistorical account' (p. 209). The omission of the words 'about rights' would I think have made that a better statement still. We have an academic tradition behind us. If we did not, there are all sorts of judgements in our work and in relation to the daily running of a university that we should be unable to make. The tradition has enough fineness in it, and universities have gone on long enough through good times and bad, for a sound assessment to be made about their state of health at a given time. And the state of British universities during the present century up to 1965 was such that we can count ourselves fortunate in the kind of going concern that we inherited. If anybody cannot look appreciatively at this tradition and recognize that the standards which had grown up, the well-tried arrangements in these institutions and the general decency of their style of administration are, or were, things to be cherished; if he cannot see the importance of, one can hardly any longer speak of maintaining those standards, but at any rate resisting their further erosion; if he cannot see how deplorable it is that the effective functioning and orderly working of our universities should be impeded by ministerial manipulators from outside and disrupted by the manipulators of students' unions from within—then he will not be put in a position to see it by a 'theory' of academic freedom, whether Brown's or Searle's or any other.

Both of these theories are about *rights*. I emphasize this because I do not think it should be taken for granted that issues concerning academic freedom have to be, or can most illuminatingly be, discussed in terms of rights. In connection with the freedom which the theories are intended to justify there are things that I would say academics certainly ought to uphold (for instance the conception of what it is to be a senior member of a university and what on the other hand it is to be *in statu pupillari*) and things they should do everything they can to stop (for instance the behaviour of students who treat visitors on the precinct in a way that disgraces a university). But what would somebody be adding if he were to say, 'Yes, the staffs of universities ought to . . . and what is more they have a right to'? It sounds like an endorsement from another position and maybe the thought is that in trying to do what they ought to do academics should be afforded all possible assistance by those in civic office or in leading positions in other walks of life—which is intelligible enough without any reference to a right. Similarly, when Phillips Griffiths links the 'rights' of academics to 'the common good' which he says we have a duty to contribute to (pp. 222–4), I cannot see that what he says about this in the first half of his paper adds substance to what is pungently said in the second half about the protective duty of university authorities and their failure to meet it 'because they have been inadvertent, lazy, muddled-headed and intimidated' (p. 233). He has in mind at that point the shouting down and physical assaulting of people like Eysenck and Jensen, but I think he may perhaps be underestimating the problem that violence on the premises presents to university authorities who are not like night club owners with body-guards and bouncers on the payroll and find it difficult, especially in a university of any size, to identify the particular culprits (who quite often come from elsewhere).

Brown had already referred to the type of investigation in which Jensen and Eysenck engage or are thought to engage. He suggested tentatively that there is a type of belief which people arguably ought to hold for reasons other than those bearing on its truth or falsity; and he cited as a possible example 'the belief that races do not differ genetically in respect of their ability' (pp. 219–20). The reason why he thinks it arguable that people ought to hold this belief has to do with the 'ability [of racialism] to thrive on almost any piece of evidence which points to something like an essential difference between an out-group and the in-group. Members of group A who dislike members of group B will fear them the more if they have reason to believe that group B are in some way genetically superior and despise them the more if they have reason to believe the contrary.' I would not have supposed that the thriving of racialism in places where it does thrive had much to do with anything's being thought to be evidence for something, and Brown's argument noticeably presupposes that the dislike together with the fear or despisal are already there. I wonder if he was meaning to include himself among the people who ought . . . (there is a question as to how they *can*: did Brown have in mind that it would be as the result of propaganda? If so, by whom? And why should anyone swallow it?).

Why, I want to ask, in connection with the enquiries Jensen and Eysenck are concerned with, should any belief be entertained one way or the other about races differing genetically in respect of their ability—genetically or non-genetically for that matter? What puzzles me particularly is not that anyone might think they do but rather that *if* he thinks they do he should think so *in this connection* on the ground of what might emerge from the enquiries. Now there are some who, possibly for reasons that are *mutatis mutandis* of the kind mentioned by Brown, would say that people ought to hold the belief that individuals do not differ in ability. That this belief should be encouraged and that the differences should be wrapped in a fog of concealment, as happens in certain schools, strikes me as a pathetic sop to the social—pathetic because it is *a matter of common understanding* that individuals do differ from each other in ability, sometimes very markedly. Is there then any common understanding that we can also be said to have about differences in ability between races? To a certain extent there is; and it is important to be clear both about the extent and also about the limits. The life of a race is on an entirely different time scale from that of the life of an individual. We can recognize that there are differences of ability between races to the extent that at one period of time or another certain races, or at any rate certain peoples, *have* shown themselves to be conspicuously able, talented, gifted by comparison with others—this much clearly belongs to common understanding and is manifest from their achievements. Among the foremost are the Greeks and the Jews, the Chinese and the Italians (anyone who wishes can have the idle fun of adding others to make up a cricket team). It is evident that in general there are periods of flowering and periods of decline. In the case of peoples who, in so far as we can identify them, did not flower, or who have yet to flower, or who might have more than one flowering, we are in the main without any notion of what they might have been or might in future be. Despite what we can see in history, we should acknowledge ourselves to be highly ignorant about all this, and not with the kind of ignorance that is to any significant extent remediable. What would have been learned, from some analogue of a twentieth-century intelligence test performed in pre-Homeric days, about the potentiality of the Greeks? An intelligence test on, for instance American Negroes *circa* 1970, whatever race or admixture of races they may be, will only tell us something, no matter what the test might correlate with, about whatever its limited parameters can convey concerning their situation at that given time in that particular place out of all their possible history. They changed their abode, or rather had it changed for them, by violence in the past and there can be change in it again, as there can for others too for better or worse.

4

Education and Values

Suppose we begin by asking where good and ill, and other distinctions of value, make an entry into our minds and lives. It would be natural to distinguish initially between two broad areas in which values make their appearance: on the one hand the context of a person's dealings with his fellow human beings and on the other hand the context of his engagement with the world of things. Of course there is a very thorough interpenetration between the two areas. A person's embroilment with the world, with the stuff of reality, is at its highest pitch of intensity when he is energetically working at something; when he is executing a task or carrying on a pursuit in which others also are engaged; when he is related to a craft or art or science or mode of understanding that belongs to the life of his people and forms part of the culture of his country. And goodness has most of a chance to enter in when the work he is doing can take on something of the character of a vocation, so that he can be glad that he is placed where he is, and love the work, and share his love of it with others.

As I said though, one can draw a distinction between the sphere of human dealings and the sphere of a person's relationship to his work; and in each of them the evaluative terms which are the vehicles of our thought and feeling make a formidable array, ranging from the very general contrasts between good and ill or better and worse or right and wrong, to contrasts with a more determinate significance, such as (if we are considering the dealings of one person with another) generous and mean, fair and foul, straight and crooked, compassionate, brutal, mean and so on. There is a considerable degree of overlapping between the terms of judgements that are used in the two spheres. For instance you get the contrast between fine and rotten or between decent and shabby in arts and sciences, in intellectual ideas and in conceptions of craftsmanship, just as you do in matters of personal behaviour. In both cases alike there are traditions by which we can be guided and great exemplars whose lives and doings are touchstones, giving strength to the currency of our language and providing us with paradigms for its use.

In distinguishing the two broad areas I have indicated, we need to pay attention to the modes of communication which exist between them and through which ideational trafficking goes on from each to the other—particularly in the direction I now want to mention. From arts and disciplines that have any virtue in them, we do not learn only about the difference between good and ill as it stands within those arts and disciplines. In literature especially, so long as it has any seriousness, there are to be found highways of edification concerning what enhances and what depresses the quality of our relationships, insights into the nature of vanity and stupidity, of dignity and nobility, enlightenment about the struggle between good and evil and what the faces of human good and evil characteristically are. This is the most obvious mode of communication between the two contexts and it has generally been put first by those who have spoken well on the theme of literature and life. But of no less significance is the fact that our slothful minds and senses can be animated, both by the arts and their related studies and by scientific enquiries alike, so that we respond to the beauty of the world. This response may come about through an invasion of our spirit by the gladness and the sense of wonder that has expressed itself in the creative work of others. Or it may come about through the patient attention to what we have before us in some humble exercise of our own. But whichever way it happens, whichever way the beauty manages to make an entrance into our lives, our natures are helped to be less crabbed. When however we are not trained to appreciate standards of work and expression, and when we have not been taught to exercise them at least to some degree in activities of our own, then assuredly we suffer for it, for we are deprived of a passageway for something that we have to feed on if we are to flourish and grow.

Because of the connections I have indicated, the educator, whose immediate concern is with the values residing in the context of studies and pursuits, is in a vital way a contributor to the values of the context of human dealings and of human life quite generally.

Recurring to the parameters of evaluation, the actual terms of judgement we use—I mean for instance the fact that a man's demeanour towards his neighbour and his manner of working at a craft are both alike to be weighed on the scales of better to worse or fine to shoddy—it is obvious that while the more general terms of evaluation tend to be common to both spheres, many of the more specific terms do not. 'Compassionate' and 'spiteful' for example belong in the context of dealings between persons. 'Generous', 'mean' and 'brutal' go along with them, though there are transferred senses in which some of these terms are applied in the other context too. 'Accurate' and 'inaccurate' however are among the value-predicates that are only at home in the context of work and pursuits. And when 'right' and 'wrong' occur there too, they bear senses connected with those of 'accurate' and 'inaccurate'. We speak for instance of getting it right and getting it wrong. So, as you can see, there is a difference of slant; and it has to do with the entrance into the 'pursuits and studies' context of precisely those considerations which make it both possible and necessary that there should be teaching in a more or less formal sense.

As we well know, provided we have not been put off by a gaseous theory according to which the personality can be developed directly whether on its intellectual side or any other, we are concerned in the sphere of teaching with the implanting of abilities to do specific things: things which, especially in the earlier stages, can be practised and learned by imitation and according to instructions. Even when we have moved well forward from the earlier stages we remain predominantly in the realm of that which has been demarcated and established—where there are differences of character between subjects, where there are bodies of knowledge to be assimilated, where there are clear enough borderlines between the unproblematic and the problematic and where, when there are problems, they are problems with an ascertainable intellectual history—problems in relation to which there are methods of investigation that the enquirer has to come to terms with, manners of procedure that in each case have their origins and their standards; so that it makes sense to speak of getting the matter right as opposed to getting it wrong, of competence *versus* incompetence, care *versus* slipshodness, coming to grips with the business or just dabbling with it, obtaining a degree of control as opposed to fluking one's way through.

Values rest on differences. This is not just accidentally the case; it is a conceptual necessity. And the differences I have just mentioned—getting it right/getting it wrong, competence/incompetence, care/slipshodness, well-versed/ill-versed, getting to grips/dabbling, obtaining control/fluking one's way through—these differences, together with any others that go along with them, could do with being summed up in a single broad idea. So I shall summarize them in the way Plato would have done by speaking of *mastery*: mastery as opposed to the free man's penal servitude of having nothing within his grasp.

The degree of mastery that is possible in a given case may be very limited. Naturally it will vary according to the degree of maturity and the type of background of those who are being taught, the time available, the nature of the subject and, not least, the powers of the teacher. It will be different at each stage of education. But either a degree of mastery of something is aimed at or it is not. And if it is not, then a vacuum is created for vanity to occupy (the vanity will be an amalgam of that of the milieu and that of the child himself, in one proportion or another according to whether it be socialization or free expression that is particularly gone in for).

Following Plato, I am proposing mastery, together with the foundations of the possibility of it, as the mediating idea for our understanding of the relation between education and values—or for our understanding of the value of education, as I could equally have put it. I do not mean the mastery of just anything but rather of things which have enough in them (or which lead on to and facilitate other things which have enough in them) to occupy a person's consciousness and absorb a substantial portion of his energies; things which afford enough scope for there to be an indefinite progression of work, with the possibility always of advancement and the growth of comprehension and the natural joy that attends the exercise of a human faculty.

Mastery is an open-ended concept. What it focuses upon is an ideal and not an actual resting place. Yet in all fields there are people who can be said without hesitation to possess it, and not in any qualified sense either. To be sure they are rare.

But by the specification of an appropriate relative level, mastery, together with the sense of achievement that attends it, at once becomes something for the generality. In an established institution, for instance in a school that has not been messed about by changes imposed from outside for non-educational reasons, it can and should be made to mean something pretty determinate in relation to each rung of the ladder. In advocating that this should as far as possible be done, I am not speaking with an eye to high flyers or the academic interests of universities. What I have said applies no less, but if anything even more, to the non-grammar streams, to schools where the curricular emphasis is on crafts, and to remedial teaching.

I wonder what would be your most favoured candidate in a competition for the title of 'The first or most basic educational proposition'? I should be very interested to know and we shall have an opportunity to compare notes shortly. In order to be in the running at all, whatever proposition you put forward would have to be something obvious. However, a good deal can hang on the question of which proposition out of a number of obvious propositions might deserve to be put first. And coming to assign a primacy to one educational proposition over another can make a deal of difference to one's demeanour as a teacher. For instance, 'You can't make a silk purse out of a sow's ear' would be a good example of an obvious educational proposition. But is that the proposition you would want to put *first*?

The observations with which I began this evening, about the way distinctions of value relate to each other in their different spheres, have led me to a suggestion first as to what the basic educational *concept* is, namely mastery, and secondly to a proposal that I should like to go on to make now for the basic educational *proposition*. It is an evaluative proposition, or in other words a proposition with a 'should' in it, and I would state it by saying that there is a mastery of a relative kind which, however modest the standard might in some cases have to be, should be made available, be transmitted and as far as possible reached, at every educational level.

There are two points that I would emphasize about this proposition. First, it does no violence to the essential ideality of the concept of mastery; and secondly, while invoking standards, it does not entail but, when properly understood, positively excludes any ugly sort of competitiveness.

Regarding the first point—the consistency of my proposition with the fact that the concept of mastery focuses on an ideal—mastery always displays this feature, namely that no matter how supremely it may have been attained, the attainment has its fruition in the disclosure of further tasks. There is a bit of jargon, useful in the philosophy of mind and invented by Professor Ryle, according to which certain terms are called 'task words' and contrasted with 'achievement words'. Such is the relation in which fighting stands to winning and searching to finding. But the idea of mastery is not well explicated by this contrast, for it is an achievement that never annihilates the task. It is a finding in which an essential part of what is found is that there is more to seek. The reason why mastery has this property is that the achievement is not external to the task. Hence that combination of unbowing independence with humility towards the subject which noticeably characterizes the masters.

That there should be a non-accidental association between true mastery and an ethical demeanour brings me to the second point I wanted to make, which was made by Plato and is that mastery, whether by this one means mastery *simpliciter* or the mastery that is related to a limited ability and grade, has nothing to do with entering into a competitive struggle. Masters do not compete against other masters. On the contrary, those who value and respect mastery, no matter whether they happen to have attainments to their credit or whether they are studying and practising on the way, are united in common tasks and bound by their mutual love of the same work. Any other attitude would testify to ignorance and infidelity. So if the educational situation should take on any of the characteristics of a rat race, then however this may be brought about it is not the transmission of standards or the insistence on their upkeep that does it, but something else; and as standards rest on differences I would say that those who trot out the words 'rat race' automatically whenever they spy selection, that is differentiation, are mostly self-deceivers putting up a front. The rat race which does exist is associated with the pursuit of advancement in the sense of getting on in the world, betterment according to the vulgar conception, the essence of which was summed up by Plato in the word *pleonexia*—having more, or as people often call it nowadays, 'getting what one is entitled to': whereas the idea of mastery, of the progression by stages through relative degrees of understanding and attainment, relates to betterment, not in the sophistical sense, but the absolute and serious sense of getting better and being better. Unlike the ascendency in which others are done down, this kind of rising is in principle open to all. No one is excluded so long as he is educable and the object of the exercise is not to get on top of other people but to get on top of the task.

But although here there really is unlimited 'room at the top', not all will go equally far. That there are differences of ability and energy is a fact of life and only harm is done by covering it with flannel. Suppose a youth looks over his shoulder enviously at something another can do, instead of being glad of what *he* can do and seeking to improve on that. If he is thus disposed, or if his parents are thus disposed, the disposition is not removed but only pandered to by the clouding of truths about differences. Nobody is in this way helped to *do* anything and to be glad of what he can do. And attention is diverted from the real problem, which is the provision and allocation of appropriate forms of education, of curricula which will do justice to the varying kinds of ability that young people have, and which will accordingly contain different blends and ratios between the intellectual or theoretical on the one hand and on the other hand the manually orientated and practical where beyond a certain point the development of skills would be largely by apprenticeship.

In our officiation over the various levels of relative mastery, we are concerned as teachers with the conditions of a possibility which has still to be categorized in its deepest aspect. I shall now try to say what I most of all want to say about it.

It is the possibility of coming into an inheritance. It has to do with no less a question than whether a man can be at home in the world—whether he can find it a good world despite the ill. Not that I am supposing there is a kind of education that could guarantee the outcome, but rather this: that by being brought into contact with forms of understanding and apprehension in which some good is to be encountered, some wonder to be seen, whether in nature or the work of human beings, a person might be helped to see the beauty of reality, helped to live more fully, helped to be glad he is alive. The expression knocking at my mind here is 'nourishment of the soul'. Casals, at the age of ninety-three, wrote the following:

For the past 80 years I have started each day in the same manner. It is not a mechanical routine but something essential to my daily life. I go to the piano, and I play two preludes and fugues of Bach. I cannot think of doing otherwise. It is a sort of benediction on the house. But that is not its only meaning for me. It is a re-discovery of the world of which I have the joy of being a part. It fills me with awareness of the wonder of life, with a feeling of the incredible marvel of being a human being . . .

I do not think a day has passed in my life in which I have failed to look with fresh amazement at the miracle of nature.

If you continue to work and to absorb the beauty in the world about you, you find that age does not necessarily mean getting old . . .

But this absorption in the beauty of nature, this source of vitality and spiritual energy that Casals tapped in his work—how many can it be for?

That only a very few would ever be in his position as an artist is obvious enough. Nevertheless the conception I am presenting with his help is of the greatest importance for the spirit of all that we as teachers try to do, no matter at what level we may happen to be operating and no matter what we may encounter in the way of imperviousness and undermining influences. I do not underestimate the gloominess of some educational situations. If I am asked how Casals' conception can affect the daily routine of a snail-paced and struggling progression through the rudiments of number and language, in a difficult school, among children who have no common background, whose grasp of the written and perhaps even of the spoken word is tenuous, and where the teaching is liable to constant interruption by misbehaviour—if I am asked how the conception of the soul's nourishment can make any difference to *that*, I should prefer to answer simply that it helps to get some sanctity into the proceedings, helps the educator to carry on without despair in the face of his difficulties, rather than suggest the picture of a golden mountain being infallibly jacked up at enormous distance by a mechanism of levers with infinitely small notches. The patience that is called for here is not a matter of being prepared to bide a very long time for results; it is rather of the kind that must exclude any concern about results.

'And at the end of that halting, stumbling progression,' someone might add, 'with examinations scraped through or failed, comes the factory, the office and the shop, where more often than not the conditions of work, and even more the character of the work itself, are such that it cannot possibly take on the aspect of a vocation; but instead, the soul is sacrificed for the sake of the wage-packet.'

I know: and it is exactly my point that educators are concerned with a possibility which in bad times is apt to be frustrated anyhow. I only wish to add two more things. First that you can never be sure what each of the individuals whom you teach will turn out to be capable of and find a way of doing—especially if the teaching be carried on under the influence of the conception I was considering. And secondly, there is a realm of the caught which, while it is impalpable by comparison with the formally taught, is of incalculable worth. I think that whether there is going to be anything much to be caught, and if so what, must depend on the conceptual background against which the teaching is taking place, on the demeanour and way of thinking of the one who teaches in respect of good and ill. What I have been saying this evening, especially towards the end, has pointed to a way of looking at the matter and to a kind of hopefulness that it would be idle to try to entertain otherwise than in conjunction with the belief in a value, in a kind of goodness, that is absolute. The question whether there is such a value belongs to pure ethics: it is exceedingly difficult to talk about and I shall not attempt to go on about it now.

5
Education and the Spirit

I hope my title did not evoke the Geni and the Lamp. Tales of Genis are attractive and an edifying moral sometimes is attached. But the notion of spirit as signifying a non-human personality endowed with occult powers by which on being conjured up it accomplishes at our bidding transformations excluded by the laws of nature—such a notion amounts only to a combination of wish-fulfilment and spurious technology; if any moral attaches to the story, it is not to be found in *that*.

But spirit can be associated with strength in a profounder way, in which case the connection must be with a different conception of power from the one just mentioned. It follows that the idea of spirit must be different too and we cannot take it to be something summonable up directly. It can still be responsible for great things but they will not be wreaked with quasi-mechanical immediacy—only through a span of time. And along with the requirement of time, a vulnerability enters in. That which, if we are lucky and have patience, may flower can also die or never come to anything.

I am thinking of what it means to speak of the spirit of a country, or of those who belong to a particular region in a country or who are united by some institutional form of association—for example a group who in cognizance of each other's existence engage in the same mode of scientific enquiry at a particular epoch. Or take a guild of craftsmen, a regiment, a football team, a school or college. These and other institutions that might be instanced as logically appropriate entities for a spirit to be ascribable to them are not of course always found in the condition and endowed with the quality, the degree of character, that impresses us in such a way that we would say they have a spirit—spirit *simpliciter* or a spirit of a particular kind, expressions of which we can point out to each other whether or not we also find ourselves able to capture what it is in words. But one context in which we very readily allude to the spirit of the people of a country is when we are contemplating a work of art that strikes us as wonderful, not necessarily because it enshrines something universal in humanity (it might not do that), but because it expresses in a particularly pure way *their* character. Take the music of Berlioz for example: if anything expresses the spirit of France surely that does. Or to offer another example, there are passages in Schumann of which I would say that the goodness of the German spirit is expressed there (to which I shall add that Schumann knew what he was about in conceiving the idea of the Davidsbund).

The judgements we utter in attributing a spirit are obviously judgements of value, sometimes aesthetic only; but usually they are ethical as well and among the most serious ethical observations we make. We cannot make them at second hand. When we accept as true what another has said, it is a truth we have to see for ourselves. But the voicing of a judgement is not the vital thing. The kind of understanding open to us here is such that we can (and most often do) have it without being able to say what it is we understand. It is an understanding that is not exhausted in whatever the discursive intelligence manages to render explicit, even when someone comes out with a form of words that seems to hit off exactly the nature of the spiritual quality before us. For the words can only do this when the spirit has already in a non-discursive way made itself familiar through our dealings with it and when it has already come to mean something to our hearts.

I hope I am managing to give you the hang of what an understanding of spirits amounts to without encouraging you to hypostatize the term 'spirit'. I don't take this word to be the name of a class of invisible substances. As for the term 'non-discursive' which I used a moment ago in categorizing the kind of understanding we have, when we have it, of the spirit of something—I could also have used the term 'non-theoretical'; but anyway by 'non-discursive' I meant 'unformulatable in discourse of the kind which by a series of statements expounds a subject in an itemizing, orderly, argumentative way'. One could equally use the term 'non-propositional', especially in so far as one thinks of propositions as vehicles of factuality, bald specifications of states of affairs; and it would be in keeping with this notion of a proposition to add that a poem does not consist in a set of propositions. Poetry and other forms of art are the most natural vehicles of expression for the amalgam of recognition and response, of awareness and appreciation, that constitutes our understanding of a spirit. From an educational standpoint I take the most significant case of this to be in fact the understanding of the spirit of a people as manifested in their literature, the style of their art, their *res gestae*, their demeanour in the face of adversity, their ways of working and thinking more generally. And while the feeling for the fineness in a civilization, which this understanding mainly amounts to, is not the same thing as being able to categorize it as thus or thus and does not demand the kind of analytical acumen which goes along with that, nevertheless it is tantamount to having a sense of worth, because above all else it is a matter of responding towards something wonderful, responding to it with respect and coming to feel at home with it. This relationship with a spiritual heritage that exists independently confers an identity and wholeness on the spirit of the one who enters into it, especially when the relationship is with the spirit of his own country and its past.

What then gets in the way? All sorts of things; but in general the factors that make it difficult for an individual to acquire what in principle he already possesses through having been born and brought up as a Frenchman or an Englishman or whatever it may be, in a land with a history where there have been strong traditions—the factors that prevent him from relating himself to the spirit of his people are the very same as those which weaken and corrupt that spirit anyway. Before considering some of these factors, notice that when we admire a nation's spirit we ascribe what we see there to the folk as a whole, and justifiably because its presence can be recognized in one form or another among people of every walk of life. They will not be without their share of rogues and wretches, but then the elements of worseness too are found in every walk of life. There will be those whose development has been arrested by their circumstances—you would take this naturally as a reference to material circumstances and so *inter alia* it is; however I do not mean only material circumstances since broken homes for instance exist in every milieu and may well be less prevalent among the poor than among the relatively affluent in a country. By subjecting the many to servitude and taking their leisure away, a tyrannical few can cripple the spirit of a people. Nevertheless it is entirely false to suggest that 'spirit' is a class phenomenon (the style of political theorizing which associates value with the interest of a particular class is itself both a cause and effect of spiritual decay). That a programme for the elimination of penury by redistributing resources should be governmental policy in any country where there is concern with social justice is one thing. Nevertheless the concentration of effort upon raising 'the standard of living' whether of the country as a whole or of a sector (the working class, say) is not at all the same as a concern for the spirit but leads to the killing of it, more or less in proportion to the extent that the programme is successful; because it universalizes the obsession with material gain, so that all the rest end up with the same anti-spiritual preoccupation with money as is already endemic among the investment-managing, property-speculating sections of the bourgeoisie.

Turning to what I believe is the central aspect of spiritual decline, we have noted that the manner in which spirits are affected makes apposite the biological metaphors of growing, dying and—let me add now—the need for roots. That last phrase, 'The Need for Roots', happens to be the English translator's rendering of the title of a book by Simone Weil which she called 'L'Enracinement'. In a discussion of the phenomenon of uprootedness in towns, she speaks about the past in the following terms:

It would be useless to turn one's back on the past in order simply to concentrate on the future. It is a dangerous illusion to believe that such a thing is even possible. The opposition of future to past or past to future is absurd. The future brings us nothing, gives us nothing; it is we who in order to build it have to give it everything, our very life. But to be able to give, one has to possess; and we possess no other life, no other living sap, than the treasures stored up from the past and digested, assimilated and created afresh by us. Of all the human soul's needs, none is more vital than this one of the past.

Love of the past has nothing to do with any reactionary political attitude. Like all human activities, revolution draws all its vigour from a tradition.

Universities suffer nowadays from would-be revolutionaries who, not having mastered a tradition, are consequently without understanding of what they ought to be revolting against and why.

Simone Weil says, 'The destruction of the past is perhaps the greatest of all crimes'—a remark which itself is strongly expressive of a spirit. Expressive of another spirit would be the rejoinder that surely the past like everything else is a mixture of good, bad and mainly indifferent; that relics are just relics, not as such worth keeping; customs outlive their usefulness, traditions hang on, frustrating progress and denying possibilities. The second spirit is superficial by comparison with the first and dangerous too.

It may be observed that Simone Weil's remark has nothing to offer those locked in a history of misery through enslavement. But to take two obvious cases, Spartan Helots and the Africans transported in the slave trade to America, she does direct attention to what the violation that put them into their affliction consisted in—namely in tearing them away from their roots, so that they were put out of contact with their past. I believe that the Indian caste system too, maintained and developed as it was over centuries by a gross religion, could not have got started but for the Aryan conquest of a native people who already had a flourishing and rooted culture —their real past to which a false past for them was grafted on. It would be a bad misunderstanding to take Simone Weil to be recommending contentment with their lot to those who have been long enough in a state of oppression for that to constitute all they can remember of their past.

Yet the objection I am calling superficial seems to be such a compound of common sense and logic that one may wonder how the conceptual question it poses can be met. I mean how—if we put oppression on one side—still, how is it possible that the past with its mixture of good and evil should have a value just in being what it is, which makes a human being's relation to it incalculably precious to him despite the ill?

That generally speaking practices which stand the test of time are good is true I think, but not exactly relevant to the point at issue—the value of the past as such. A consideration that bears strongly upon it is the following. Age has a remarkable power of conferring beauty on things; which it does in a way that nothing else can. And beauty is food for the spirit. Think of the way a building that initially had no merit falls gradually into harmony with its surroundings and takes on character and dignity as it comes to belong to the past. That we find beauty there, that this kind of beauty should exist for us and be something that can profoundly move us, is connected with the relationship in which we stand, not to particular things, but to the world as a whole; it is connected with our being able to have the experience of wondering at the world—an experience that Wittgenstein compared with wondering at a tautology; it is connected with the beauty of the world and with the possibility of the world's being an object of love, a 'spiritual object' so to speak. These connections bring me to the vital part of the answer I would give to one who professes scepticism about the absolute value of the past. The historical institutions most intimately bound up with a people's language stand in the position of a *datum* in relation to their lives which transcends ordinary good and evil in a sense analogous to that in which the existence of the world does, and which might be expressed by saying that unless the world were given—or if God had not created the world, to put it religiously—there would *be* no good or evil; there would be nothing to be born into. So far from there being anything fanciful about this analogy, the idea of dispensing with the past is like the idea of dispensing with the necessity of the world in two senses simultaneously: first in the sense that the world as a whole has, so far as we are concerned, a necessary being (whether or not we entertain the religious thought that God could abolish it); and secondly in the sense that the world contains necessities within itself (it is also the locus of chances but the necessities have to come first). Losing the past then is like losing what is fixed and firm in the world and being left with only possibility, only a 'perhaps' as it were, instead. And to the retort that possibility is fine because possibility is freedom, the answer is that the alleged freedom is illusory in the absence of a past because there is nothing to base it on.

A small but good example of an institution bound up with a people's language and endowed with the kind of significance just explained would be our own traditional modes of measurement and exchange, jettisoned by shoddy politicians in their unsanctioned selling of English birthright for a mess of European pottage. In an article called 'The New Inflation: Its Theory and Practice', E. J. Mishan writes:

The currency conversion came in 1971. The case for it in terms of economic efficiency alone is doubtful. Indeed it is more than doubtful since the changeover to a decimal currency (in which one new penny was equal to $2\frac{2}{5}$ old pennies) had the predictable effect of giving a perceptible fillip to the upward drift of prices. Yet economic efficiency is but one consideration. There are others, seemingly less tangible but no less potent, of sentiment, pride, and custom. Pounds, shillings, and pence are not merely convenient units of account and currency. They are also an essential part of John Bull's accoutrements, an extension of Britain's personality. Our national system of weights and measures, our pints and yards, our acres and fathoms, which are now to be thrown into limbo as so much jetsam, are also part of our Anglo-Saxon heritage. They ring familiar to our ears as church bells. They are resonant with centuries of British history. They are part of our language and our literature. And in a world in which familiar landmarks are vanishing, in which, as a result of rapid world communication and mass tourism, differences in accent and architecture, differences in character and custom, are everywhere being ironed out, there is much to be said for holding on tenaciously to these peculiar manifestations of a national persona. But, on yet another issue of deep national concern, the government made no pretence even of consulting the feelings of the British people.

Encounter, May 1974

On top of this comes the comprehensivization of local government into faceless, slab-like units in which old loyalties and the pride in belonging to a place will vanish. The physical destruction of the past both in towns and in the countryside will continue (because it lines the pockets of the Road Haulage Federation) and a minor aspect of this, worth mentioning because it is entirely characteristic, is the way that early on in the process the country got littered with road signs of an alien and strident nature, dulling to English sensibility.

The root-cutters have wrought their destruction for the sake of growth, but growth only in the economic sense.

The notion that economic expansion is an economic phenomenon sounds like a tautology but is in an important way false. Dr Mishan sees with a clarity rare among economists that the pursuit of expansion has causes and consequences of a spiritual character and that among the growth-induced factors in our spiritual decline is:

. . . the new pop culture, which emerged partly in response to an affluence-begotten youth market with a commercial emphasis on excitement, on stylised violence and carnality; a pop culture sporting a permissive 'own thing' ethic that is antithetic to traditional values and, more generally, to social order. ('R. D. Laing and the Death Circuit', *Encounter*, August 1968, p. 45)

I will mention just two more matters before closing my sample-box of things that come between the rising generation and its heritage. One is the influence of modish practitioners of psychiatry who officiate at the demise of marriage and the family and make out that what our tradition has called normal is a product of repression: 'selling a schizoid fraud' to quote David Holbrook's description of R. D. Laing. Laing while professing compassion gives himself away in 'The Bird of Paradise' by his diction, which is partly that of a tout but above all the language of violence. Which brings me to my second point: the growth of violence—the vandalism, the slashings and batterings that have nothing to do with robbery. Why does it happen? The perpetrators are not exculpated by the possibility of a general explanation along the following lines. It is a fact of nature that those who are tormented lash out and if they cannot hurt the source of torment in return, either because it is too strong or they cannot identify it, they hurt someone else instead. Now spirits can be wounded and are being wounded today in a way that does not put them in a state of conscious torment—so they do not know what is happening to them—but which greatly worsens them and stimulates the reaction just mentioned. Being unable to pass the evil back they pass it on, only in a different form. The non-physical violence done to them is converted into the physical violence they do.

I like putting the boot in—I get relief from it.—Roy Coldham, 17-year-old Manchester United football fan, after being fined £50.

If we asked, 'Relief from what?', he would be unable to say; but the malice that got into him and was vented in the way it was did not leave him intact: he became an evil person and bore the responsibility for it because, as he knew in his heart, he could have forgone the relief.

The foregoing observations were directed to the problem of acquiring a spiritual inheritance: I had asked what gets in the way and was offering the sketch of an answer. Suppose that having seen enough of what gets in the way we ask what helps.

Ought not the reply, or part of it, to be, 'Schools, colleges, universities . . .'? But these are among the institutions most affected and weakened by the factors we have been considering. Here too the past has been destroyed and continues to be destroyed. Schools which had a character and history, even if only a modest one, have been deprived of their identity. Reorganization into cumbersomely large units has broken loyalties, taken away a sense of place and turned an increasing proportion of teachers into administrators. There is an upsurge of indiscipline and in places violence in the schools. The circumstances put a premium, or at least they seem to do so, on substitutes for teaching. But the substitutes—for which there are various names like pastoral care, development of the personality, socialization, integration—only help to mislocate the problem, glossing over its depth and encouraging the thought that an answer might be found in tea and sympathy or psychology or the fostering of a social pull-together: as though the tide we are drifting on could be diverted by people pulling themselves together on it. In fact the substitutes for teaching were spawned by a style of educational theorizing that from its inception was flattering a trend.

Even where subject-teaching has been well maintained, schools reflect when they ought to resist the movements going on around them: for instance, only in a period of decline in the use of language could there be courses carrying the cachet of a famous university's name that proceed with the teaching of inflected languages as though their grammars scarcely existed.

So we live at a time when teachers to whom their country's spirit means anything are, or ought to be, in opposition; and unless they are lucky, the drift of their own establishments will have to be included in what they oppose.

The answer to my question, 'What helps?' is not (save for relatively few exceptions) educational institutions. Moreover similar considerations apply to teachers taken as a body. In any case a collectivity of teachers cannot bring influence to bear on a collectivity of the taught. However it is possible for them to do something as individuals, for other individuals or for small groups.

It will be clear that when I spoke of teachers in the role of opposition I did not have in mind for instance voting at meetings on principle against proposals destined to be carried anyway: the opposition is a spiritual one. But spiritual oppositions do have a principle. The most famous illustration of it I suppose is the injunction to turn the other cheek, but in that form it implies a passivity that could have no place in the present context. The generic idea is that of meeting evil with good. Teachers in England have not for a long time and until recently had much evil to meet. Now, the idea of adaptation to changing needs requires to be given a fundamental interpretation. In the customary superficial talk, 'changing needs' has been largely a euphemism for deterioration and the official response has been one of accommodation. In contrast with this, the principle governing spiritual dealings says that you do not face a lowering situation by lowering your sights but only by raising them.

An alternative expression for the principle would be to assert simply that nothing but the best is good enough. In relation to the problem of rootlessness I believe we should interpret this very much as Simone Weil interprets it, namely as an injunction to concentrate on making available to those whom we teach the very best and most beautiful things we know, and as far as possible only these things. There will not be many, so in principle it should be possible to call attention to them—or to those which are most accessible, bearing in mind the stage of education we happen to be concerned with—often enough for them to become familiar, and be accepted, and take on a status approaching that of natural surroundings for the minds of the recipients. Not that the minds we have to deal with are *tabulae rasae*: still, by persistence good coinage can be made within the classroom to take the place of the bad.

I think it is the primary school teacher today who is best placed to achieve something. The conception of early education put forward by Plato is well known but apt to strike readers, or skimmers, of that part of the *Republic* as intransigent and remote. I do not know why, since it seems to me that he was right in his belief about the power of certain pieces of music and poetry to breathe spiritual dispositions into people; and right also in his belief that such influences can, and with help do, catch on early. Platonic scholars are unable to say much about the differences of mode to which Plato attached importance and the little they do say tends to obscure the issue. Plato lived as we do in an age of decline. The popular music and song of his time was feeble and enfeebling. A relatively small amount of different stuff was available which could still communicate a strength and goodness of spirit. But that point alone does not fully give us the hang of why he should have wanted virtually just one kind of melody alone and one kind of verse alone to be heard. Consider another expression of the same idea, which is to be found in Nadezhda Mandelstam's remarkable memoir, *Hope Against Hope*:

In his youth M. always carefully weighed his words—it was only later that he tended toward levity. In 1919, when he was still very young, he once told me that there was no need at all to have a lot of books, and that it was best to read one book all one's life.

In what he said about reading only one book, M. was condemning something he loathed—namely, the mechanical absorption of incompatible things, the impaired sense of discrimination which he described in his 'Fourth Prose' as 'omni-tolerance' ('Look what has happened to Mother Philology—once so full-blooded . . . and now so omni-tolerant').

The first time I heard M. denounce the omnivorous approach was in 1919, in Kiev, when he criticized Briusov for his poems about different historical epochs, comparing them to gaudy Chinese lanterns. If such a comparison sprang to mind, M. concluded, it meant that Briusov was really lukewarm about everything, and that he looked at history as an idle spectator. I don't remember his exact words, but this was the sense of what he said. Later on, he and Akhmatova used to dismiss this kind of stuff as 'the story of the nations down the ages.' M. always knew, or at least tried to know, whether he should say 'yes' or 'no' to something. All his views gravitated to one pole or the other, and to this extent he was a kind of dualist, believing in the ancient doctrine of good and evil as the twin foundations of existence. Poets can never be indifferent to good and evil, and they can never say that all that exists is rational.

I think I know the kind of thing I would want to do if I were a teacher in a primary school. It would be the same *mutatis mutandis* as what I take my task to be at present.

6
Morality and the Two Worlds Concept

The idea of an antithesis between two worlds, the outer world and the inner, between the realm of objects and occurrences which physicists or zoologists study and the realm of the mind in which are to be sought the processes, and perhaps the immediate objects, of thought and reflection, knowledge and remembrance, feeling and desire—this idea is the thread out of which a large part of the history of philosophy has been woven and it is only recently that investigations into its composition have led to some reluctance to spin more of it. Moral philosophy has been in a different situation *vis-a-vis* the two worlds concept from that of some other branches of philosophical enquiry, for instance the philosophy of perception, which as traditionally conceived could scarcely have existed without it. Without it, no *philosophical* theories of perception—as distinct from scientific theories embodying laws about the behaviour of light, the functioning of the eye and so on—could ever have come to be formulated. Theories of morals, on the other hand, invite a division into those in which the inner–outer distinction plays a role of vital importance and those in which it is present only as an incidental feature. This division is, I believe, the most deeply rooted of all the divisions it is possible to make between moral philosophies, and it puts into the same hemisphere two luminaries who might otherwise (*cp.* E. A. Gellner's paper in *Proceedings of the Aristotelian Society*, 1954) be regarded as standing at opposite poles from one another—

Kierkegaard and Kant. These two, together with Plato, are the outstanding exponents of the two worlds thesis in moral philosophy, of the point of view which connects the quest for goodness with inwardness. I shall try, in what follows, to compare and put into some sort of perspective the behaviour of the inner-outer dichotomy in a selection of their writings.

In Kierkegaard's *Stages on Life's Way* there is a treatment of the question: What is the difference between being married to a woman and simply living with her, however happy and successful and fraught with love one's life with her may be? Kierkegaard is in no doubt that a crucial distinction is to be drawn between these two conditions, although to judge from appearances, to judge from any external or outward standpoint, no difference may be discernible. A couple whose relationship is of the second kind might be pillars of respectability; the woman might wear a ring on her finger, both of them might have sworn an oath and signed a book, have gone through some ritual in a church. These are the commonly accepted criteria of marriage: they make a relationship a marriage in the aesthetic, the legal, the civic, the officially religious sense, but they do not turn it into a marriage of the kind about which Kierkegaard wishes to speak. And if this be lacking he holds that the couple, for all their conformity with convention, for all their success and their happiness, will be living thoughtlessly, their relationship founded upon what he calls a worldly-minded deification of existence; which, he says, is perdition. Marriage, in the sense in which he wishes to use the term, is a *telos*, a supreme work of freedom. It is not something immediate but implies a resolution. Love, though it can prompt, does not resolve. Hence there is a gap between love's immediacy and marriage. This gap is bridgeable only by a resolution. Kierkegaard insists moreover that the resolution must be on hand from the beginning and that a marriage cannot be regarded as something capable of growing up by degrees after a couple have lived together for some time. If the resolution be not there from the start then something has come amiss and in his view something irredeemable. A seduction has taken place instead of a marriage.

The resolution about which Kierkegaard is speaking must be one of a special kind. He cannot be speaking of a decision simply to terminate a situation in which a number of different courses of action have presented themselves for consideration; not of a proposal, howsoever firmly made and far-seeing, to take a plunge in one direction rather than another: for how could that produce a marriage as distinct from an indefinitely prolonged association? It looks as if the resolution must be in some sense a generalized one, not a resolution to do just this or just that in this or another situation and subject to these or other conditions. It must be an unconditional resolution. Kierkegaard says of it that it has nothing to do with probability, nothing to do with the upshot. It is not, in other words, a resolution whose actuality or effectiveness is judgeable in terms of what it accomplishes: it is not concerned at all with what is outward, with one's success or progress in the world. It is an eternal resolution as well as one that is made at a time. In it, so Kierkegaard says, a bond of union is forged between the pagan and the spiritual, between love and reality. To be capable of making it one needs reflection and also faith.

To be capable of making it—but what is this? To be capable of doing what? If there is nothing specific, no one deed rather than another to be performed, what difference can remain between the person who makes the resolution and the person who does not? There surely has to be something which the former does or achieves and which the latter does not. But to the question, *What does the resolution achieve?* only two answers are allowed to be given. First, the resolution puts the maker of it into a relationship with eternity. Second, it achieves nothing: there is nothing in the world that it achieves, that it enables one to grasp. In the world—the external world—one ventures all; one suffers; one's attitude is to be that of resignation. All the ends that are here to be achieved one dismisses from view, for they are only relative ends. As far as the eternal is concerned, and that is the only absolute end, the whole of time and existence is a period of striving (*Unscientific Postscript* Ch. IV, Sec. IIA).

What the existing individual must do in making his eternal resolution, therefore, is to strive or will, and to will absolutely, while renouncing all acquisition for himself. What he wills is in fact this renunciation. But the question we wish to be answered is: In just what way does he will it, in what does his willing of it consist? This is indeed the great question for Kierkegaard also. But whereas our problem here, in asking this question, is that of investigating the sense, if any, that can be attached to the idea of an eternal resolution, the problem for Kierkegaard is that of how to live—of how an individual may put himself, in his temporal existence, into a relationship with eternity. There is one solution which could be offered and which he appears to rebut with peculiar force by using, as an example of an eternal resolution, the resolution to marry. This is the suggestion that the individual may solve his problem by sitting motionless in a monastery, though that is one possible way of construing inwardness and seemingly the most radical form of renunciation of the relative ends of the world. The rejection of relative ends must be encompassed, Kierkegaard believes, in action, not through inactivity. Now although he does not actually say this, it seems to me that a directive that might from his point of view be given to anyone who should ask how he is to will in action an eternal resolution, be it willed in connection with marriage or in any other connection, is the directive that he should do whatever he does entirely for the good of it and not do anything that cannot be done for the good of it. In other words (somewhat Irish-sounding words perhaps), to reject relative ends, to eschew the doing of anything for the sake of a worldly end, is to treat the doing of everything as an end in itself. In this way alone would it be possible in one's doings in the world to achieve the requisite freedom from the world and hence a relationship with the eternal. In so far as one's doings cease to be doings for the sake of some end then the less, in a sense, do they amount to doing—at the very least they no longer amount to bringing about—and the more they approximate to taking things as they are, or indeed to suffering. And it is in suffering that the freedom is said to be greatest and that the world and the eternal come closest together.

Let me return to Kierkegaard's point that the resolution is the outcome of reflection. He also speaks, like Socrates, of the necessity for recollection. What reflection and recollection lead to in this context is self-knowledge: the precept for one who would attain inwardness is *gnōthi seauton* and this is attained by an 'inner' or 'internal' examination. But the self-examination called for is not what would be suggested by the introspection that is the legacy of Lockeian inner sense. It would be a radical misunderstanding to suppose that self-knowledge could consist, on the one hand of any kind of intuitive awareness or self-authenticating experience of what is going on in one, or on the other hand that it could result from an experimental enquiry. It is not attainable in a scientifically diagnostic way, has nothing to do with psychological investigation. There is not here, as in many other contexts, the identification of knowledge with certainty; for it is (so Kierkegaard affirms) a searching, not a conclusion, and it is carried on with fear and trembling. To some extent undoubtedly self-knowledge can be identified with insight into the motives from which one acts, though Kierkegaard characteristically declines to sanction this identification explicitly. But awareness of what one is (of one's motives as they are) would be impossible without a conception of what one might have been or might become (a conception of one's motives as they ought to be—the conception of the ethical reality in accordance with which the maker of an eternal resolution strives and wills). Accordingly the search, in so far as it establishes anything, is said by Kierkegaard to establish that one is guilty and a sinner; and this result was foreshadowed from the start. As to the validity of the result, one's guarantee is the quality of the search. The quality of one's relationship to a *telos* is the guarantee of the absoluteness of that *telos*. It is one's relationship to eternity that defines it as eternity (*Unscientific Postscript*).

I have tried to indicate, in the foregoing remarks about Kierkegaard, something of the relationship between the conceptual dichotomy of Inner and Outer and the notions of Striving or Willing, End or Result, the Need to do Something Specific, Eternity, Freedom, Knowledge and Motive (I shall want to consider later the way in which the notion of Happiness fits into this scheme of relationships). I am not supposing that Kant exercised much influence upon Kierkegaard directly, or precisely in the direction which this comparison might seem to suggest, but there is nevertheless to be found in Kant's *Groundwork of the Metaphysic of Morals* a set of conceptual relationships which corresponds quite closely to the one I have so far outlined.

The contrast between the inner and the outer is drawn in Kant's famous opening remark that the only thing that can conceivably be called good without qualification is a good will. This will is contrasted with talents, with gifts of nature and fortune, with power, riches, honour, health and general well-being. A good will is not good, says Kant, because of what it effects or accomplishes, not through its aptness for the attainment of some proposed end (its existence has nothing to do with the upshot, to use Kierkegaard's expression). As the bearer of unconditional value the will is thus, for Kant, a denizen of the inner world; but it is also conceived as an agent whose activity impinges on the outer, where it can suffer hindrance at the hand of nature. Kant might well have said of the good will what Kierkegaard said of a resolution such as the resolution to marry, namely that it unites the temporal with the eternal. He says in fact that the will stands at the parting of the ways, where it is subject to two distinct and opposing influences—an internal influence, for which another name is the motive of duty, and the external influence of inclination. In so far however as it is at the beck of inclination, determined by alien causes, it is unfree: and this amounts to saying that it is unfree in so far as its activity is geared to the production of any desired end or result. To be an entirely free will the will must be an entirely inward will. Freedom is not to be found in the realm of phenomena (the outer world) where everything is determined, but belongs to the noumenal (which amounts to the eternal and is also to be equated with the inner world) where too there is determination, but of another kind—the will's rational determination to be a good will, the determination to legislate in accordance with the moral law.

The question one may now be tempted to ask of Kant is: What does the moral law enjoin us to do? His critics have grumbled that he fails to tell us. He provides a formulation of the moral law in imperative terms, but all that the imperative seems to say is: Obey the moral law!—or to put this in the form Kant reached *via* an analysis of what he took to be involved in the notion of a law, namely universality: Act only on that maxim through which you can at the same time will that it should become a universal law.

From the standpoint of Kant's position it is not a defect that he should be unable to deduce as a consequence of his premisses any specific type of action that we must always do or avoid. To make such a stipulation as a condition of morality would be tantamount to assessing the goodness of the will from an external standpoint, judging it from the point of view of its achievements or results. For Kant to do this would be for him to contradict himself; and in so far as he tries to do this he actually does contradict himself. To know, in so far as you can know it, that your will is good is not to know that this in particular is to be done or that in particular avoided:[1] to search in this direction is to search in the outer world, which is the wrong direction. Instead you are required to look inward; to

[1] This is not to say that the good man can be indifferent to, and under no necessity to discharge, actual obligations that may be placed upon him —which would be an absurd thesis to maintain. The point is rather that the nature of goodness is such that it cannot be grasped piecemeal. The task is not like that of learning the dates of the kings of England, a matter of having one's attention drawn to an increasing number of 'moral facts', or the gradual cataloguing of more and more prohibitions and licences, with the idea that one would understand all there was to know about morality after every conceivable example had been enumerated. ('Nothing could be more fatal to morality than that we should wish to derive it from examples.')

know yourself; to ensure that your motive is not one of inclination, i.e. that you are not doing whatever you do for the sake of something to be got out of it, but rather for its own sake. Kant's practical imperative—So act as to treat humanity, whether in your own person or in any other, always as an end and never simply as a means—is thus a consequence of his premises in a way that the categorical imperative, that is, the imperative about universalization, is not. The latter is really a gigantic kink in the argument, a distraction that gets introduced because *inter alia* Kant, not being content to regard moral determination (the manner in which the good will is determined to will) simply as the negation of a determination to obtain some sort of advantage for oneself (which is what the subjection of the will to inclination and the forces of nature amounts to), insists on conceiving it as a kind of parallel shadow of this—a conformability to a non-natural counterpart of the law or laws of phenomena.

Kant's use of the contrast between the inner and the outer in his moral philosophy for the purpose of saying something about the difference between a person who is morally serious and a person who is not, cannot be separated from the use of this contrast elsewhere in pointing to the difference between a human being and a machine. One of the effects of the double use of the same dichotomy is to secure that these two distinctions merge conceptually into a single contrast. Hence the two equations which are to be found in Kant, first between the will that is not good and the will that is not free—which is one way of assimilating the non-moral man to the robot; secondly the equation of the good will with rationality, the thesis that ill will is somehow a deficiency of knowledge or understanding—again the defect of the robot. An appearance of these two equations has been noticed already in Kierkegaard. With regard to the second, since obviously the idea that orientation towards goodness is a matter of reason or understanding is not confined to moral theories in which the contrast between the inner and the outer is prominent, I want here to direct attention towards the difference in the sort of connection that is made between understanding and the aspiration to goodness, or else in the sort of reason with which the aspiration is connected, when a moral theory centres itself upon this conceptual dichotomy.

In the late Professor G. C. Field's book *Moral Theory* a chapter entitled 'The Kantian Fallacy in Other Forms' begins with the following words:

No one, except his immediate disciples, has attempted to take over and defend Kant's system in all its details. No later writer of any importance has accepted the proposition that goodness simply means universality, in Kant's sense. But, as we have seen, that theory is only the result of a more fundamental error. And this fundamental error, as we shall find, reappears in many different forms in later writers. The fundamental objection to the theory is that it fails to fulfil one of the fundamental conditions of any correct account of the moral fact. Whatever goodness is, it is at least in some way a reason for action, a reason for pursuing those things where it is present and avoiding those where it is absent. And any account of it which fails to show why it should be a reason for action, still more an account which describes it in such a way that it could not possibly be a reason for action, stands condemned.

In his suggestion that goodness according to Kant 'simply means universality' I believe that Field was diverting the attention of his students from what is most important in Kant's moral philosophy: however his 'fatal objection to the theory' happens not to be contingent upon pre-eminence being given to the categorical imperative and it is with this objection that we are now concerned. Goodness is not, in Kant's opinion, *a reason* (for action, for the pursuit of anything); it is—*reason*. The indefinite article, the absence of which Field condemned, constitutes the dividing line between the standpoint of Socrates, Plato and Kant on the one hand and the standpoint of Aristotle and the Utilitarians on the other. To Kant the problem: How can reason be practical? meant something different from what it meant to Aristotle. It was not for Kant the problem: How can reason be or become practical reason?

(How is *phronēsis* attainable by a rational animal?), but rather:
What is the connection between pure reason and morality?
Hence Kant's persistent use of that odd-sounding juxtaposi-
tion 'pure practical reason'. His answer to the question was, in
brief, that reason and morality are connected internally—the
connection is not to be sought in the outer world but in the
inner. The nature of the reason here determines and is determined by the nature of the connection.

As a synonym for 'pure reason' Kant used the term 'a priori
reason' and the significance of these terms is to be found
primarily in what they deny. Pure reason is that which contains no admixture of the empirical. It has nothing to do with
one's ability to manage a household for example. It is no sort
of capacity to cope in a discriminating fashion with matters
that are variable and contingent; is no sort of skill in fact. It is
not *savoir-faire* which one might acquire by experience, by
knocking about the world. It is not something that is exercised
about the means of securing an end (contrast *Nic. Eth.* II 6, 9;
III 3; VI 5–11). It is, in short, the very antithesis of *prudence*, as
phronēsis may be rendered accurately enough into English. The
prudent man takes out insurance policies: the man who is
seriously concerned with the ethical, Kierkegaard said, must
risk all. So far from having to do with insight into the circumstances of this or that time and place, pure reason focuses itself
upon the timeless, the eternal. The knowledge with which
Socrates equated virtue, when he rejected the mention of
particular instances of things to be done or not done as irrelevant to an understanding of the nature of virtue, is thus akin to
Kant's pure reason. It is not, to use the Platonic mode of
expression, knowledge of the world of many particulars, but
knowledge of one thing only—the Form of the Good.

Field's criticism of Kant is reminiscent of the objection
brought by Aristotle against the belief that the way to an
understanding of morality lay through the Theory of Forms:
'Even granting that the good which is predicated of different
things were somehow a unity or that it somehow stood by
itself, still it clearly would not be something that man can

practice or possess' (*Nic. Eth.* I, 6). Aristotle, as H. W. B. Joseph remarked, 'was more interested in the multiplicity of virtues than in the unity of virtue', and Plato's reformulation of the Socratic thesis seemed to him only to throw into relief its inherent absurdity. Supposing the Form of the Good to signify a remote and gaseous super-entity, he decided that Plato had portrayed goodness as something that could have no bearing on life. But this was not how Plato thought of the independence and self-sufficiency of goodness (the idea that he was not all the time concerned most seriously with life were an absurdity indeed): nor does the eternal seem to have signified for Kierkegaard any kind of gaseous realm.

The conception of goodness as an eternal Form, with the attendant conception of life's wisdom as other-worldly wisdom, is the expression of an attitude to life which Aristotle failed to get inside in the way a person whose outlook is non-religious is apt to make no sense of religion. In fact the Platonic, the Kantian and the Kierkegaardian conception of morality, with its reference to Forms, to Noumena and to the Eternal, may as well be called outright the religious[2] conception of morality. It is characteristic of religious utterances that they should require an attitude to the world to be expressed by speaking of something beyond the world. Yet this way of stating the matter runs us into trouble immediately. For in speaking of an attitude to the world we meant an attitude to the entire universe, to the world as a whole. But how can it be possible logically to speak of something beyond the world as a whole? How indeed could a language even *seem* to refer to something beyond the world in that sense, except to someone who had misunderstood it? The terms 'world' or 'universe' could just possibly have been employed equivocally in our statement, being used on their second appearance in the way

---

[2] I have not forgotten that Kierkegaard distinguishes between the ethical and the religious: I think that despite all the complications it is still possible to regard him as having presented in the end only one great antithesis, one *either/or*—the choice between various kinds of frivolity and the ethico-religious mode of life.

an astronomer might use them (there would be a great deal for language to refer to beyond that). Such an equivocation would permit sense to emerge from the statement. But only, it seems, by forcing us straight back on the distinction between the inner and the outer. For the world *qua* subject of astronomical and other scientific investigations is the outer world as opposed to the inner world. If it be only the outer world that Forms, Noumena, Eternity—or God—can be said properly to be beyond, then, how can the reference to Forms and the rest be anything more than a reduplication of the already existent reference to the inner?

Plato equates the unworldly, formal unity of virtue with an inward unity: *dikaiosunē* is a state of the soul. And there is a Christian saying that the Kingdom of God is within you —which obviously depends for its acceptability on what else is said alongside it: imagine a Christian's reaction to the suggestion that the Kingdom of God were *only* within him. In fact arguably it was never a good saying for a Christian to utter, for the reason that it is a statement the devil himself could use. Somewhat similarly, if Plato's assertion that *dikaiosunē* is a state of the soul had stood by itself, unaided by any reference to the Forms, it could readily have been taken over by a Protagoras and perverted into what is virtually the antithesis of Plato's intention—*metron dikaiosunēs estin anthrōpos*. Kierkegaard, when he advocates the cultivation of inwardness, is sensible of the fact that there is more than one possible form of inwardness. The genuine has to be distinguished from the spurious: it is only one kind of inwardness that puts one into a relationship with the eternal. Truth is to be identified with subjectivity, but the Kierkegaardian species of subjectivity is vastly different from Hume's kind wherein 'a thousand different sentiments, excited by the same object, are all right'. The references by Plato, Kant and Kierkegaard to Forms, Noumena and the Eternal, whatever else they may involve, are thus a cardinal qualification as well as a reinforcement of the distinction between the inner and the outer in its relation to ethics. In one way they add greatly to the difficulty of understanding the connection between goodness and the inner, but in another way they are the safeguard against its being misunderstood.

Plato insisted that the man in whom knowledge of the good was dominant—that is, the just man—was the happiest; and Aristotle, in condemning Plato's good as a thing which had become somehow separated from human desire and satisfaction, may seem to have ignored this. I say he *may seem* to, because I think that in fact he did not ignore it but made his objection notwithstanding. An error of H. A. Prichard provides the clue. Prichard thought that Plato wanted to justify morality by showing it to be profitable: he thought that Plato thus provided 'perhaps the most significant instance' of the mistake on which moral philosophy rested (*Mind*, 1912, p. 22; reprinted in *Moral Obligation*, p. 2). Prichard regarded a confusion between morality and expediency as the most radica[l] mistake a moral philosopher could make and he was perce[p]tive enough in his contention that if the task of moral ph[ilo]sophy be taken to be that of supplying *a reason* why we sh[ould] act in the ways we think we ought to act then there can[not be] such thing as moral philosophy. But in the case of [Plato he] jammed the cap down over the wrong head. Socrate[s is not] made to answer Thrasymachus by saying that jus[tice pays in] the sense that Thrasymachus had maintained t[hat injustice] paid. It is because Plato was concerned to a[void and was] largely successful in avoiding the mistake att[ributed to him] by Prichard that his standpoint seemed u[nacceptable to] Aristotle.

It appeared impossible to Prichard that [in being] concerned about rightness and duty one c[ould at the same time] be deeply concerned about oneself. He [did not need to con]sider very closely what happiness me[ant or in] what way it was connected with vir[tue: the contrast was] made and that was enough. The j[ustice which led] Plato to be concerned about him[self was not worthy of] him: so Plato's moral philosop[hy was tainted with] utility. But if this taint was [

philosophy, it was also to be found in—of all people—Kant's. In his lecture on *Duty and Interest* (p. 4) we find Prichard observing in a shocked tone that even Kant insisted that duty and interest were intimately connected—the connection in question being not, of course, that between my duty and other people's interest but that between my duty and my personal interest. Kant says, towards the end of the *Groundwork*, that to make the nature of the interest we have in morality comprehensible is an impossibility identical with the 'subjective impossibility of *explaining* freedom of will' (Paton's trans., p. 128). Autonomy and personal interest thus go together: it is *self-interest* that is equated with heteronomy. He affirms in another passage that the interest which morality has for us is the highest possible interest, though it 'carries with it no interest in mere states', by which he means, as Paton notes, agreeable states of affairs and states of feeling (pp. 117 and 144 of Paton's translation).

Where Kant thus speaks of our interest in morality he could equally, had he wished, have spoken of our happiness. He refrained from this, I believe, because he recognized that the latter term was most commonly used and understood in the sense of external well-being, the Aristotelian *eu zēn kai prattein*; that it was used to signify something in the world whose nature can be pointed out—some 'mere state', as he put it (*cf* his reference in Ch. I of the *Groundwork* to 'health and that complete well-being and contentment with one's state that goes by the name of happiness'). Using the term himself therefore in conformity with the prevailing notion, he asserted that happiness, as something which our inclinations are designed to further, is connected with morality only through the existence of indirect duty: one has a duty to assure one's own happiness because unsatisfied wants are a temptation to transgression. When however he affirms that in striving to be a moral one is concerned with one's interest and with one's possible interest, though without being selfishly concerned, Kant is in close agreement with Plato and Kierkegaard. man is concerned about his own happiness according to Plato—infinitely concerned, says Kierkegaard; but he is not feathering his nest or seeking a benefit. Since this crucial distinction eluded Prichard it is no wonder that he was hard put to it to find any moral philosophy that did not rest on a mistake.

The battle against utilitarian and aesthetic misconceptions of morality had reduced Prichard to a state of siege. All he could advocate was a sort of scorched earth policy; moral philosophy had better be given up, he was inclined to say. Kant was on the offensive even if in deploying his forces he got into cramped positions. Plato and Kierkegaard wielded an unrestrictive armoury. The position of happiness as well as reason, in relation to the problem of living in the way one ought to live, was not in the least to be played down. Instead, the inner-outer dichotomy was employed in order to split each of these concepts into two, so that with the one part jettisoned and the other magnified their connection with morality might be reinforced. Discrete and variable reasoning was supplanted by a rationality perilously hard of attainment but of an infrangible kind: the happiness of the most superior type of worldly existence imaginable was dismissed for the sake of a *telos* of a different order—a happiness which would be inward and eternal. The pragmatic conception of ethics whose attractiveness over its rivals seemed to reside in its teleological outlook was thus represented as having failed to be teleological enough.

This same process of splitting and partial jettisoning was already in operation upon the notion of goodness at the beginning of the *Groundwork* where Kant, contrasting the goodness of the will with other goods, allowed only the good will to be called good *unconditionally*. Particularly instructive in this connection is the passage in the *Gorgias* (469B) where Socrates defines the moral standpoint with extraordinary conciseness by means of a distinction between two kinds of badness, asserting that it is worse to do harm than to suffer it—a contention which is received with incredulity by Polus for whom 'better' and 'worse' have no other significance than 'more expedient' and 'less expedient'. It should be observed that there is no question here of measurement. If I were faced with the alternative between injuring another and suffering injury myself, it would not become less wrong for me to injure him in so far as the injury I might avoid became commensurate with the injury he might suffer, nor would it cease to be wrong at the point at which the injury I might avoid became greater than the injury he might suffer, even if such an assessment were possible. Those who said that everybody was to count as one might just as well have said, from Socrates' point of view, that nobody was to count as anything (for if each of us is to count as one then nobody can count for more than I do, nobody's pains can be more important than mine). The transition from egoism to morality is not to be accomplished by converting 'expedient for me' into 'expedient for the aggregate'. What Socrates does is to replace 'good for me' in the sense of 'expedient for me' by another kind of good, the soul's goodness, which is not merely still *my* good, but is more mine than before since nothing external can deprive me of it.

In the *Nicomachean Ethics* the contrast between goods of the soul and bodily goods, also between goods of the soul and external goods, is prominent enough (1098b 13), but it has now been altered in force. This is mainly the consequence of Aristotle's insistence that happiness should be something *ostensive*—a definite and palpable objective which could be located in some describable pattern of activity, some public and non-subjective state of affairs. In Aristotle's moral philosophy therefore the scope of the distinction between the inner and the outer or soul and body is restricted to differentiating between various types of desirable situations. Its sphere of operation lies within the bounds of what Kierkegaard would call the aesthetic plane. The difference between Socrates and a fool or pig as it presents itself to Mill is also that kind of difference.

Aristotle's conception of happiness was not indeed so wholeheartedly naturalistic as that of Bentham, who more than anybody else tried to treat it as a commodity of plainly measurable dimensions and seemed to dream of himself running a kind of social power station from which he could generate huge amounts of this commodity to huge numbers at small cost. Still, Aristotle's good was commercial enough for him to share in some degree the remarkable capacity of the Utilitarians and their modern successors for knowing what was good for other people. What I mean is this: Aristotle, who had been more interested in the multiplicity of virtues than in the unity of virtue, ended up—paradoxically enough—by wanting to put everyone into the strait-jacket of a single happy life. For *theōria* (whether it fulfilled all his earlier stipulations or not) was put forward as his candidate for *the* happy life. No matter who you were, this was the life for you; this was your ultimate end, the place where your happiness lay. On the other hand Plato, who believed that virtue was a unity, did not recommend everyone to live the same kind of life. Quite the reverse, for in Plato's view happiness cannot be defined as a life whose activity conforms to this or that indicable pattern; happiness is something inward. Hence if you ask Plato what you are actually to do, the response is *ta heautou prattein*; each is to live his own life and nobody else's.

7

Is Goodness a Mystery?

For understandable reasons people get the impression that philosophy is a wholly mysterious business. But the relation between philosophy and mystery is mostly like the relation between air and a vacuum. And if mysteries are cultivated by philosophers, they are cultivated rather in the way that crimes are by sleuths—for the sake of their unravelling and with the aim of giving an account of them, so that our thoughts may become free from entanglement and the mind be set at peace.

But in pursuing this endeavour one may become struck by the sense of a difference in kind among mysteries, some of which present themselves as offering a more than accidental resistance to explanation. I am speaking now of a difference within philosophy and not of something that is the mark of any philosophical difficulty whatever. For there is a sense in which all distinctly philosophical perplexity is non-accidental, or of a necessary character, by comparison with the perplexity that is engendered by a murder mystery for instance; and this point could be expressed by saying that the former sort of perplexity is conceptual while the latter is not. But having recognized this difference, one may find oneself brought up against a kind of difficulty, within the realm of the conceptually perplexing, that offers such a peculiar resistance to explanation that other conceptual difficulties will then seem to be rather accidental again by comparison. Of course when you are presented with something that you think to be not just accidentally mysterious but necessarily mysterious, there is always the danger that you have fallen into an obscurantist muddle. But while this is one of the worst sorts of muddle that can occur in philosophy, it is by no means the worst thing possible in philosophy. Far worse is the superficiality that conceives nothing to be unfathomable because it has fished only in coastal waters. In any case the kind of philosophical work that is most worth having has always tended to come from those in whom a sense of mystery has been nurtured and kept alive.

Here is part of a conversation that took place forty years ago. The speaker is Wittgenstein:

> Schlick says that theological ethics contains two conceptions of the essence of the Good. According to the more superficial interpretation, the Good is good because God wills it; according to the deeper interpretation, God wills the Good because it is good.
>
> I think that the first conception is the deeper one; Good is what God orders. For this cuts off the path to any and every explanation 'why' it is good, while the second conception is precisely the superficial, the rationalistic one, which proceeds as if what is good could still be given some foundation.

This opinion of the early Wittgenstein (and I don't suppose he would ever have gone back on it) does not just run counter to a view expressed by Schlick. It amounts to an attack on the possibility of doing any moral philosophy at all in the most widely accepted manner. For it has generally been thought to be the task of moral philosophy to examine the judgements that are commonly made about the goodness or badness of things and actions with a view to establishing a foundation for some of these judgements. And it has generally been thought to be very much a part of the business to try to explain what constitutes goodness or accounts for its existence. But in the conversation I have quoted Wittgenstein intimates that to proceed as if this could be done is to proceed according to a superficial conception.

It might at once be objected that the idea of explaining judgements of value—saying wherein the goodness or the badness consists—is a perfectly familiar idea both inside and outside philosophy. But I should wonder here whether the examples that the objector might have in mind would include judgements of relative value as well as judgements of absolute value. Wittgenstein drew a firm distinction between these two kinds of judgement. He saw no difficulty at all in the idea of explaining the relative kind and what he had to say about the two conceptions of theological ethics related only to judgements of absolute value. In an ethics lecture belonging to the same period (written in 1929 or 1930 and published in *The Philosophical Review* in 1965) he explained the distinction between relative and absolute value as follows. Expressions like 'good', 'important' and 'right' are used, he said, in two very different senses:

If for instance I say that this is a *good* chair this means that the chair serves a certain predetermined purpose and the word good here has only meaning so far as this purpose has been previously fixed upon. In fact the word good in the relative sense simply means coming up to a certain predetermined standard. Thus when we say that this man is a good pianist we mean that he can play pieces of a certain degree of difficulty with a certain degree of dexterity. And similarly if I say that it is *important* for me not to catch cold I mean that catching a cold produces certain describable disturbances in my life and if I say that this is the *right* road I mean that it's the right road relative to a certain goal. Used in this way these expressions don't present any difficult or deep problems. But this is not how Ethics uses them. Supposing that I could play tennis and one of you saw me playing and said 'Well, you play pretty badly' and suppose I answered 'I know, I'm playing badly but I don't want to play any better', all the other man could say would be 'Ah, then that's all right'. But suppose I had told one of you a preposterous lie and he came up to me and said 'You're behaving like a beast' and then I were to say 'I know I behave badly, but then I don't want to behave any better', could he then say 'Ah, then that's all right'? Certainly not; he would say 'Well, you *ought* to want to behave better'. Here you have an absolute judgement of value, whereas the first instance was one of relative judgement.

One possible reaction to the remarks I have just quoted might be the following: Granting the distinction between relative and absolute value and confining ourselves to cases where we hold something to be absolutely fine and wonderful (or the reverse), still we surely are familiar with the idea of explaining our judgements. For instance in the case of works of literature or pieces of music we may call attention to the way the story unfolds or the way the themes and passages in the musical composition are put together. We can point here to a variety of elements in combination. And in the case of actions likewise there will often be a variety of conspiring considerations to be mentioned—how the person came to do whatever he did, what the action led to (especially, it might be urged, in the way of misery or happiness to other human beings), or the need that it answered, and then perhaps the adversity in the circumstances or the temptation that was overcome, and so on.

I do not know how Wittgenstein would have responded to this objection. I should myself agree that it is often possible to mention separately certain elements or considerations the presence of which in combination has led to the placing of an absolute value upon some action for good or ill. For instance I might say, in the case of a deed that has struck me as wonderful, that it was not only the courage but even more the magnanimity of it; or in the case of another action I might say that there was an element of duplicity and also of meanness alongside the brutality. In speaking thus I should be substituting more specific terms of evaluation for the unspecific term with which perhaps I had begun. What I should be doing here would be distinguishing and characterizing certain forms or typical faces of good and evil. But I should not be making plain what makes them forms of good and evil, nor should I be offering any explanation of the nature of that of which these forms are forms—I should not be explaining this however much detail I were able to go into. Suppose for example that I spoke of someone who, while he was himself in a vulnerable position, had disregarded his own danger in the exertions by which he succeeded in getting a victim of injustice out of harm's way. In so describing what he did I should be employing evaluative terms anyway; and if someone were then to ask what was so good about it I should think there must be something wrong with him. I should certainly not try to tell him what was good about it and if I were to try I should not succeed. To understand the description I gave is to understand it already as the description of a deed on which an absolute value is placed. I mean especially the part about getting a victim of injustice out of harm's way, for the vulnerability of the agent and the exertions involved are significant considerations only to the extent that they bear on this. Otherwise they might have amounted to nothing more than a stunt. Or again, suppose there had been some special temptation to be overcome, which had also been mentioned as a factor contributing to the fineness of what was done. This likewise presupposes the assignment of an absolute value to the deed: otherwise I could not have spoken intelligibly of a temptation.

It is true that through the disclosure of further details or by paying attention to the surrounds of an action one can often enough be brought to change one's judgement. It is possible also to compare different cases and sometimes to see writ large in one what was writ small and hence difficult to discern in another. Or a comment from someone else might enable one to see what one could not see before and perhaps might never have seen on one's own. But once, whether after much or little consideration and help of this and other sorts, I have been forcibly struck by the splendidness or the dreadfulness of something I have seen and I register this by characterizing the action in one way or another according to its significance for good or ill, and I am then requested by someone to say what the good or the ill of it amounts to, and he does not mean this as a request to have any more details described to him or to be told about any further repercussions of what transpired, but he wishes to be told (so he says) what the good is or what the ill is in itself, or what the nature of it is: then I simply do not know what to reply. And my situation is a queer and perplexing one, in that I can see—as it would be natural for me to say—I can see the good or the evil without difficulty; I see it in the action. I recognize quite clearly *that* it is there. But *what* it is I cannot for the life of me explain.

So a mental fog descends and what precipitates the fog is not just the fact that I find myself unable to make plain something that I feel I ought to be able to make plain, but also the fact that the nature of my inability is itself not plain. Suppose I felt frustrated at my inability to lift a dumb-bell or to calculate the volume of a pyramid; there the sort of ability that is required would be perfectly clear to me and if I lacked it I should lack it only accidentally. But in the present case I find myself unable to do something and I do not have even a moderately clear idea of what it is that I cannot do.

When I say that I do not know what is wanted by the man who asks for the explanation of the goodness—and neither, I think, does he—I mean that I cannot imagine what would be conceptually appropriate, though I am aware of numerous proposed answers that are conceptually inappropriate. The history of moral philosophy is full of them. It also contains important negative findings, among which the following three are due to Plato: first that goodness does not consist in or depend upon pleasure, although counterfeit forms of it are commonly generated by an attachment to pleasure. For as Plato put it, some men are brave out of a kind of cowardice and temperate out of self-indulgence: they barter pleasure for pleasure, but there is no more virtue in this than in being a money-changer. The second negative finding of Plato I wish to mention is that goodness has nothing to do with getting on or getting more, nothing to do with consumption, aggrandisement or the glamour of worldly esteem. His third finding was that goodness is not a conventional creation and does not consist in following the prevailing *mores* or being within some social swim.

But then in relation to the kind of example I was considering—and we all know of such—where a man does something marvellous that is in no way a dictate of office or a thing that is generally expected and where he displays not just courage or devotion but conspicuous selflessness, it should be perfectly

plain that none of the three sophistical conceptions which
Plato threw out is seriously in the running as an explanatory
possibility. Nobody's pleasure is being considered, least of all
'the pleasure of the greatest number' (whatever that could
mean—numbers don't come into it); there is no concern with
prestige or with advancement; while as to conventionality,
nothing marvellous was ever conventional.

Leaving Plato on one side, the movements that have most
often been made in the history of philosophy towards a positive explanation of absolute goodness have taken as their
signpost the fact that judgements of relative value are explain-
able and the kind of explanation that can be given for them has
been used as a model from which to extrapolate. Now goodness of a relative sort is characteristically associated with a set
of notions among which the chief are *function*, *role*, *purpose*, *aim*
and *desire*. For example, a good knife is one that serves its
purpose; its function is to cut and if you desire that function to
be performed it is a good thing to have. Cutting is doubtless an
aim that you will only have at certain times and even then it
will be subordinate to some more comprehensive aim like
upholstering, which in turn will be comprised within the more
general aim of furniture-making, which again is only a relative
aim since perhaps you only do it for a living. And as to why
you are doing that you may say 'Well one has to keep one's
head above water' or 'Goodness knows what it's all about,'
whereupon the whole progression is brought to a stop. But if
one could go on and speak intelligibly of the aim in living: if
one could speak of a desire or objective so general and comprehensive that it included everything, then one would have a
purpose that was no longer relative. And a good that had its
role on the level of that purpose would no longer be a relative
good but would be an absolute good; indeed it would be *the*
absolute good and it would have its explanation in that all-
embracing purpose. This was how Aristotle reasoned. I shall
call it the goal-seeking explanation of value. There are variants
upon it which dispense with the notion of a single ultimate
purpose—and this is an advantage because, as soon as you try

to specify the ultimate purpose, whatever you come up with will be bound to be either obscure on account of its abstractness, or if not obscure then contestable precisely in so far as it is specific and hence exclusive. Aristotle said that the goal was Contemplation, and there might be a way of taking this in which it would contain profundity: but then it would have to be made compatible with much else that he did not say; whereas what he did say about it is strongly suggestive of scholarly pursuits which are plainly not suitable for everybody. He did not connect contemplation with either the beauty of the world or the pain and evil in it; and while he emphasized the pleasure to be had from contemplating, it was only in a quite separate context that he spoke of love.

The variants of the goal-seeking arguments that dispense with the notion of a single ultimate aim postulate an irreducible plurality of desires. These are supposed to form a kind of psychological democracy and the problem of absolute value then presents itself as a problem of organization—the task of achieving harmony and a stable balance. For instance, according to the theory of value put forward by I. A. Richards in his *Principles of Literary Criticism*, 'Anything is valuable which will satisfy an appetency without involving the frustration of some equal or *more important* appetency; in other words, the only reason which can be given for not satisfying a desire is that more important desires will thereby be thwarted.' The importance of an appetency or impulse is then defined as 'the extent of the disturbance of other impulses in the individual's activities which the thwarting of the impulse involved.' There are variations on the argument which try to get the harmony of purpose into the picture from the start by postulating a common objective or concern that is supposed to be connected with the nature of society or shared among mankind as a whole. This is sometimes identified as the good *of* society, or the human good.

So when I speak of the goal-seeking explanation of value I am referring altogether to a very large family of positions. I reject the whole family. For the recognition of an absolute

value, as in the case I mentioned earlier, where one is struck by
the egregious fineness of an action like the rescue of an innocent person who is harmed or wronged—acknowledgement
of the goodness of such an action involves the awareness of a
demand that can as readily obstruct as further any purpose
howsoever elevated and irrespective of whether the purpose
be conceived as private or communal. And instead of its being
the case that anything could come to have absolute value by
being related to a superordinate purpose, purposes that are not
subordinate to other purposes call for assessment from the
standpoint of absolute value just as they do when they are
merely subordinate. The same applies to desires, unless the
desire in question is already an aspiration for absolute good.
But in that event it would be impossible to explain the nature
of the aspiration otherwise than by reference to the goodness
towards which it is directed (I do not say we have no means of
indicating the direction: this might be done by citing exemplifications of the goodness or alternatively by means of negative stipulations like those I gave earlier from Plato).

In regard to the branch of the goal-seeking argument which
posits as the absolute value a good that is thought to be in or of
society, I cannot see what this position amounts to other than
the placing of a value upon association as such, or the belief
that it is absolutely good just to keep things going. The objection is that whether or not there is a value in association will
depend upon the nature and worth of that in which you are
associated. It could be said perhaps that what you are associated in is the carrying on of the life of your people and country,
the upholding of its traditions and the maintenance of its
institutions. And I do indeed think that the capacity to love
one's country and its past, when untainted by jingoism or
fondness for 'gloire', is not unconnected with the capacity to
have an aspiration for absolute good that I spoke of a moment
ago—if only because it is an example of a kind of love which
while being something outside oneself, and therefore taking
one out of oneself, at the same time helps one to find onself.
However there will be in one's country and its life a mixture of

good and ill, and while this does not mean that one loves the country only in a qualified way, still if the good were not present or were exiguous by comparison with the ill, then one could not love it, except chauvinistically.

There has been an attempt to make non-relative goodness intelligible by recourse to the idea of 'what is required for the carrying on of *any* human life'. Although I shall contend that this idea ends up in the same boat as the goal-seeking argument, it is not really a species of it, for it is not said that the maintenance of some kind of human life is what we are ultimately aiming at, but rather that whatever we attach absolute value to and call a virtue or a moral requirement always makes a kind of difference to life that extends beyond the immediate occasion. Virtues and moral requirements are in their non-special character akin to the laws of logic. They run through the entire fabric of life. There has to be honour, just as there has to be logic, among thieves. And it might be said that whatever is covered by the term 'honour' here is inescapably a value. No form of human life is possible in which for instance truthfulness would not in general be accounted a virtue. (Peter Winch, 'Nature and Convention', *Proceedings of the Aristotelian Society*, 1959–60.)

I shall call this the life-form argument. The version just sketched was so slanted as to support a qualified absolutism. But the mainstream of life-form argumentation flows in the direction of moral relativism, thus: Somebody who was so used to counting and to giving and receiving the correct change that this was second nature to him would probably find it unimaginable that there might be folk who could get along without this—folk to whom commerce was important I mean. And yet, so long as they engaged in some practice which, while it need not be counting, nevertheless fulfilled, perhaps in a truncated way, the same sort of role and had consequences analogous to those of counting, then commercial dealings among them could still flourish and even be virtually all that interested them. It could well suffice for the needs of such a people if, in place of numerals, they had say just three locutions in their language, corresponding to 'large', 'small' and 'an amount'. And if they had a conception of giving change it might bear no resemblance to what we understand by 'the right change' or 'honest change' but might rather suggest 'doing somebody down whenever one can get away with it'. Now if you should be reluctant to credit these people (as thus far described) with a sense of moral value, an enthusiast for life-form arguments will rush to correct you. For there is something on which they place a value: that they do so, and what it is they value, is shown in the way they carry on. It may not be what you or I value, but then a value is whatever the way of life makes it. Looking at the other life you may say gloomily, 'What a life!' But from the standpoint of their life the same can be said about yours. At this bedrock level we come up against an irreducible relativism. And the user of the life-form argument might comment further upon the sense of your judgement 'What a life!' by saying that you are here looking at things on which a value is placed within the other life—things which, as it seems to you, give a certain colour to that life. You are judging them, however, in terms of ideas and connections that exist and have meaning only within your own form of life. And this is necessarily to misunderstand, to misconstrue the sense of, what you are misguidedly presuming to judge.

Such is the sound that is made when a life-form argument blows its horn. The first version I gave, with its qualifiedly absolutist twist, need not be considered incompatible with what I called the main-stream version. Some relativities are less relative than others. But the possible differences between versions of the life-form argument are in any case not vital so far as I can see, because all versions boil down in the end to the position that placing an absolute value upon something—or as I should prefer to say because it fits certain cases very much better, seeing that there is an absolute value in something, or being struck by the absolute value of something—is the same as favouring it or otherwise supporting it (registering a choice, influencing someone in respect of it, and so on) against a background of arrangements composed of a nexus of natural and institutional needs. In short, the existence of the value is reduced to a matter of there being an approval and the approval is made intelligible by the background. What is illuminating here, and what makes life-form arguments attractive, is the idea that approval can be explained by reference to its surrounds. This is a notable advance on David Hume and I shall return to the respect in which it is an advance because I want to give life-form arguments all the praise they deserve. But first a word about Hume—the classical exponent of 'approval ethics' in its purest form.

Hume's position is arrived at by taking a short cut in the direction in which functionalist accounts of value carry us in any case. What I mean is this. The procedure whereby positive explanations of absolute value have most often been attempted has been, as I have said, by extrapolation from the instrumental explanations that are ordinarily given of relative goodness. In this procedure the distinction between absolute and relative gets lost; and not surprisingly, because there is a relativizing tendency in the very idea of an absolute value's being what it is in virtue of its having a function or role. Furthermore, in the goal-seeking explanation or in the role-playing explanation of absolute goodness, the instrumental concept of function is knitted together with the psychological concept of wanting. However, in order that this conceptual link with wanting should be explanatory, the wanting must be already a datum. In other words an anchoring point must be found among existing wants, and this imports into the explanation a self-centredness or social-centredness which again relativizes the value. Now in order to reach self- (or social-) centredness by a short cut, you do not need to begin by thinking of function. Instead you adopt a contemplative standpoint (which I should want to say is the right approach to absolute value so far as that goes). You also have a scientific outlook (which should have been left hanging on the door of the physics building). You then make the following observation: Good and evil do not have a nature in the way that material substances or material properties do, and there is no possible mode of enquiry analogous to a physical enquiry into what that nature may be. There is nothing at all analogous to getting a piece of the stuff on a bench and weighing it or putting it in a machine and bombarding it. Whatever might be disclosed by such methods, the difference between good and ill is not of *that* kind. Thus far the observation is correct, and this is the juncture at which Hume's short cut is taken. For his conception of a real difference is limited by a scientistic presupposition to the kind of difference that cannot here be observed. So he slides from 'no relevant difference of that sort in the objects' to 'no relevant difference in the objects'; and in order now to account for the difference between good and ill he has to withdraw his attention from the objects and turn it elsewhere. But where can he turn it other than towards the subjective? For mind and matter together exhaust the realm of the knowable: hence what cannot be discovered in the material has to be discovered in the mental, that is, within the self. Hume believed that he did discover it there in the shape of feelings, or sentiments of praise and blame. Yet these inside events, or any others that he could have discovered, were after all only further facts—facts just as flat as those outside and equally incapable of explaining an absolute value. (This point was made by Wittgenstein in the lecture from which I earlier quoted.)

One way of meeting the difficulty would be to find something non-factual in the territory that Hume had his eye on. The idea of producing a non-factuality which is at the same time not a nothing may sound Irish, but the way it has actually been done is as follows. Hume focussed attention on praising and blaming. Now praising is an act we perform and it is different from simply stating. To praise is not to describe whatever is being praised, nor is it to assert that there is some element present in the object. *A fortiori* it is not to assert that there is in it the element or property of goodness—whatever that could mean: for the point is precisely that to say that something is good is the same as to praise it. No wonder then that the *fact* of goodness proved difficult to track down: that

any fact-describing was going on at all was an illusory idea
fostered by the surface form of certain expressions. It might be
added by an advocate of this view that there are limits to what
we can intelligibly praise or go for: that generally we choose
things or commend them in so far as certain standards are
satisfied. We have *criteria*: and the question why our criteria are
what they are might be answered by a life-form argument. But
howsoever the position be developed it remains essentially
Humeian. Approval or one of its surrogates is still the heart of
the matter and the advance on Hume consists first in reclassify-
ing approval as a species of performance (whereas Hume had
classified it as a feeling) and then in backing it up with a relative
explanation.

An altogether more radical line of development beyond
Hume might appear to be opened up by the following argument. The objection to be surmounted was that all Hume
could possibly find when he turned from the valued object to
the person doing the valuing was just another tideless factual
sea. But this objection was itself a product of the very scientism by which Hume's own thinking was crippled. When
scientistic prejudice is put aside it can be seen that facts are not
all equally flat and indeed that the concept of factual flatness is
fishy altogether. It goes along with the idea that the domain of
the factual is analysable ultimately into a set of discrete units
which can in principle stand by themselves and be what they
are no matter what the rest of the territory is like. But that
there is something wrong with this idea is shown by examples
like the following from G. E. M. Anscombe, *Analysis*, 1959.
Suppose your grocer has delivered the stuff you ordered,
enclosing his bill. If that is a fact, then in the circumstances
which obtain it is a fact that you owe him payment. If in fact
you don't pay him you are behaving *badly*, and that too is a
fact. However, this last fact unlike the first can be stated only
by employing an evaluative term and in stating it you can be
said to have made an ethical judgement. Or switching to the
language of perception, it can be seen in the facts that your
behaviour was bad. To see this in the behaviour is a matter of

grasping the relation in which your action (or failure to act) stands towards its surrounds.

But I want to say that in this line of advance although the scientism, the atomism, has gone the spirit of Hume remains —transfigured. For the Humeian inner centre of personal approval has now been externalized and expanded into a syndrome of shared proceedings in which actions have their institutionally charted consequences and elicit institutionally appropriate reactions; so that chains are formed and patterns of carrying on to which sense and a sort of necessity attach. The sense and necessity are conceptual but the agents do not always conform—they do not always do as they should; somewhat as in arithmetic the outcome of a calculation in leading to a particular result is conceptually necessary but the clerk does not always do it as he should. He may fail for accidental reasons or otherwise, but anyway it is no accident that what he should do is what it is. And not altogether dissimilarly, what you should do and what it is reprehensible of you not to do after you have received your groceries, is non-accidentally what *it* is, given an appropriate background of life ways.

The argument here then is what I have called a life-form argument, and arguments of this family are powerful: so powerful that I would credit them with the capability of accounting for 90 per cent of all ethical phenomena. They can show how ethical concepts first get off the ground; they can indicate the situations in which evaluative language is taught and learned; they can help us to see in regard to a particular society why certain choices rather than others should present themselves and why it should be possible for what is called a virtue to be exercised in one particular way but not in another; they could go on to account, I should think, for every kind of customary and mediocre goodness. It might then look as if this were all the ethical could contain, whereas absolute value is something different and remains unaccounted for.

Consider for instance the life-form argument in the version which concludes that it is impossible to conceive a human life in which truthfulness would not be generally regarded as a virtue. This conclusion is soothing to the intelligence as long as you do not enquire into the concept of virtue that is being employed. But ask what concept it is—or to put the question in another way, ask what sort of truthfulness might be at issue—and immediately your attention is caught by what the argument does not do. For the argument neither claims nor implies that truthfulness must exist to the same degree and have the same significance in all societies or among all the people in a particular society. Well then, if the concern of some of them for truth be such that they would hazard all their prospects for it there is something as yet to be accounted for. For the only truth thus far explained is the sort that is told in the degree to which it supports the surrounding organization or gets you by without disrupting the existing social pattern. All that is necessary for this is a modicum of truth or something that approaches it yet keeps its distance, a conventional sort of standard truthfulness but anyway a relative truthfulness—even if it be arguable that in some society, in view of the advanced state of commerce say, the standard might have to be very precise or very subtle. I should be sceptical about 'the standard', but anyhow my point is that alongside it there could co-exist for at least some people in the society a concern with truth of an altogether different character, in which *not to falsify* became a spiritual demeanour. Where then could this spirit come from?

The possibility of anything in the way of spirituality could still be said to depend on the form of life that a man was living. However, the concept of a form of life that is brought in here would have to differ from the one previously employed. For the life-style of an individual is now in question, not that of a community, and it will not just be a question of whether the institutions to which he is related are of one sort or another but also of the manner of the relationship; not just a matter of which life-games he is playing but of how they are being played and of how the way he goes about things in one game bears upon his way of proceeding in another. This formulation of the point though is of limited help, because to speak of the way he does whatever he does and to consider it as a unity comes very close to speaking of the way he relates himself, or tries to relate himself, to the world as a whole; which is something that the game-playing image hardly fits at all.

It will indeed make an enormous difference if the other individuals whom he encounters and the institutions which shape his growth are of one sort rather than another. Hence I should agree if it were maintained as an off-shoot of the life-form argument that the concern with truth which I have contrasted with the conventional and time-serving kind has to do with the importance of specific institutions, in particular the non-utilitarian arts and the carrying on of enquiries both scientific and non-scientific. However, these institutions are susceptible to debasement. Enquiries trivialize themselves in subservience to exploitation and the arts are commuted into instruments of gratification. The more they gratify the more they falsify and they proliferate with cancerous fecundity while in this state. So it is not their popularity but the presence or absence of anything absolutely good in them and the degree of attachment people have to whatever is absolutely good in them that makes the difference. To get the hang of this spiritual possibility further connections must be made; and they must be of a sort that will swing attention back from societal considerations to the orientation of individuals, that is to say towards something that concerns each individual separately.

I think that the attainment of, or the attachment to, anything absolutely good in the non-utilitarian arts, and in other institutions, has to do with what it is to wonder at the world. If this be so, there is a connection between concern for truth and wondering at the world. And if wondering at the world is connected, as I believe it is when it has any profundity, with seeing the beauty of the world and having a respect for what is given, then truth has to do with beauty and with the cherishing of things. Also, since to wonder at the world is to wonder at a mystery, concern for truth has to do with being related to mystery. These are not the connections that I find users of the life-form argument making, though Plato made them and so did Wittgenstein in his ethics lecture. They are in a sense explanatory—and the more that can be shown about the possible modes of connection in each case the more powerfully illuminating they might become—but in the sense only that they try to hold together the different forms of, or encounters with, absolute value so that goodness might be apprehended as a unity. Why this goodness is what it is or why it should be present at all is left as the mystery it needs must be. When explanations are attempted of *this*, a movement of thought takes place of which I have offered illustrations. The positions I have rejected were rather roughly sketched, but maybe it was enough for the self-defeating principle to be discernible in them. To put it in a word, these explanations only relativize the value. And there comes a time—which for me had better be now—when one wants to say 'Let's close the whole chapter.'

In that ethics lecture of Wittgenstein, which I have meant my ethics lecture this evening to be not an exegesis of but a small tribute to, there is a passage that exactly expresses my feeling about explanations of goodness. The passage does not have to be changed much although the considerations that led up to it were in some respects very different from those I have put before you. Here is the passage with the appropriate changes put in: 'I see as it were in a flash of light, not only that no explanation I can think of would do to explain what I mean by absolute value, but that I would reject every explanation that anybody could possibly suggest, *ab initio*, on the ground of its significance.'

8

Good and Evil in Action

Nobody I think would want to deny that in order to understand what it is for actions to be good or evil it is necessary to relate them to something outside them and to consider the relation of good or evil in action to what we recognize as good or bad outside. This being so, the natural order of procedure in ethics would seem to be first to attempt a characterization of the good and bad that lies outside and then to consider the relations in which action might stand towards it. Hence the theoretical attractiveness of Utilitarian accounts. However, although these have the merit of so proceeding, it is not the fact that they have this merit which characterizes them especially as what they are, but rather the manner in which the connection between value and action is established. Take any version you like—J. S. Mill's or maybe G. E. Moore's which has been called Ideal Utilitarianism, or perhaps the theory sketched by Von Wright in his book *The Varieties of Goodness*. In each case the relationship that is reckoned to hold between actions and the good or ill lying outside them, and postulated as the relationship in virtue of which goodness and evil come to belong to actions, is the relationship of cause to effect or, when looked at from the standpoint of intention, means to result.

There is no doubt that actions can stand in causal relationships to good or evil and be judged to be terrible or the reverse on account of it or partly on account of it. Nevertheless it seems to me that Utilitarianism gives us a myopic, misleading view of the way that good and evil enter into action (a view which cannot be put right by adding a rider about the agent's morality being dependent upon motive) and that it fosters misunderstanding about our relation to good and evil more generally, misunderstanding about the ways we are related to our actions and misunderstanding about what it is for a human being to act in the world at all.

The first thing to observe about the causal view is that it puts an obstacle in the path of ascribing to actions any good or evil of their own. There is only the consequential good or evil which (by an external operation, so to say) they produce, and the actions themselves have to shine in the borrowed light of that—an idea expressed by Von Wright in his doctrine that there are various forms of goodness but moral goodness is not one of them. Moral goodness, he says, has to be accounted for in terms of some other form of the good; it is to be defined in terms of *the beneficial*, which he classes as a sub-form of utilitarian goodness (*Varieties of Goodness*, pp. 18 and 119). 'The utilitarian goodness of an individual act or of an act-category depends solely upon a causal relation to some end of action' (p. 117). Von Wright goes on to make the following 'suggestions of how the moral value of a human act may be considered a "function" of the way in which this act affects the good of various beings favourably or adversely' (p. 121):

an act is morally good, if and only if it does good to at least one being and does not do bad (harm) to any being; and an act is morally bad, if and only if it does bad (harm) to at least one being.

And then he brings in the notion of intention, offering definitions of morally good and morally bad intention and modifying his account by the observation that 'it is characteristic of the logical complications of the concepts, which we have been discussing, that the notion of a morally good or bad act is secondary to the notion of a morally good or bad intention (will) in acting, which in its turn is secondary to the notion of a good or bad, i.e. beneficial or harmful, thing' (p. 130).

Von Wright's proposal to *define* the good of action in terms of what it is outside has a certain affinity with the tendency in the philosophy of mathematics to harden up the truth that numerical expressions would not have the sense that they do within mathematics unless they also had a use outside into the idea that a number, as something mathematical, might actually be *defined* as signifying a group or class of entities, for instance Russell's class of all classes that are similar to a given class.

The draining off from actions of any good or evil of their own is connected with two other features of Utilitarianism which are themselves mutually related. The first is that, among the relationships that exist between actions and outside good or outside evil, the only one regarded by Utilitarianism as fundamental is the relationship to a good or evil that lies ahead of the action or supplies an objective that lies ahead. The second feature is that actions take on the character of instruments, or vehicles of efficacy, on account of their causal role in relation to the objective.

On the Utilitarian view, as I have said, action relates itself to good or evil by bringing about an alteration of one kind or another to something that lies in front. No adequate account is taken of actions as reactions to alterations that have already occurred or (what is not the same thing) as answers to actions already performed, as responses to evil and good encountered or received, and as modes of recognition—especially the recognizing of, or the refusal to recognize, a limit.

Examples of evil in response: responding to weakness by taking advantage; responding to another person's misfortune, physical oddity, maladroitness, feebleness, intellectual simplicity and so on by making him a butt or in any other way that resembles the pecking of birds at the weakest member of the flock; responding to misfortune or ill treatment by kicking the cat; wreaking vengeance; responding hubristically to being elevated in power; responding cantankerously to authority; responding to another's achievement by detraction, slander or other behaviour expressive of envy; exacting one's pound of flesh. And now I can give an equal number of examples of goodness in response at one stroke by asking you to consider the idea of refraining from these things, all of which somehow lend themselves to being done with ease and human natural-ness in connection with pretty well any pursuit. Refraining might figure in a Utilitarian account as the avoidance of harm or the production of harm, but hardly as demeanour with any positive goodness in it, a goodness that can be great in view of what may have gone before.

It is sometimes argued against Utilitarianism that actions and consequences can be looked at separately and that when detached from their consequences and imagined as being done on their own some actions at least can be judged to be odious as they stand. This argument has a strong *ad hominem* force because the Utilitarian view itself makes the consequences in principle detachable, but it is not what I am at present urging. On the contrary, I hold it to be a defect of Utilitarianism that it would in general permit the consequences of actions to be considered in detachment from them. Often enough it makes sense to consider the consequences separately, but more often I would say—and this applies to my examples above of action patterns which are evil as responses—that of course these things have evil consequences, or at least they do unless the agent is very lucky, and the evil consequences are internal to the nature of the actions. They may have incidental conse-quences too, or non-consequences, that are external to their nature. The distinction I am drawing here between internal and external consequences is not the distinction between consequences that are intended and consequences that are unintended. By an internal consequence I mean one that, life being what it is, is more or less bound to ensue: in the over-whelming majority of cases it does ensue and this is not an accidental matter. For example the child who has been made a butt at school and not been injured by it is, if he exists, exceptional. Instances of this type of connection are written into our language. Thus brutality brutalizes. Discourage-ment—I am thinking of what a teacher might do—discour-ages, that is, leads non-accidentally though not always to

discouragement, whereas upholding a high standard sometimes does so incidentally. And a teacher can believe himself to
be engaged in the second when all he is doing is the first. He
may also be doing it in response to something without realiz-
ing that either: for example, having had a thesis of his own at
one time rejected, he may make it almost impossible for a
pupil ever to complete one satisfactorily.

The behaviour just mentioned would be a manifestation of
wounded vanity; which brings me to a further important
feature of the patterns I have given of evil in response, namely
that generally they are expressions of something. They flow
from a certain posture. It may be a facet of the agent's character
that he should regularly take up this posture or he may have
fallen into it on an isolated occasion; but however this may be,
the relation between the action and what it is an expression of
is again, I want to say, internal. Putting this point alongside
my previous point about the internality of the consequences, I
am asserting then that in general, where there is a significance
for good or ill, agent, action and consequences are connected
together internally. For instance if a man is envious or can-
tankerous, actions with an evil shape to them do not just
happen to flow from him and they do not just happen to have
evil consequences.

In connection with Von Wright's statement that the moral,
that is, utilitarian, goodness of an act or act-category depends
on the causal relation in which it stands to some end, I have
remarked already that an action becomes on this view an
instrument: as though in principle there could have been
something else—a piece of wire there instead. Works of art
are put in a corresponding position by Utilitarian-Idealist
accounts of aesthetics which make out that the only true
bearers of aesthetic value, the only things that possess this
value in themselves, are *experiences* and that the works have it
only in a derivative sense on the strength of the experiences
they produce. If the value resided simply in the existence of the
experience then it would not matter if it were brought about
by sticking an electrode into the brain. The work of art has

here been reduced to a contingent device and it would be possible in principle to abolish all works of art without taking anything of aesthetic value away from the world. Similarly if Von Wright's view of the status of 'moral' good and evil were true then all human agents could disappear and robots take their place without diminishing by one iota the prevailing amount of 'moral' value; for the same borrowed good or borrowed evil could exist in a mechanism.

As instruments, actions are peculiarly *ad hoc*, intrinsically characterless and empty of significance. Unlike chisels and pincers they are made up and expended on the spot. I would not want to say it is never like that: think of the publicity stunts and other capers that go on in the business world when people are promoting something. However, I could not invite you to consider the special idea of human action as promotion or manipulative efficacy unless we already had some different basic idea of it. And this basic idea is not something we might build up to by starting with efficacy or starting from a source of energy that *has* efficacy, and then grafting an intention onto that. Actions do not originate in and come out of human beings in the way that sunrays originate in and are emitted by the sun. Generally speaking a human being is *in* his actions somewhat as a bird is in flight.

The flight of a bird normally has its place in one or another mode of behaviour manifested by the species or by birds in general, such as migration, nest-building, mating, rearing the young, and other things which we cannot necessarily link with a biological purpose but are just something that a particular kind of bird does, like singing in a certain way at sundown on the edge of its territory and then flying back to its nest. Very often, though not always, a bird flies in response to another bird's behaviour, to a regular terrestrial phenomenon or to an adventitious noise or movement that has no natural connection with bird-life.

Human actions too have a place normally within practices and dealings of multifarious kinds which go on in connection with institutions belonging to the form of existence that

human life is; and the respects in which the comparison between a human being in action and a bird on the wing is
illuminating could be elaborated upon—I am thinking here of
the fact that both kinds of biped, feathered and featherless, are
creatures of flesh and blood, and of matters to do with that,
particularly the capacity of both of them to feel pain and have
other sorts of sensation: it is in this connection that the issue of
the relation between action and perception enters in, and the
relation between action and perception should not I think be
regarded as a contingent one. But let me move onwards to
something about human action which is of vital importance
for the relation of a human being in action to good and evil and
which the comparison with a bird in flight leaves out. It goes
along with language and is connected with the ability to say
something in a language. I touched on it earlier when I said that
actions often are expressions of something (envy for instance).
They are expressive in more or less the same sort of way as
what a man says may be expressive of something.

Presupposed to the notion of that which is expressed in
what a man says is the notion of his saying something, as
distinct from going through the motions of saying it and also
presupposed is the notion of what it is that he is saying.
Correspondingly, though not exactly similarly, the notion of
an action's being expressive of something presupposes an idea
of what it is that the agent is doing which is distinct from the
idea of the motions he is going through or the movements his
body is making or the alterations in the environment he is
causing. What the man is saying is governed—not entirely
because for instance he may be speaking ironically, but largely
governed—by the language, that is, by the meanings that the
words he uses have in the language and the way the words are
put together; whereas there is nothing of which actions are
composed in the way that sentences are composed of words
and no structure that actions have in the way that sentences
have a structure. But just as there are differing degrees to
which a man can be present in what he says and different ways
in which he may fail or decline to put himself into what he

says, so too it is with what he does. Much of our speech is a matter of chiming in with something. And with actions similarly there is a great deal of swimming with the tide, of being caught up in activities: in fact we engage together in corporate actions in a way we do not utter communal statements or sub-statements that go to make up corporate complex statements. Still when we speak, whether it is a matter of chiming in or not, we are almost always talking *to* somebody, not manifesting vocal behaviour: speech in other words is a form of action in which we typically act towards this or that individual or in relation to certain people rather than others. And that is how it generally is with actions when they are something for good or ill. On the Utilitarian account, however, an action enters the world like a stone's being projected into a pool, creating ripples all round and causing everything in the ambience collectively to bob about. Hence the characteristic allusion to amounts and numbers—the greatest happiness, the balance of pleasure over pain, everybody to count and count as one. Von Wright speaks of doing good or harm 'to at least one being'.

I am not contending that the idea of doing good or harm by itself has less importance for ethics than Von Wright takes it to have. Rather: I am concerned to detach it from its Utilitarian surrounds and to supply other associations and further vocabulary. An exemplary instance of great evil, paradigmatic simultaneously of evil suffered and evil done, is the ruination of a life. The language of harm and harming, at least as Von Wright uses it, is too weak to accommodate this, though not so hopelessly inadequate as Mill's talk of pleasure and pain. I would speak rather of destruction and destructiveness—evil as the destruction of something given as a blessing, the spoiling of a miracle.

Also, while I objected to the Utilitarian reduction of actions to vehicles of efficacy, I think there is nevertheless illumination to be got from regarding actions as vehicles—not of efficacy but of good and evil. For actions that are good or evil, in their relation to the evil and good that lies outside them, work very often like transformers (the idea I am using here is from Simone Weil): they can be thought of as *loci* of more or less creative transformation, through which good and evil pass en route from one location to another and in which various conversions of value into value take place—one kind of evil into another, one kind of good into another, good into evil and evil into good. What comes out is sometimes in a kind of proportion to what goes in but more often not. The footballer kicks his opponent who promptly kicks him back. The company director suffers a hangover and threatens the manager who sacks the junior clerk whose mother depends on him. One kind of suffering, through the mediation of action, is transformed into another, which in turn gives rise to an action of greater ferocity, and evil accumulates as the rocket passes down the line.

The transformation that was wrought on a terrible scale by Iago was one in which the goodness located in Othello's nobility, in Desdemona's innocent beauty and their mutual love and happiness was looked at, seen as the wonder that it was, and in hatred obliterated. Sometimes the good to which strongly evil actions are destructive responses lies in something done to the agent, who bites the hand that feeds him. This was not particularly so in Iago's case, but I suppose it was an element in it. Great goodness on the other hand characteristically consists in repaying evil with good and in other creative transformations that work in the opposite sense from the evil ones—like rescuing the victim of an evil-doer or toiling in a wilderness of aridity and adversity to create a work of beauty.

I have categorized actions as creative transformations, but when they convert good into evil there is point in calling them decreative. To ruin a life no talent or prolonged hard work over a period of years is required, although a sophistical sort of art and application was brought to bear on it by Iago—spurious creativity. Man is said religiously to have been created in God's image: the creativity of goodness can be thought of as a simulacrum of the divine creation of the world and the decreativity of evil as the work of the devil that opposes this.

In my remarks about transformations, I was sketching a kind of geometry of some relations between good ..nd evil in action and the evil and good that lies outside. Nothing was implied about intentions; for example it was not implied that in the case of good actions there is the intention to benefit or intending of 'good for somebody for its own sake' which Von Wright thinks there has to be (*Varieties of Goodness*, p. 128). So far as I can see, there is no single mode of mentality or type of belief whereby agents are brought into relation with the good and evil residing in the forms of action that lie within their capability. As to the kind of mediating idea by which signally evil action may be guided, in Iago's case for example there could have been inner-life fantasies about his own psychological insight and superior power by comparison with Othello's simplicity and limitation (the ordinariness of a man with an Achilles heel). I would like to conclude by presenting an example from literature which shows one guiding idea or perspective that a man can have when his demeanour is greatly good. It shows us also the demeanour of another man who is guided by an inferior, impure version of the same idea.

Joseph Conrad's short story, *The Duel* (from *A Set of Six*) contains a remarkable portrayal of human fineness. My summary will convey nothing about Conrad's way of telling the story. It is about two cavalry officers in the Napoleonic Wars whose lives become entangled through a combination of stupidity, accident, misunderstanding and call of duty, whereby one of them, Lieut. D'Hubert, who is A.D.C. to a General, is sent to arrest the other, whose name is Feraud, for duelling with a civilian and finds himself challenged to a duel by the man of his own rank against whom he has to take action on the General's order. In this, the first of their duels, D'Hubert, who is the superior swordsman, wounds his adversary in the course of avoiding killing him. Feraud, after an interval for recuperation, issues a second challenge; much to D'Hubert's annoyance for he is an ambitious and highly professional officer—getting involved in duels is not good for his career. In their second duel D'Hubert suffers a mishap and is seriously wounded. Feraud is advised by his friends to make peace but will not quiet his enmity. D'Hubert, after he has recovered, is made a Captain. As duelling is not countenanced between officers of unequal rank, Feraud must contain himself until he also gets a promotion, whereupon he challenges D'Hubert again. Their third duel is fought to a standstill: both survive. D'Hubert is stricken by the imbecility of it all, but Feraud precipitates a further encounter, which however hardly gets going because the challenger is blinded by blood from a superficial head wound. The two officers are then posted to different theatres of war and years elapse before they find themselves together again as Colonels without regiments in the retreat from Moscow.

Both show bravery in the retreat and emerge alive. D'Hubert is made a General. It is now a habit with Feraud to blacken D'Hubert's name: '*that* man never loved the Emperor'. But soon there is a change of regime and Feraud, who also has been made a General, comes in for the attentions of the Special Commission. Twenty Bonapartist commanders who are considered politically dangerous are to be made an example of. D'Hubert, on sick-leave, learns that Feraud's name is on the list of those to be shot. He hears about this at the same time as he hears about the detestable reputation he has acquired, thanks to Feraud, for being an intriguing dandy who never loved the Emperor. For the first time in his life he does resort to intrigue and with a man for whom he has particular distaste—Fouché, the artisan of the Second Restoration. He tells Fouché that Feraud is not dangerous; but he is hardly able to give any account, either to Fouché or to himself, of the reason why it is important to him to get Feraud's name off the list. He just says that, 'There is between us an intimate connection of a nature which makes it a point of honour with me to try . . .' His request is granted. 'I have nearly died there,' D'Hubert says afterwards, '. . . of nausea.'

So the uncomprehending Feraud carries on with his life as an unemployed officer, haunting the streets of a small town where people raise their hats to him as he passes by. 'That's poor General Feraud. His heart is broken. Behold how he loved the Emperor.' Sitting in a café one day he explodes with curses at the news that D'Hubert has been offered a command. 'There's a pomaded, curled staff-officer,' he says, looking round the faces, 'darling of . . . the marshalls who sold their father for a handful of English gold. He will find out presently that I am alive yet.' So he sends his seconds to D'Hubert, who has just got engaged to be married. The ensuing duel, their last, is fought with pistols in a wood through which the adversaries stalk each other. The outcome is that for a third time D'Hubert finds himself with the power of life or death over Feraud; and this time he is determined to ensure that there shall be no more inroads into his life from that quarter. Of what Conrad has D'Hubert do for a solution, after he has restrained the anger that would have killed Feraud and also 'recoiled from humiliating by a show of generosity this unreasonable being', I shall say only that the justice meted to Feraud has an elevated kind of artistry about it, in keeping with D'Hubert's nature, and the effect of it is that Feraud is bound over on his word of honour. Later D'Hubert writes to him, offering friendship and proposing that the slate be wiped clean. But Feraud remains as unopen to reconciliation as ever and the story ends with D'Hubert's sending him secret payments of money because he has lost his pension.

Von Wright's account of the relation between agent, action and value would require us to suppose that when D'Hubert did what he did for Feraud at the end, and when he saved him from being shot earlier, an intention to benefit or to do 'good for its own sake' must have been there—*must* have been because a psychological attribution of this sort is, on his account, theoretically necessary in order to get goodness into any relation with an agent (in so far as the rest of the theory permits this to happen, for however firmly the agent may intend to do good for its own sake there still cannot be any goodness *in* his doings because they only become good through being causally linked to goods external to them).

Now D'Hubert of course was a benefactor to Feraud and knew it (which however is to say nothing about what was before his mind); also he acted with intent, that is, deliberately. Putting these two propositions together does not make him an intender to benefit unless a compositional fallacy is involved, and the idea that this was what he was in relation to Feraud affords no insight into his manner of behaviour, into the way his doings were guided, into the spirit of what he did.

Conrad concludes his story with a conversation between the recently wedded couple, in which D'Hubert's attitude to his last bit of dealing with Feraud is beautifully brought out. 'My dear, I had the right to blow his brains out; but as I didn't we can't let him starve.' What D'Hubert is proposing to do presents itself to him as an obligation, which—as he puts it with deprecating humour—arises out of something he failed to do before. As things have turned out he has become, or regards himself as having become, responsible for Feraud. It should be noted in this connection that, to the extent to which a man acts from compulsion, so the scope for the idea of intending a result diminishes. Because of the forward-looking element that it incorporates, Von Wright's theory is incapable of capturing the goodness that resides in the spirit of an action—a purity or highness which attaches to actions only when they are elicited as responses to situations. 'Compulsion' was the word I used a moment ago, but unlike external compulsions, this is a compulsion under which a man can act in character: indeed it can sensibly be claimed that in just such cases a man's action is most fully his.

It belongs then to D'Hubert's understanding of what he is doing that Feraud stands towards him at this stage in the relation of a dependant, somewhat as a child is for a parent; and D'Hubert can no more think of himself as acting with the intention of benefiting Feraud than a parent can think this about the feeding and clothing of his child. Conrad adds a further element: 'We must take care of him, secretly, to the end of his days. Don't I owe him the most ecstatic moment of my life? . . . Over the fields, two miles, running all the way.' The allusion is to the way the woman who then came running disclosed on that occasion her love for him. In his gratitude for the revelation D'Hubert can be glad that Feraud existed and be thankful for his attentions, so that what he is doing for Feraud now takes on the aspect of a return. But even if it did not have this aspect he would still be thinking of it as something due to Feraud from him *in honour*—and I put it in this ambivalent way deliberately: there is an obscurity that needs to be preserved as to whose exactly is the honour. The theme that holds Conrad's story together from start to finish is this idea of honour.

I have concentrated thus far on the act of generosity at the end, but the sense that D'Hubert's intervention to save Feraud from the firing squad had for him emerges equally clearly in the story. Among the ideas that surrounded this action was D'Hubert's disgust (p. 196) at what had come over his country. The thought was inescapable that Feraud's death would bring him peace, but he could not allow his peace to be purchased in this fashion. He had to avert the ignominy that would be his if he failed to preserve a life that had become closely related—and related over a matter of honour—to his own. So again we find that in Conrad's story, the space that might have been occupied by the notion of intending the beneficial has been taken up by something else—by a set of thoughts relating to the idea of that which must in all honour be done and that which cannot in all honour be done.

This honour, which in its requirements provides the orientation for all D'Hubert's dealings with Feraud, is simultaneously on the one hand D'Hubert's own honour or honourableness, and on the other hand it is the honour of, or the honour which is due to, another man. The other man could thus far be almost any other man; but it is important for the story that he happens to be a man who is in many respects like D'Hubert himself—like him in being an officer of the army and like him in being, mainly in a different way but partly also in the same way, another man of honour. Moreover, and this too is important for the story, he is someone with whom D'Hubert has become personally involved, in a manner which

again has to do with honour—in the first place with the
honour of the regiment as this is seen through D'Hubert's own
eyes, and secondly with Feraud's honour, where once more
there is an ambivalence between in this case Feraud's personal
honour (or that which is due to himself from himself so to
speak) and the passionate concern that he in particular has for
the honour of his regiment. 'Was I to let a sauerkraut-eating
civilian wipe his boots on the uniform of the 7th Hussars?'
D'Hubert warmed to the sentiment as coming from a man
after his own heart; but because D'Hubert had been less than
tactful in the way he had communicated the General's order,
Feraud was seized with the notion that honour had to be
vindicated in a duel. From these origins, the affair grew into a
cause celèbre as the result of a perverse escalation in Feraud's
sense of what honour required. But a condition of its being
kept alive was the way that honour entered into D'Hubert's
thinking also.

With Feraud, honour becomes an obsession. And self-
deception enters as the sense of honour ceases to take its proper
objects and turns into something else. Feraud goes on challenging D'Hubert as though it were a simple matter of honour, but after a certain point it becomes clear (to the observer)
that honour can never be satisfied—like desire when it turns
into addiction. It is as though there is something, not so much
in the circumstances as in his own character, that Feraud
cannot rise above; so he creates for himself the substitute task
of trying to rise above D'Hubert, hoping somehow to show
him to be the worse man but not succeeding, envying his
goodness while disclaiming knowledge of it. The man whose
character can be seen deteriorating is still someone whose
word is his bond, whose bravery is outstanding and who keeps
unswervingly to old loyalties. Though tarnished with corrup-
tion Feraud's sense of honour never was, and never becomes,
false all through.

In contrast with Feraud's conception of honour, which is
entangled in a vanity that increasingly distorts it, D'Hubert's is
rooted in respect rather than pride and linked with a sensibility

and generosity of spirit which enables him to continue to see in the man with whom he is dealing a dignity greater than is suggested by anything that comes out of him. In so dignifying Feraud, disproportionately to his desert, D'Hubert dignifies himself and gathers the strength, not only to remain patient under the burden of difficulty created for him by Feraud's animosity, but to decline all opportunity of gaining advantage from his attacker's faults and misfortunes. He behaves as though the feud were anything but a sordid thing, as though the circumstances were altogether finer than they are. Though it does not go equally deep, the concern of both of these men with honour is equally intense. Feraud cannot very well see this because of the inclination to locate all the honour within himself. D'Hubert can see it because for him honour is something that has an independent existence. Such a conception allows no separation off into distinct categories of two sorts of good, *allotrion agathon* (the good that serves others) on the one hand and self-beneficial good on the other—categories which, when once they have been dissociated, can never be brought back into any satisfactory relationship with each other.

9

Absolute Ethics, Mathematics and the Impossibility of Politics

The idea of absolute goodness and the idea of an absolute requirement tend nowadays to be viewed with suspicion in the world of English-speaking philosophy. The tendency is well rooted and has not just arisen by osmosis from the temper of the times. There are various lines of thought, all of them attractive, by which a recent or contemporary academic practitioner of the subject could have been induced into scepticism about an ethics of absolute conceptions.

For one thing, the use in an absolute sense of 'good' and 'must' presents a problem at the level of linguistic machinery; and many will have had a philosophical training that disposes them to turn for a solution[1] to what is called the performative element in discourse, to the dictionary's reminder that 'good' is the most general adjective of commendation, to a distinction between two types of meaning ('prescriptive' and 'descriptive') and an account of the possible modes of relation between them when they are simultaneously present. A likely outcome of such considerations will be the verdict that the idea of the reality of absolute value is a shadow cast by two factors which in combination do constitute the criteria of the ethical, namely prescriptiveness and universalizability. Or the opponent of absolute ethics may have found a petrol station in Popperian reflections on the distinction between a 'closed' and 'open'

[1] For an alternative possibility derived from Wittgenstein see Cora Diamond: 'Secondary Sense', *Proceedings of the Aristotelian Society*, 1967–8.

society, so that he associates absolutism with putting the clock back and the attempted stifling of freedom and egality. Or again he might have observed the extent to which Wittgenstein's later philosophy is directed towards the eradication of metaphysical 'musts' and their replacement by 'it does not have to be so', and having appreciated the force of this in other connections he might assume it to be applicable to the idea of absolute value in ethics.

Then there is a further range of possible reflections—on the nature of tabu, the genesis of historical phenomena such as the Inquisition, the psychology of obsessional neurosis, the odiousness of much that has been taken by different peoples at different times to be absolutely good or absolutely required—all of which conspire to support the theses that belief in the possibility of absolute judgements is bound up with invincible surety about his own rightness or righteousness on the part of the judger, and that the terribleness of so many of these judgements is a consequence of their 'absoluteness'.

Yet it seems to me that nothing here comes in the category of what has to be. There is the diagnosis that absolute injunctions and prohibitions are both intelligible and justified or sanctified in the context, but only in the context, of a decalogue where their prototypes have been handed down by the voice of revelation for the benefit of those brought up in the one true religion. And there is the charge that absolute judgements impart a bogus finality into discussion where the issues can only rationally be decided by reference to consequences in which there is no finality. But nothing whatever of all this, I want to say, *has to be true* of absolute judgements in ethics.

Absolute judgements are not all of the same kind and in the case of some it is possible for the subject to be trivial without the judgement's failing to be absolute on that account. But I am concerned with those in ethics which are either instances of, or else are in one way or another related to, the recognition that something is magnificent; that in some action or suffering there was pure goodness; where this recognition is not a matter of giving anyone or anything a pat on the back, least of all with the overtones of the evaluatory G.P. ('prescribing'), but where the realization is elicited or forced on the observer by that in the face of which the judgement is voiced and there is no question of degree or comparison. Such a judgement is in one sense not a judgement at all—it does not confer anything, does not assign a top grading, but is like exclaiming at a revelation. And the witness, if he speaks, speaks without appealing, somewhat as the thing itself did to him. It is not a common phenomenon like its spurious counterparts, the 'vibrations' which are rife in collective surroundings where they are transmitted by various sorts of conscious or unconscious artifice. The latter can make powerful and deranging impacts, whipping the response into a frenzy, whereas what is seen by the beholder of goodness stirs something in him deeply without giving him the feeling of being close to it.

While obviously there are those who never make judgements in the way I have described, there certainly are such judgements; that is to say there are people who do make them and who therefore believe there is something absolute although they might not express this belief in any other way. When it is a position held reflectively, I take the idea that there is such a thing as absolute goodness to signify at least a refusal to go along with reductionist accounts of the nature of absolute judgements. It does not have to signify more. But I think that nearly every holder of this position will say it does, although when he tries to indicate what else it signifies he runs into confusion or runs out of gas.

Absolute goodness *is something*, to use Plato's phraseology; and he made the point that it is not a thing among things in the world. We get an apprehension of it only by seeing the world, or some of the things that are in the world in a certain light. And while we can turn or be turned in its direction, we do not ourselves supply the light: it is, Plato said, the goodness that provides the light (*Republic* 508E–509C). His achievement in the face of the difficulty of giving expression to this vision or reading of the world is almost unique among philosophers. Maybe the dearth of others has to do with the fact that the difficulty is more than an intellectual one. But unless someone manages to give the vision expression he cannot have it strongly and it calls for expression otherwise than in words; I mean in a non-verbal as well as verbal way. The general throng of us get no more than a flickering of it.

That belief in absolutes is not the same as, and so does not have to go along with, surety that one is right in particular cases was recognized by Plato and provided for in his epistemology. In Plato's terminology, the absolutely good was a Form and in the case of anything that had this status we could aspire to understanding. Particulars on the other hand were subject to a drift which along with their manyness made it impossible for us to comprehend them fully or be cognisant of all their repercussions on each other.

Plato also recognized—it was one of his cardinal insights —that the problem of spurious semblances ran right through ethics. There is such a thing as the absolutism of the Cave. For in the cave, relative light is taken for absolute light; images are taken for reality and made the subject of a consequentialist style of (both natural and political) science. The images gyrate. There is an interest in forecasting outcomes and planning accordingly. Some people are adept at this. Getting to be adept at it is the limit of what they can achieve, and so in a way they reach their absolute—by the standards of the cave.

The monstrosities perpetrated by people in the belief that they had to can look like a powerful reason in favour of relating oneself to one's moral views as though they were akin to hypotheses subject to falsification. But I see no cogency in this or even any argument. When you learned of these monstrosities were you not utterly horrified and did you not absolutely condemn them? I doubt if absoluteness of conception opens the door to anything like as much evil as consequentialism does—at least it does not unless twisted into an eschatological shape in which it *combines with* consequentialism.

In any case, the 'liberal' inclination to find something morally amiss with the idea of an absolute attitude from fear of what it could lead to, does not retain its grip when attention is shifted from the abysmal to the wonderful—to things of staggering beauty, actions of an order of magnanimity such that no degree can be assigned to them or comparison made; save in so far as they could be contrasted with relative versions of what they manifest absolutely. Consider the difference between rendering what is due when this is conceived in terms of equilibrium or compensation and on the other hand going on giving, forgiving, turning the other cheek . . . where repaying evil with good is the only kind of repayment there is; or the difference between cupboard love, arising from need and contingent on satisfaction, and on the other hand what was expressed by Spinoza when he said: he who loves God will not expect God to love him in return. I would be surprised if someone said he were unable to see anything but power worship in Spinoza's observation or that he could not catch the hang of it at all because of difficulty in understanding the 'God' part. He need not feel particularly called upon to attach credence or sense to that part: in place of the first occurrence he could substitute 'absolutely' and for the second 'anyone or anything'.

It is remarkable how seeing the point of one absolute conception can pave the way for the introduction of others. Plato arrived at the conception of absolute being, or of an absolute being. He got there by more than one route and partly perhaps as a result of confusion. But I would not say he was confused in finding a connection between the problem of the foundation of absolute conceptions and the problem of the genesis of the world. If you speak of creation here and if you compare the idea of creation with the idea of transformation or one thing's becoming another, being made out of another within the world, then you see that creation is an instance of an absolute conception. And if you spoke of the Creator of the world you would be speaking of an absolute being. You would not be able to assert of such a being anything other than absolute predicates. It does not follow from this that there is something about absolute predicates which makes it unfitting for them to be predicated of anything other than absolute beings. I do not think it possible to argue directly from the existence of absolute predicates to the existence of any absolute being if only because absolute predicates can be intelligibly predicated of relative subjects, as when in certain ethical judgements, they are of human beings or the actions of human beings. Yet the inclination to make this connection is not stupid and when absolute qualities are attributed to human beings it is natural already to introduce the idea of 'that which is eternal in a human being' and to associate the absolute quality with that, namely with the soul. The idea of eternal or absolute being can encourage a type of speculation I am disposed to dismiss as pseudo-scientific. Nevertheless there is profundity in these games with absolute conceptions: I am not sure how far we can significantly proceed with them but I do want to assert that in the absence of absolute conceptions there can be nothing profound in ethics.

If, by way of offering a reason for not entertaining absolute conceptions, someone were to suggest that the problem of false semblances in ethics is exacerbated or indeed in its most intractable aspects created by their presence, my reply would be that in a sense this is perfectly true, but by declining to attach sense to absolute conceptions you would not get yourself out of that problem; you would still be in trouble through it although you might not know it. Here there is light to be got by turning to Plato again and considering aspects of the relationship he believed to exist between ethics and mathematics.

In the course of a dialogue concerning the problem of false semblances Plato remarked, to people whom he charged with self-deception, 'You neglect geometry' (*Gorgias* 508A). He was addressing those who did not see goodness as distinct: in particular they did not see it as something distinct from pleasure. Equally they did not see goodness as independent of the will and antithetical to assertion of the self. They were engaged in the pursuit of more (*pleonexia*), and not necessarily for themselves alone—perhaps this was so in the conversation to which I am alluding, but Plato was mindful of the variant in which they want more for the generality and so put themselves at the service of the social. He was not recommending mastership of a specialized study but inviting them to attend to certain general features of geometry in the way that one should attend to general features of things in philosophy.

They would find in geometry something with an unchanging nature of its own over and against theirs, which put demands on them rather than being amenable to any they might try to place on it. They would see the power and scope of geometry and marvel at the beauty of its unfolding. Reflecting on the nature of this power they would see that while it had to do with the order of the cosmos it was *a power without force*; that all the possibilities in geometry were possibilities within limits—indeed that they were possibilities arising out of limits. They would see that the limit of each component line depended on where it was placed.

In geometry there was a type of equality that had nothing to do with quantity; thus for instance the equilaterality of a triangle has consequences for that triangle no matter how large or small it may be. And in any case a line was not to be considered as an aggregate of units: the discovery of incommensurables had put paid to that. Yet these lines could stand in a relationship of fellowship or kinship (*koinōnia*) to other lines with which they were not commensurable: they could do this although there was no common denominator. In fact the whole of geometry could be viewed as a study of *koinōnia*—of the higher possibilities within limits open to men as they try to live together.

The plane is the limit of the solid; it is not that to which three dimensions are reducible. In the solid there is a necessary plurality of planes. Life too is a composition on many planes.

Geometry supplies the model for an ethics which when set alongside the ethics of advantage, can be seen to have an incomparably greater profundity and power. Of such a kind would be the ideal power and control over life which we cannot achieve but of which exercising all the material power at our disposal (which we do not achieve either) is the spurious semblance. The former would be an absolute and the latter is a relative power.

What gives to the problem of spurious semblances its depth is the fact that in many circumstances the relative presents itself as indistinguishable from the absolute. When the pursuer of advantage is fighting his way up it is obvious that his power is only relative and we should not think of calling it anything else however vigorous he may be. But once he has got to the top and become a dictator, his power is 'absolute' (we call it that because we no longer see any relativity in it). He has absolute power in the state. And in this connection Plato's comparison between the state and the soul is instructive. In the soul, there is a demand of the ego which to all appearances may be indistinguishable from a requirement of absolute value: it presents itself with the same absoluteness once the ego has got on top. The complete egoist then is a man of 'absolute conceptions'. In this way the problem of false semblances makes an inroad into the nature and style of absolute conceptions. However, the help that geometry can give keeps pace. Considerations such as I have mentioned, relating both to what is so *within* geometry and to the attitude called for *by* geometry, can together supply criteria.

Turning now to the bearing of the connection between ethics and mathematics upon the impossibility of politics, I have a confession to make. When I first used to read Plato (and it was mainly the *Republic* we studied) it seemed to me that his running mathematical concepts and ethical concepts together and according them such closely parallel treatment in the Theory of Forms was attributable to a constellation of misunderstandings—Socratic prejudice about the nature of definition (or in other words the treatment of all concepts as closed), the 'Fido'—Fido fallacy as Ryle used to call it (or in other words the treatment of all words that look like names as names), the assimilation of the logical grammar of 'know' to that of 'see', misapprehension suggested by the substantival use in Greek of the definite article plus neuter case of an adjective, and so on. How, I wondered, otherwise than as a result of confusions such as these, could Plato have come to entertain the peculiar idea that ethics and mathematics might have much to do with each other? I wonder now at my obtuseness, for it is not as though there is only one kind of ethics, nor is there only one kind of mathematics; and it takes but a moment's reflection to realize that the most popular and readily digestible of all ethical theories in existence is one that requires mathematical terms for its expression: greatest happiness *of the greatest number* . . . everybody to *count as 1*. So I had had no reason to think that Plato's recourse to something in mathematics when he wanted to expound the ethical was the result of any of those confusions even if he did commit them. What I should have been attending to was the type of mathematics with which his ethics was associated and to the difference between that type of mathematics and the type which entered into the other sort of ethics.

Utilitarianism belongs to the family of ethical positions that Plato opposed (you will recall my reference to the consequentialism of the cave). In the dialogue in which he alludes to the power of geometry, Plato says it is better to suffer evil than to do it. In this fundamental ethical proposition it is the sense of 'better' that he believes geometry might help us to understand. When you see that in doing such-and-such a thing you will be harming someone you are brought up against a limit. Evil is the unlimited range of points lying outside the circle of action drawn by the geometry of goodness. But here there is no question of numbers, of counting. For a Utilitarian on the other hand there is, and the agent counts himself as one for a start. So what sense is he going to make of Plato's proposition? He cannot use the term 'better' as Plato does in an absolute sense, and when the relative sense is substituted the proposition ceases to be necessarily true. It makes a difference whether those who are going to be harmed are one or many (if many, how many?) and a further difference if effects (whether direct or indirect) outweigh the harm. Suppose there were no further effects and only one person were harmed and the harm to him were less than that which would come to the agent if the agent were to refrain from doing the harm. In that case Plato's proposition would be judged false, though this is a misleading way of putting the matter: it ceased at once to be Plato's proposition when it began to be judged from the Utilitarian standpoint.

The difference between these two kinds of ethics is accentuated by the fact that the association of consequentialism with arithmetic, that is to say with numbers, is one that characteristically brings in *large* numbers. On Plato's geometrical view, the limits to what you can do include limits that depend on where you are placed, and there are both limits and facilities that arise from special relationships in which you might or might not stand towards other people in the picture. On the consequentialist view, all is facility so to speak, because your lines of possible action extend without interruption into every corner of the globe, affecting people you do not see and have no knowledge of. The sense of place drops out when you try to tot up the balance of good and evil as this stands over the world. Consider the proposition that there are 10^{18} turps of evil—I borrow this unit of evil, the 'turp', and the proposition containing it, from Alvin Plantinga's *God, Freedom and Evil* (p. 63): he introduces it just to help along a discussion—but anyway suppose, if you think you can, that there are in the world ten to the eighteenth turps of evil. With this amount around and a scheme for reducing it to ten to the ninth you do not hesitate to throw in ten cubed of your own. So those who stand in your way can be shot if there is no more room in the mental hospitals.

Arithmetic is the mathematics of consequentialism and consequentialism is the ethics of politics. I would put the point more strongly and say that politics, particularly in the modern sense of large-scale administration, is the perfection (*Die Perfektion*) of consequentialist ethics. Consider this in relation to the factors of power and compromise.

From among the various aspects of the connection between

politics and power take the simple fact that an individual in politics has to have power if he is to do anything significant. But then this is exactly the theoretical position in any context of an individual who tries to approach the ideal of doing what is morally right according to the Utilitarian conception. His lines of possible action extend ideally to the limits of society as I said before; and now I am adding the further point that in order to make them actually do so—or rather, in order that his doings should even remotely square with the ethical theory, he needs power; and the power he needs is a substantial power over affairs, the power to effect social changes.

Again, in politics you must compromise, and often this has to do with the balance of power. Among the many aspects of the relation between politics and compromise, the significant one for ethics is that you have to compromise with evil. You come to agreement with it, make concessions to it for example in striking bargains with evil powers; but I am concerned with the fact that you cannot avoid doing evil yourself. The customary ways of alluding to this, or describing the transactions that involve it, disguise the fact while testifying to the inevitability. Evil-doing in politics is called taking whatever steps are necessary to safeguard P or make the world safe for Q where P and Q are things that people would agree to be worth making sacrifices for. But compromise with evil has its roots in consequentialist ethics, and politics only provides the natural setting for its full fruition. For consequentialism is an ethics that sanctions the doing of evil: it lets in propositions like 'This is an evil thing to do but I am justified' and 'It is evil but I must do it'.

Plato would have regarded these as crooked propositions: 'It is evil but I must do it' means 'I must not do it but I must do it', which is a contradiction. And of course the consequentialist would hardly assert the first proposition *sans phrase* (the second he would not assert at all). He always tacks another proposition on with the aid of a connective thus: 'It is evil but I must do it in order that so-and-so'; and attention is shifted to the further proposition. Still that does not get round the contradiction: it does not even seem to make it disappear, though there are conceptual devices which can help in this direction—for example the use of the expression '*prima facie* obligation'.

The contradiction never does disappear and the Platonist too will add a rider to the original proposition—but only after negating and indeed reversing the second 'must', thus 'It is evil (which means I must not do it) and so I must not do it however great and real the benefit that was to accrue.' The moral geometry which puts the doing of evil outside the agent's limit, while providing him with infinite space in which to suffer when others do it, puts a limitation also on the good that he can achieve. Much that would otherwise have been possible, especially the most spectacular, world-historical part of it, has to be forgone; and this too is at the cost of suffering—his own and other people's.

Absolute ethics is the ethics of forgoing, and politics belongs for over-determined reasons to the pursuits that have to be forgone.

The objection many people will raise against this position is that by retreating from politics you leave the way clear for usurpers within or aggressors from outside. These are consequentialist considerations but they will not be ignored by the Absolutist on that account (it is from his point of view especially that consequences have to be faced) and they are bound up in any case with considerations of an absolute kind. For you do not start with a clean sheet: there will already be commitments, to preserve institutions and to look after individuals, and since you cannot do this if you retreat, what is being contemplated puts you in a dilemma. If you find yourself obliged to abdicate you are involved in a moral contradiction.

Plato pressed the analogy with geometry to the point of thinking it might be possible in principle for an ethics of absolute conceptions to be so worked out as to form a system that would be free from contradiction. He recognized that for this you would have to start with a clean sheet—as with his *Republic* where there is no possibility of any transition to it, no possibility of any existing state's becoming it, but only of various stages of deterioration. And I suppose that since the rulers of the Ideal Republic would have nothing to achieve, because it was already there, and no consequences to consider because they would make no changes for there to be consequences of, they could operate at that limit of politics which is also non-politics and hence have an absolute ethics. Their absolute ethics would not require them to withdraw from politics because of the political vacuity of the kind of ruling they were doing.

But in the world, absolute ethics by requiring withdrawal from politics creates a dilemma, and in general it creates dilemmas that otherwise might not be deemed to arise. Moreover, whether or not the dilemmas would be such from an alternative standpoint, the difficulty they present is exacerbated by the kind of consistency that an absolute ethics demands, to the point of seeming to render the agent's position completely hopeless; whereas the consequentialist invariably hopes to bring about something. Consider the following example from Professor Bernard Williams:

A visitor arrives at a South American town to find a firing squad about to shoot twenty Indians as a reprisal for acts of protest against the government. The captain of the militia offers the visitor a 'guest's privilege' of shooting one Indian on the understanding that if he does so the rest will be set free, but if he does not, all twenty will be shot. There is no chance of the visitor's overwhelming the captain by force, so what should he do? Utilitarianism answers that he ought to kill the Indian. And Williams comments on the fact that Utilitarianism not only gives this answer but gives it as the obvious answer: he does not find it obvious himself.

The visitor is (it can be taken for granted) very much concerned and engaged; he is well-intentioned and courageous; he wants with all his heart to do the best he can. Does that mean he could go either way, could agree to shoot the Indian or decline, and be as good a person as it is possible to conceive? No: I want to put it to you that there is something which if it

were to be written into the example as a piece of information
about the visitor—a categorization of the sort of man he
was—would make his position clear, or clear at any rate in the
respect that is vital for the present discussion. There are or
there have been in human history people, very few admittedly,
of such marvellous goodness that they have been regarded as
saints. And you cannot imagine a saint shooting that Indian.
Nor is it imaginable that a saint would do nothing either; for
the man I am calling a saint would face the consequences and
engage in the suffering in a way that is different from the way
an ordinary man would, and his presence would not be without its impact on the outcome. It goes against the grain to try
to predict what such a man might say and do. But then we
have already been stifling our sense of the repellant in contemplating Williams' example at all and I do not believe I say this
out of squeamishness. In order to proceed further I have to
quote the heart of it again, this time using Williams' words:

'. . . since Jim is an honoured visitor from another land, the captain is
happy to offer him a guest's privilege of killing one of the Indians
himself. If Jim accepts, then as a special mark of the occasion, the
other Indians will be let off. Of course, if Jim refuses, then there is no
special occasion, and Pedro here will do what he was about to
do . . .' (Williams in Smart and Williams: *Utilitarianism For and
Against*, p. 98).

What is the meaning of this bland tone? Who is this captain?
What is this alleged *honouring* of the visitor with the *happy* idea
of such a *privilege* as is spoken of? I do not think we should take
the dressing in our stride so to speak for the sake of the
example. Rather we should consider the role it plays, which is
that of providing a 'plausible' background—though I have to
put the word 'plausible' in quotes because I do not find much
plausibility in the example myself—against which a man
might straightforwardly and naturally say (might utter the
threat): 'either you kill this one man or I shall kill twenty'. In
fact the idea of the 'honoured guest's privilege' takes the place
of what we call at home the motive for the blackmail; but it

does so in a way that makes the association with blackmail seem irrelevant, and in this way it provides the framework from within which the vistor's predicament is represented. Whether he is going to do what the captain invites him to do is then the question—though to say this makes it look as if we knew exactly what the question was and how we were to take it.

At the time when I began thinking about this example the Government of Southern Ireland was facing the question whether to do what the kidnappers of Dr Herrema had invited them to do, that is, release three murderous prisoners from the jail in which they were lawfully held. If the prisoners were not released, the kidnappers said they would kill Dr Herrema within 48 hours. One of the techniques which police employ in such cases is to consider the situation from the standpoint of the blackmailers' ideas and try to maintain a dialogue with them. What the Irish Government to its credit did not do was consider the nature of the problem and try to formulate its own ethical position from the standpoint of the ideas and terminology of those who had presented it with the problem.

Williams' example is fanciful (I do not suggest he thought it anything else), and that point *simpliciter* I would further emphasize because speculation about what in particular some essay of the imagination might be doing within a fanciful example could draw us away from what I think is the source of the sense of outrage at being asked to contemplate this example and other examples of a similar kind ('Either you torture the child or I will blow up the world'). The sort of make-believe involved is different from that which occurs when a playwright of the stature to do it shows us something from which we can learn. When Shakespeare for example presents characters imaginatively in their entanglements with evil, our sense of the reality of our own relationship to both evil and good is heightened, whereas here we are drawn into an exercise of fancy about just that relationship. It is a kind of temptation: that is what the revulsion is about.

To return to the rider which I asked you to consider being

written into Williams' example, namely that the visitor might conceivably turn out to be a saint: although it goes against the grain to try to suggest what a saint in such a circumstance might say or do, I suppose that maybe he would manage somehow to take the place of the one Indian; or if he could not get himself shot instead of him, perhaps he would make sure that he was shot along with him or else as the first of the twenty. That is if the Captain had not thus far been given pause, for there is what a saint might say to be thought of as well as what he might do, and being spoken to by a saint would not be like being spoken to by an ordinary person; so perhaps it would not then be so much a matter of what the Captain might or might not do, as what the men in his company were prepared to do, and what the bystanders might be moved to do, after having seen and heard a saint.

However, predicting goes against the grain in all this, as I said. And the reason is not that it is in the present case an exercise of fancy—real predicting would be worse—but that to entertain predictive notions is to be involved in thoughts about consequences; whereas in the case of the difference, the impact I called it, that a saint would make, none of those affected would any more than the saint himself have thoughts of the consequences.

Jonathan Glover, who has discussed Williams' example in an Aristotelian Society Symposium (1975), believes, as Williams himself appeared to do, that what is central to people's resistance to consequentialist morality is a concern for personal integrity (p. 184). Glover redescribes this as 'a possessive attitude to one's own virtue' (p. 186)—a diagnosis which would represent someone who differed from the consequentialist, in that he found it absolutely impossible to shoot the Indian, as just some other kind of consequentialist (one who counted his own property highly): if he were to shoot the Indian his personal integrity would be shattered. There are men who might have that thought, but this is another of those things that do not have to be so. Could you imagine a saint's thinking about his personal integrity? Any more than you could imagine a saint's thinking about the problem as the straightforward consequentialist would?

As a matter of fact I find it hard to imagine a saint's having any theoretical ethics whatever: at least if he had one I do not suppose it would contribute to his saintliness. On the other hand if he did have one, it is clear that it would have to be an ethics of absolute conceptions. I brought in the idea of the saint because for all the difference between them there is this significant point of contact between the position of a saint and the position of an ordinary person who has absolute conceptions if he is true to them. Neither could shoot the Indian. The impossibility here is the impossibility of politics.

10
Suicide

I am concerned with the subject as an ethico-religious problem. Is suicide all right or isn't it; and if it isn't, why not?

The question should not be assumed to be susceptible of an answer in the way the question whether arsenic is poisonous is susceptible of an answer (which would be *the* answer to the question). Moreover in the case of arsenic the question what it is, and the question whether it is poisonous, are separable questions: you can know that arsenic is poisonous without having analysed its nature. But to know or believe that suicide is objectionable *is* to have analysed its nature or construed its significance in one way rather than another. So let us not ask at the outset whether suicide is objectionable as though we already knew perfectly well what it was (which we don't), but let us rather approach the problem by asking what it might *mean* to commit suicide—or simply, What *is* suicide? I do not think it is just one thing and I do not expect to get very far with the question.

Durkheim, whose book on suicide is one of the classics of sociology, seems to me not to have understood what suicide is. He believed that in order to avoid being prejudiced the enquirer into human behaviour should never go by what people think ('the confused impressions of the crowd') but should make comparisons and look for the common properties of actions as a botanist or zoologist distinguished objective common properties among flowers and fruits, fish and insects (*Suicide*, trans. Spaulding and Simpson, London, 1952, pp.

41–2). Durkheim thought it a condition of the possibility of investigation that systems of human behaviour should be capable of being identified and classified as one thing or another quite independently of any reference to the agents' ideas. And since intentions involve ideas, he declined to allow that the question whether a man was a suicide could be settled in the negative by the discovery that he did not intend to take his life:

. . . if the intention of self-destruction alone constituted suicide, the name suicide could not be given to facts which, despite apparent differences, are fundamentally identical with those always called suicide and which could not be otherwise described without discarding the term. The soldier facing certain death to save his regiment does not wish to die, and yet is he not as much the author of his death as the manufacturer or merchant who kills himself to avoid bankruptcy? This holds true for the martyr dying for his faith, the mother sacrificing herself for her child, etc. Whether death is accepted merely as an unfortunate consequence, but inevitable given the purpose, or is actally itself sought and desired, in either case the person renounces existence, and the various methods of doing so can be only varieties of a single class (p. 43).

On this account of the matter it looks as if we have to say that a man who exposes himself to mortal danger, for whatever reason and whatever the circumstances, is exposing himself to suicide. Well, why not? Isn't it enough that the man should know what he is doing?

The common quality of all these possible forms of supreme renunciation is that the determining act is performed advisedly; that at the moment of acting the victim knows the certain result of his conduct, no matter what reason may have led him to act thus. . . . We may say then conclusively: the term *suicide is applied to all cases of death resulting directly or indirectly from a positive or negative act of the victim himself which he knows will produce this result* (p. 44).

Durkheim here ignores the problem of how the investigator, especially one who is supposed to be collecting data in the spirit of a botanist, can judge whether or not a man knows what he is doing. And in trying to make the applicability of the term 'suicide' to martyrdom turn upon this, he simply begs the question of *what* it is that the martyr is doing; for of this we are only entitled to say thus far that he goes to his death.

Though the martyr may go willingly to a death which he foresees, it is a death which has been decided upon for him first by someone else. Whether he now makes things easy or difficult for the decider is hardly to the point. He might accept the decision as justice and so in a way concur with it, assisting its implementation out of duty, as Socrates did. Socrates took the cup of hemlock and drank it, and thereby might be said strictly to have died by his own hand. Yet even this cannot make a man a suicide, given the fact that his death was not decreed by him. In the case of the mother who dies while rescuing her child from a blazing building, the death is not decided upon at all, inevitable though her action might cause it to be. Similarly with the soldier facing certain death to save his regiment, of whom Durkheim remarks that he does not wish to die. He would not necessarily be a suicide even if he did wish to die—to die well or just to die. For to wish that death might come, to hope that it will soon come, is still not to decree that one shall die. Socrates had a wish for death and thought it his business as a philosopher to 'practise dying' (*Phaedo*, 64A); but not to practise suicide, which he said should be committed by no one (*Phaedo*, 62A).

However I can imagine an objector insisting that there is a logical entailment which I have not got round between 'Socrates knowingly and deliberately drank the poison' and 'Socrates killed himself, that is, was a suicide'. One way of meeting this objection would be to accept the entailment and invoke the idea that in killing himself a man may be at the same time doing something else. Thus in killing himself by taking hemlock Socrates was also doing something else which belonged to the role of a state prisoner and formed part of the procedure for judicial execution in Athens. And the additional factor makes (so it might be said) a radical difference to the ethico-religious status of the self-slaughter. But although this has an illuminating sound the illumination is spurious because the alleged entailment between Socrates' taking of the hemlock and his committing suicide is non-existent. Taking hemlock does not, in the context of an Athenian judicial execution, amount to slaughtering oneself: in this circumstance it is no more an act of suicide than the condemned man's walk to the scaffold was in our society.

If the suggestion be that Socrates was a man bent on self-destruction to whom the advent of his execution came in handy, then that is a different matter. But I should think the innuendo impossible to account for save as a misinterpretation of the fact that Socrates did in a certain sense wish to die. Hence he was able to take the poison gladly as the fulfilment of his wish. However, anyone construing that wish as a pointer towards suicide would be taking it for something other than it was through failing to relate it to its surrounds.

Though he did not go in for theology, Socrates thought it well said that mortals are the chattels of the Gods (*Phaedo*, 62B). 'Wouldn't you be angry,' he went on, 'if one of your chattels should kill itself when you had not indicated that you wanted it to die?' Socrates, then, did not wish to die before it was time for him to die. He did not wish to run away from anything. And it certainly cannot be said of him that he wished to die because he found no sense in living. On the contrary the sense he found in living was what on the one hand made him reject suicide and on the other hand enabled him to look on death, whenever it should come, as something to be welcomed rather than feared; hence it enabled him to die courageously. To put this another way, the sense he made of death and the sense he made of life were one and the same. A man who decides to commit suicide because he sees no sense in living cannot from this point of view be said to contemplate anything sensible in regard to his situation, for his death must be just as senseless to him as his life.

In contrast with the kind of objection that Socrates had against suicide, some of the objections to be heard against it are only of an external or accidental nature. For instance one reason, and it is a moral reason, which a man contemplating suicide might give for refraining is the fact that he has a wife and children who depend on him. However this consideration would be no more a reason against suicide than it would be a reason against his walking out on them and declining to return, so we do not learn from this example whether or not the suicide itself is especially objectionable. It would be likewise with the case of an army officer who cannot pay his gambling debts, so he wants to commit suicide, for which there are precedents anyway; but then he reflects that this would be a reprehensible thing to do because if he kills himself there will be no chance of the debts ever being repaid, whereas his duty is to try to work them off. The objection would be much the same if he were inclined to go off to live in Rhodesia under an assumed name.

I once read of an officer with gambling debts who confusedly thought he had a moral reason, not against, but in favour of shooting himself. The note he left behind contained a remark to the effect that he was choosing death rather than dishonour (at the time of writing he had not yet been found out). Now that great maxim of the military ethic, 'death rather than dishonour', is exemplified by the conduct of the sentry who declines to leave his post when he could run away to safety but stays and carries out his duty although the consequence of doing so is death. Here the death and the dishonour are genuine alternatives—if he escapes the first he incurs the second, and if he embraces the first he avoids the second. But the case of the gambling officer is not like that at all. So far from being an alternative to the disgrace incurred by his inability to pay the debts, his death by suicide is rather a consequence of that disgrace. What he ends up with is both the death and the dishonour. There might or might not have been a way out of the dishonour had he stayed alive, but at least it is clear that killing himself is no way out of it. As Socrates observes, death is not an escape from everything: if it were, it would indeed be a boon to the wicked (*Phaedo*, 107C).

There are situations, though the gambling officer's is not one of them and neither is the sentry's, in which the only way of choosing death rather than dishonour would be to kill oneself—for instance if it is dishonourable to be taken captive and the only way of avoiding capture is to kill oneself. In just this situation Greek heroes fell upon their swords. However in regard to dishonour there is a distinction to be drawn between doing and suffering. The captured hero suffers dishonour in being treated as a slave: he does not in his loss of freedom *do* anything dishonourable. He would therefore have been exhorted by Socrates not to commit suicide but to accept what comes, for Socrates believed that harm befell a man through his doing evil rather than through his suffering it (*Gorgias*, 469B).

The choice before the hero on the eve of his capture is, one might say, between suicide and *indignity*. Opting for the former he chooses both nobly and rationally according to a thoroughly serious conception. For a man who is truly a hero cannot consent to live otherwise than as a hero; and above all the servile life is not open to him. Now if a Christian were to make that choice. . . . But then you see for a Christian it could not possibly be *that* choice. The status of the alternatives would not be the same although the Christian also might be described as choosing between suicide and indignity. However, in his case opting for the indignity would not be ignoble, while opting for the suicide would amount to consigning himself to damnation.

Let us now try to explore the idea of a choice between suicide and dishonour not in the sense of suffering but of doing something terrible. Compare the Greek hero with a modern spy who on his impending capture kills himself by swallowing a pill which has been supplied for use in this emergency. I am supposing that he swallows the pill not because of the possible consequences of the capture for himself but because he knows that under torture he will inevitably betray the secrets of his comrades and his country. Though I cannot imagine Socrates saying to a man in this predicament that he must not commit suicide, there is something he might have said to him earlier, namely that anyone who is concerned about his soul should beware of engaging in this sort of spying. For it is to enter into an institution the ethics of which require that in a certain eventuality you poison yourself; and the poisoning is not transformed into something other than suicide by the institutional role as it was in Socrates' own case by the role of being a condemned man in process of execution. Still, the fact that the spy's suicide is committed as an act of self-sacrifice gives it a very different flavour from the deed of the financier who does away with himself when his empire starts to totter. The financier 'can't take it'. That is also true, though on a much deeper level, of the Greek hero, who unlike the financier dies nobly. The hero commits suicide because there is something he cannot accept for himself, namely captivity. But the spy (in this particular variant out of many possible cases) is concerned solely with the good of others. Because of this one would like to deny that his is the spirit of a suicide. The difficulty is that he has supposedly entered the spying profession, which is a suicidal game, with his eyes open: he was not compelled to enter into it. But this consideration also means that his case fails to provide me with exactly the example I was looking for: I wanted an example of a completely forced choice between suicide and the doing of something morally terrible.

It might be held by a religious person that no man is ever forced to make such a choice; that it is something a good God would never inflict on a human being. But whether or not it be religiously imaginable, it is logically possible and I can depict a case where there will be no question of the agent's having voluntarily let himself in for the outcome by postulating that he suffers and knows that he suffers from a congenital form of mental instability, as a result of which he is overtaken from time to time by irresistible impulses towards something very horrible, such as raping children. Getting himself locked up is no solution, either because no one will listen to him or because no mental hospital is secure enough to contain him during one of his fits; and his fits come upon him without warning. So he decides to kill himself.

At first it may seem possible to argue that this man is not a suicide. For does he not belong to the category of those who are called upon to sacrifice their lives for the safety of others? Most often in such cases the order of events is: salvation of the imperilled followed by death of the saver, as in shipwrecks, when the men who have made possible the escape of others are trapped on board; or else the two events are concomitant, as at a grenade-throwing practice when one of the grenades is dropped and there is no time to throw it clear, whereupon an N.C.O. falls on the grenade and with his body shields the others from its effects. Either way, what the saver here decrees is another's salvation, with the unavoidable consequence of a death for himself which he does not decree. If, as with my imaginary maniac, the saver's own death has to take place first in order that the peril to others should be averted, the characterization of what is decreed can remain exactly the same as before. To put it another way, all the man really does is to preserve someone else and his death is encompassed as a consequence of this. The peculiarity of the case is that the death has to be encompassed first and is thus an instance of an effect preceding its cause.

But now I fear that the argument has overreached itself; not in positing an effect that precedes its cause, which I should accept here as a coherent conception, but in gliding over the fact that the man's death is not encompassed *for* him—he encompassed it directly himself. This is manifestly a doing and not a suffering; hence it was false to claim that 'all he really does is to preserve someone else'. That is not all, for he kills himself.

A comparable example, not this time from the imagination, is that of the explorer, Captain Oates. On the day before his death Oates had said that he could not go on and had proposed that the rest of the party should leave him in his sleeping bag. 'That we could not do' says Scott, whose account of the upshot is as follows:

He slept through the night before last, hoping not to wake; but he woke in the morning—yesterday. It was blowing a blizzard. He said, 'I am just going outside and may be some time.' He went out into the blizzard and we have not seen him since. . . . We know that poor Oates was walking to his death, but although we tried to dissuade him, we knew it was the act of a brave man and an English gentleman (*Scott's Last Expedition*, vol. i, p. 462).

What Oates decreed was that his hard-pressed companions should be relieved of an encumbrance: of this there can be little doubt. He had borne intense suffering for weeks without complaint (Scott tells us) but remained cheerful right to the end. The sentiment that he was entitled to quit, or that anyway he was going to quit, never entered into it. Accordingly I want to deny he was a suicide, as I should have liked to do in the case of the maniac. And there is a feature of Oates's case that enables me to persist in my denial beyond the point to which I could take it in the other case. For if someone objects, 'But he killed himself', in regard to the maniac there was no answer, but in Oates's case I can say, 'No; the blizzard killed him.' Had Oates taken out a revolver and shot himself I should have agreed he was a suicide.

We are back again at the distinction between doing and suffering, which here as elsewhere is fraught with difficulty. For if a man puts his head on a railway line and claims 'I'm not going to kill myself, the train will do it', I shall reject that as a sophistical absurdity; yet I do not consider it absurd to claim that the blizzard killed Oates. But then of course neither is it absurd to claim that he killed himself by going out into the blizzard. And there is much to be said for a description that is midway between the two: 'He let the blizzard kill him.' To call one of these descriptions the right one is to say little more than 'That's how I look at it.'

Still I do not look at it arbitrarily when I say that Oates was killed by the blizzard. The indirectness of what he did in relation to the onset of his death and the entrance of time as a factor are features of the case which help to put it for me in this perspective. Yet do not time and a certain indirectness enter in as factors when a man puts his head on a railway line? They enter in, but not to the same effect because of the difference in the spirit and in the surroundings of what is done. That the blizzard is a natural phenomenon is something that makes a difference. To be sure, a man who out of sorrow drowns himself might also perhaps be said to expose himself to a natural phenomenon, but again the context and the spirit of it are different. Oates simply walks away from his companions—and in the act of doing so becomes exposed to the blizzard: he needs to put distance between himself and them and he cannot do so in any other way. He is concerned only with their relief. And he is well on the way towards death already. Such are the features of the case which in combination make it possible, though not obligatory, to say of him unsophistically what would naturally be said of a martyr, namely that he goes to his death.

The great divide among attitudes towards suicide lies between those in whose eyes this possibility is of special significance and those to whom it would not matter whether a man like Oates were held to be no suicide, or a suicide but an honourable one. The former are upholders of a religious ethics and I should call them that even though they might entertain no theological beliefs and never even mention a deity: the latter I should call humanists.

I am not suggesting that from the standpoint of an ethics untinged with religion it would have been exactly the same if Oates had shot himself. For it would have been ugly, unpleasant and messy, and hence a course to be rejected out of fastidiousness or consideration for the feelings of his companions. From the religiously ethical standpoint, however, the rejection of that course would be bound up with ideas of a different kind, about a man's relation to his life and destiny, or in other words about the soul.

Schopenhauer remarked that if there are any moral arguments against suicide they lie very deep and are not touched by ordinary ethics. An ordinary ethics is for instance one in which the idea of prudence looms large, as it did for Aristotle, or which speaks, as Kant did, about the duty of self-preservation. Schopenhauer saw something vulgar in the idea of duties to oneself no matter what were deemed to be their foundation. But Kant spoke in a different vein when he called suicide the extreme point along the line of *crimina carnis* and when he drew attention to the element of disdain for the world in Stoicism ('leave the world as you might leave a smoky room'). Both of these latter considerations of Kant connect with the point which Schopenhauer took to be central about suicide, namely that it is a phenomenon of strong assertion of will (*World as Will and Idea*, § 69). The real reason why suicide must be condemned, Schopenhauer said, had to do with self-conquest. In this idea he was at one with Socrates and not far distant from the Christian religion. A Christian perhaps might speak, not so much of conquering, but rather of dying to the self, and the most spiritual expression of the idea for him would be in prayer—particularly in such a prayer as 'Thy will, not mine, be done'.

The sanctity of life is an idea that a religious person might want to introduce in connection with suicide, but if he left the matter there he would be representing suicide as objectionable in the same way and to the same degree as murder. It is only when he thinks of life as a gift that the difference starts to emerge. For the murderer does not destroy a gift that was given *to him*; he destroys something which was given to someone else but which happens to have got in his way. This argues his crime to be from the standpoint of ordinary ethics worse than that of the suicide, of whom at least it may be said that it was his own affair. On the other hand the suicide, unlike the murderer, is—religiously speaking—necessarily an ingrate; and the ingratitude here is of no ordinary kind, for it is towards his Creator, the giver of life, to whom everything is owed. That the destruction of a life should at the same time be the act of extreme ingratitude towards the giver of a life accounts for the special horror attaching to parricide, against which there is something like the same religious feeling as there is against suicide: as if these were two different ways of getting as close as possible to deicide. Or perhaps rather it is parricide which symbolizes the destruction of God and suicide the destruction of the universe. Thus G. K. Chesterton: 'The man who kills a man, kills a man. The man who kills himself, kills all men; as far as he is concerned he wipes out the world' (*Orthodoxy: The Flag of the World*). Chesterton took himself there to be expressing the spirit of *all* suicides and in that he was mistaken. But there is no doubt that when a substitute for the end of the world is called for, suicide is the only possible one:

Dressed in flowing white robes, 26 people sat tense and silent in an upper room of a London house. Leader of the strange group was middle-aged solicitor Peter Shanning. He had given up practising law after experiencing what he called 'an amazing series of dreams'. He claimed it had been revealed to him that the world would come to an end on July 23rd, 1887, at 3 p.m. Shanning spent five years travelling the country and preaching. He gained 25 believers and they bought a house in north London. On the fatal day, they were gathered in a room, watching the clock ticking towards 3 p.m. Shanning sat quietly praying. Three o'clock came—and went. It wasn't the end of the world. But it was the end of Shanning. After his followers had left in bewilderment, he shot himself dead. (From a feature in a popular weekly paper.)

The fact that there is about suicide a kind of terribleness that ordinary, that is, non-religious, ethics fails to touch is a weakness in ordinary ethics not only from the standpoint of religion but from the standpoint of philosophy. However, there is from the standpoint of philosophy a weakness to be discerned in the religious conception of suicide also. For according to the religious conception, all suicides are (unless their minds are unsound) guilty of an identical offence and separated from non-suicides by the same gulf; so that it does not really matter what kind of a suicide a man is so long as he is one.

Now this principle of equal disvalue, as it might be called, is manifestly objectionable to the non-religious conscience, which will either wish to remain silent in the face of suicide or else will wish to attribute to it an enormous range of disvalue, and also sometimes value, in a gamut that resists compression and runs from the squalid and mindless suicides of playboys or film starlets through the pitiful suicides of the oppressed and rejected, the anguished and maddened suicides of those goaded beyond endurance, the Stoic suicides and the heroic suicides, and thence to the self-sacrificial suicides, terminating with cases that religion would doubtless not classify as suicide at all. Ordinary ethics, however, will see no point in any alternative classification because it can descry variety in suicide where religion neglects it. And in this discrimination philosophy must side with ordinary ethics. For philosophy is a distinction-drawing business which emphasizes differences and focuses the mind on variant possibilities.

Consider for just a moment some of the alternative possibilities inherent in the case of the gambling officer I mentioned earlier, who thought he was choosing death rather than dishonour. The point was then that suicide could not be the kind of escape he thought it was. But suppose he realized that there were no possibility of escape from the dishonour anyway. If so, he could divide through by the dishonour and consider whether it might not be as well for him to commit suicide in order to put an end to his misery. If that were the idea, it could be objected on the one hand that the misery might pass and on the other hand that, even supposing it did not, the idea of being put out of one's misery is below human dignity and appropriate rather to dogs and horses.

However, it might not be simply a matter of his wanting to put himself out of his misery but rather that he has got himself into an impossible situation. And this is different, for it is now being supposed that the incurring of the dishonour means he can no longer carry on his life as a soldier. This possibility is closed to him, yet no other life is conceivable: soldiering *is* his life. The morality of the society, and the military ethic in particular, might well in all seriousness prescribe suicide for just this type of case.

On this interpretation, the suicide of the gambling officer has come to resemble that of an American journalist named

Wertenbaker, who developed cancer in middle age and whose
story has been told by his wife. Here too it was not, or not
simply, a question of the man's inability to stand misery, but
of his finding it impossible to carry on living as the kind of
creature he had become. A difference between the two cases is
that the officer's life, unlike the journalist's, becomes impossible as the result of something he himself did, and this consideration would be capable of affecting the outcome in more
than one way. For on the one hand the knowledge that he has
made a mess of his life through his own fault might drive a
man to suicide out of sheer self-hatred ('he could murder
himself'; and so he does). On the other hand he might be
willing to abide by the consequences of his own folly out of a
sense of equity which would not be there to sustain him if he
thought he were the victim of a cruel and arbitrary fate. Not
that Wertenbaker entertained this thought; he wrote as follows:

Problem with death is to recognize the point at which you can die
with all your faculties, take a healthy look at the world and people as
you go out of it. Let them get you in bed, drug you or cut you, and
you become sick and afraid and disgusting, and everybody will be
glad to get rid of you. It shouldn't be such a problem if you can
remember how it was when you were young. You wouldn't give up
something for instance to add ten years to your life. All right, don't
ask for them now. You wouldn't give up drinking and love-making
and eating—and why should you have given them up? Nothing is
ever lost that has been experienced and it can all be there at the
moment of death—if you don't wait too long (Lael Tucker Wertenbaker, *Death of a Man*).

What Wertenbaker saw no sense in was prolonging his life
beyond a certain point, living on as something different from
what he had been before, as a squalid pain-wracked thing, a
dying man. It cannot be said that he found life meaningless.
Rather, the meaning he found in life was such as to justify, to
give him a reason for, doing away with himself in a certain
circumstance.

In relation to the example of Wertenbaker, Chesterton's words about wiping out the world have little grip. Wertenbaker did not want to throw back the world in its creator's face—and not just because he had no belief in a creator either: if he had been offered his life over again he would have taken it gladly.

But all of it? No, not all of it: he was not prepared to accept *the whole* of the life that had been given him. Instead he despaired of it, despaired of the existence of any power to sustain him in his predicament. That he should have reviled what his life had become was understandable. The trouble was he did not love what he reviled; he had not 'this primary and supernatural loyalty to things.'

The last few words of that religiously ethical comment are Chesterton's again and they help to make clear the point of the passage I quoted before: his remark about the suicide wiping out the world might otherwise seem to be no more than a solipsistic muddle. But still I do not see how Chesterton's sentiments could be expected to influence a man like Wertenbaker, who after all had his own kind of loyalty to things.

11

Suicide as a Social Problem: Some Reflections on Durkheim

Usually when collective tendencies or passions are spoken of we tend to regard these expressions as mere metaphors and manners of speech with no real signification but a sort of average among a certain number of individual states. They are not considered as things, forces *sui generis* which dominate the consciousness of single individuals. None the less this is their nature, as is brilliantly shown by statistics of suicide (Durkheim, *Suicide*, tr. Spaulding and Simpson, London, 1952, p. 307).

Durkheim's work was being done in the 1890s. The existence of social forces as things in themselves is not now an issue; though the nature of their existence, the kind of understanding which it is possible to have of them and the ways, if any, in which they are open to be influenced or controlled are questions quite variously understood and misunderstood.

The reason offered by Durkheim for attributing a real existence to collective forces does not seem to me at all the right one.

The proof that the reality of collective tendencies is no less than that of cosmic forces is that this reality is demonstrated in the same way, by the uniformity of effects. When we find that the number of deaths varies little from year to year, we explain this regularity by saying that mortality depends on the climate, the temperature, the nature of the soil, in brief on a certain number of material forces which remain constant through changing generations because independent of individuals. Since, therefore, moral acts such as suicide are reproduced not merely with an equal but with a greater uniformity, we must likewise admit that they depend on forces external to individuals (p. 309).

Against this I would say that realization of the fact that our lives are shaped by the interplay of ideas, by the traditions and institutions of the societies into which we are born, does not have to wait upon the results of any specialized enquiry but belongs to common understanding. This understanding is something that can be evinced without being articulated, like the possession of a historical sense with which it is closely allied. The task of making it fully articulate belongs to the philosophy of culture, *alias* epistemology. Durkheim's statistical apparatus hardly comes into the category of understanding at all, but is more like a species of technique. In modern physics, for example, a considerable intervention of technique has become necessary if the work of understanding is to be furthered. But in the present case I question whether the work of understanding is really assisted by the technique.

Durkheim presented figures for the suicide rates of most European countries, and the regional variations of the rates within these countries, over a period of something like fifty years. Distributions were given according to age, sex, religion, degree of education, and so on. It was shown that in European countries the suicide rate increased generally as age increased; that suicide was an essentially male phenomenon; that less Catholics committed suicide than Protestants and less Jews than either; that suicide increased along with the degree of education. Comparisons were made between the suicide rates of widowed and non-widowed; married, single and divorced; military and civilian; those with families and those without. Again there were corresponding patterns in all countries, e.g. more suicides among the married than the unmarried, less among women with children than among women without. Seasonal and diurnal fluctuations were noted. The national and regional suicide rates were placed alongside the rates for death, homicide, insanity and alcoholism.

During the period under investigation, the suicide rate varied much more from country to country in Europe than the death rate did, but there was comparatively little fluctuation from year to year. The figures were rising slowly but steadily everywhere and Durkheim observed that in this increase the various countries were retaining their respective distances from one another. Each had 'its own peculiar coefficient of expansion', as he put it. This stability in the European suicide rates was, in Durkheim's opinion, enough by itself to justify the conclusion that:

There is, therefore, for each people a collective force of a definite amount of energy impelling men to self-destruction. . . . Each social group really has a collective inclination for the act, quite its own, and the source of all individual inclinations, rather than their result. . . . These tendencies of the whole social body, by affecting individuals, cause them to commit suicide. The private experiences usually thought to be the proximate causes of suicide have only the influence borrowed from the victim's moral predisposition, itself an echo of the moral state of society. To explain his detachment from life the individual accuses his most immediately surrounding circumstances; life is sad to him because he is sad. Of course his sadness comes to him from without in one sense, however not from one or another incident of his career but rather from the group to which he belongs. This is why there is nothing which cannot serve as an occasion for suicide. It all depends on the intensity with which suicidogenetic causes have affected the individual (pp. 299–300).

Notice that Durkheim speaks here as if suicide were the natural and expected outcome of sadness—an assumption which will not bear examination for one moment. It could as well be assumed, since sadness is intrinsic to human life, that suicide were the natural outcome of just living. Now the question that is supposed to be getting an answer is, Why do people commit suicide, i.e. why do they do it at all and why is there so much of it? Yet given the assumption about sadness,

one might have expected Durkheim rather to be asking why
there is so *little* suicide. Why do people not commit suicide
much more readily than they do? And ought he not to be
invoking some enormously potent collective *anti-suicidal* tendencies in order to account for this?

Leaving aside the point about sadness, he could have moved
straight from his data to collective anti-suicidal tendencies for
each people just as readily as he moved to the collective suicidal tendencies. The information contained in the statistics need
only be presented in the alternative form of rates for those who
do *not* commit suicide and he would have all the necessary
'proof'—rates of something like 99·9 per cent showing the
same consistency as before. And is not the case for a collective
tendency now incomparably stronger? For when a property is
possessed by 99·9 per cent of a group one regards it as typical
of that group—just such an example might be used to explain
what the word 'typical' meant: whereas if one wished to
explain what 'atypical' meant, a phenomenon affecting 0·01
per cent of a group would do very nicely.

In truth, however, neither case is the least bit strong thus far.
From the fact that a certain small proportion of Englishmen
may be steeplejacks or ventriloquists or Dadaists or flat-
earthers it does not follow that there exists any collective
tendency impelling the populace as a whole towards steeplejacking or ventriloquism or Dadaism or the belief that the
earth is flat. On the contrary it is clear (to take just the last pair
of examples) that a considerable proportion of the population
is not in any direct contact at all with ideas about the visual arts
and is *a fortiori* impervious to the attraction of a relatively
esoteric movement within them which some artists support
but many more ignore or oppose: and it is similarly clear that
the flat-earth tendency's sphere of influence stops well short of
Plumian Professors of Astronomy. These are not tendencies
which belong to the population as a whole. And this would
make it impossible to use even the form of argument which I
suggested would have much more plausibility from the purely
numerical point of view than the one Durkheim actually uses.

The fact that 99 per cent of the population were non-Dadaists or non-flat-earthers would not be evidence for the operation of any all-pervasive anti-Dadaist or anti-flat-earth tendency. The population as a whole is not touched in one way or the other. If it be otherwise with suicide, then this is something that needs to be established; but Durkheim did nothing to establish it.

Now it could be objected that I have failed to take account of the factor that Durkheim really relied on in the case of the suicide figures, namely their *stability*—the steadiness of their rising trend over a period, together with the maintenance throughout of the same relationships between country and country. Suppose then that there were a comparable stability in the case of the examples I have just mentioned: what difference would that make? For instance, steeplejacks are probably as constant in their numbers as steeples are, and quite possibly a census of steeplejacks would show each nation to have its own distinctive, stable steeplejacking rate. But whether this were so or not, the postulation of collective steeplejacking tendencies, each permeating according to its special strength the whole of the society concerned, would still be a piece of metaphysical nonsense.

The position for which I am arguing is not that there could *never* be any sense in ascribing greater or lesser suicidogenetic tendencies to whole groups or even to whole nations. The question is, under what conditions would it be sensible and where would the justification have to come from? The reason why I say it would be metaphysical nonsense to credit Englishmen *qua* Englishmen or Germans *qua* Germans with a collective steeplejacking tendency lies in the absence of any basis for connecting the idea of steeplejacking with the idea of a particular nationality. However, suppose that the group under consideration consisted of the sons of steeplejacks and we found that a certain percentage of these became steeplejacks in Germany and some different percentage in England. In this case we could (if for some reason it were found convenient) allude without confusion to a pair of collective tendencies of different strengths. For in this case there is a basis for the appropriate connection. It resides in the intelligibility of sons following in their fathers' footsteps, which itself belongs to common understanding and could not be made a whit clearer by any figures. And this holds good as a general principle. Where we are able to attribute a collective tendency to a group of people it is a species of common understanding, the understanding we have of people, that permits us to do so and where we cannot it is the same understanding, or else the lack of it, that prevents us. The most that statistical stabilities will do for us, independently of this understanding, is to afford occasions for wonder. The ascription of suicidogenetic tendencies to whole nations then can only be justified, or even made sensible I would say, by an account of national differences *and of the relevance of these to the committing of suicide*. And by national differences I mean especially differences in the tradition and way of life, differences in the beliefs that people hold, between nation and nation.

Durkheim attributed suicidogenetic tendencies to nations without having any explanation to offer in terms of national differences. Not that he supposed his postulated tendencies to stand without need of explanation; indeed the purpose of his book was precisely to explain them. But because he took it to be demonstrated by the shape of the figures alone that there is such a thing as 'the suicidal tendency with which each society is collectively inflicted', which can be referred to without considering the nature of the society, since every society must have it just by virtue of being a society—because he thought this, he was driven to regard national differences as, if not irrelevant, at least not basic in regard to his problem. The solution had to be found in something beyond them, something that must apply to all nations whatever, some characteristic of *society as such*. To be sure, he also insisted that there was a multiplicity and diversity in the particular conditions affecting the origin of individual suicides. But then this insistence only helped to confirm for him the picture of a single over-riding social element in suicide which had to be independent of the particular conditions and stronger, more important than they were, just because the suicide rate was able to remain relatively fixed in spite of their vicissitudes. In this way the picture came to be formed of a multiplicity of non-fundamental causes of suicide masking a single basic cause which had to be operative to some degree or another in every human society. And that this basic cause was necessarily present in every society meant that it must be bound up with whatever it is that makes societies societies. Durkheim accordingly put to himself the question 'What do we need in order to have a society?' and came up with the answer 'Togetherness'—an answer of beautiful simplicity, dictated entirely by the form in which he had asked the question. From this point on, the course taken by his argument may be tabulated briefly as follows.

1 Since (as has been seen) there is a suicidogenetic tendency which every society must possess just because it is a society, and since in order to have a society all we need is togetherness, therefore the suicidogenetic tendency must be a function of togetherness.

2 But the tendency must equally be related to the nature of what is on the receiving end, that is, the individual.

3 *Question:* What then do we need in order to have an individual?
   Answer: Separateness.

4 Hence the relation between an individual and society is essentially one between a togetherness and a separateness and the social element in suicide is a matter of the togetherness affecting the separateness or *vice-versa*; and if the suicidogenetic tendency is stronger in one society than it is in another, this is because the balance between togetherness and separateness is different.

5 Togetherness, or 'society', is good although it is possible, exceptionally, to have too much of it.

6 Suicide is bad, and where there is any of it at all, but especially where it is increasing, one should think, not in

terms of a balance, but of an imbalance between togetherness and separateness.
7 In regard to the suicides of modern Europe the imbalance
takes the form of a deficiency of togetherness. 'Society,
weak and disturbed, lets too many persons escape too completely from its influence' (p. 373). But there is also a kind of
suicide, for instance Suttee, of which society may approve,
and where you get this the imbalance has gone the other
way: however it is a phenomenon that belongs particularly
to lower societies.

'The salutary sentiment of solidarity' (p. 374) is what Durkheim thought we must 'reimpress' on man in order to meet the
menace of increasing suicide in contemporary societies.
(Don't ask who the 'we' are.)

. . . the only remedy for the ill is to restore enough consistency to
social groups for them to obtain a firmer grip on the individual, and
for him to feel himself bound to them. He must feel himself more
solidary with a collective existence which precedes him in time,
which survives him, and which encompasses him at all points. If this
occurs, he will no longer find the only aim of his conduct in himself,
and, understanding that he is the instrument of a purpose greater
than himself, he will see that he is not without significance. Life will
resume meaning in his eyes, because it will recover its natural aim
and orientation (pp. 373–4).

'Life', says Durkheim, 'will resume meaning.' But this
meaning which life can have and which may yet be lost—what
account is to be given of it? I should not blame anyone who
tried for failing to produce one. Durkheim did not see there
was any necessity to try. So far as the mutual solidarity goes,
could there not be as much solidarity among men in the loss of
this meaning as in the preservation of it?
A man may cease to see sense in life and commit suicide
tragically under the weight of some overwhelming disaster
and there may be no others who share his predicament or are
even in any way touched by it. But also, a man may see no

sense in living because not only the kind of life that *he* is compelled to live but the entire way of life that is going on around him has lost or is losing its sense. One can think of this latter as a tragedy overtaking a group or community. No form of society is possible in which a disaster with suicide as the outcome might not overtake a man, but I would consider suicide to be, or to involve, a social problem only when it came into the second of these two categories, whatever else it might be besides. If the sense of life becomes lost to an individual while all around him are maintaining it and are not being threatened, this is no social problem. If a whole community or section of a community starts to lose it then there is a social problem. But how should we characterize the sort of understanding which a whole community might start to lose?

What I have here to say is only very rough. But in criticizing Durkheim's attitude to his statistics at the start I referred to the understanding involved in the awareness we have of our traditions and contended that only this kind of understanding could justify the ascription of collective tendencies to groups: you can allude to the character of a nation, for example, only on the basis of this kind of understanding. And you do not have to be learned necessarily, not a *savant*, in order to have it. Any man who finds some task worthy of effort and for whom there is a sphere in which he is aware of what it is for things to be done in the way that they ought to be done must have at least the beginnings of this understanding; though whether it be possible for him to have more than a glimmering of it will depend not just on the strength of his interest but on the dignity of the task itself. Here I am imagining it to be a craft connected perhaps with agriculture where the various operations performed as a part of the craft can be seen by the worker to have their point within it, and the craft as a whole its point in regard to the maintenance of the life shared by his community.

This is not at all the same as Durkheim's conception of 'serving society', i.e. doing something for the sake of a collectivity as opposed to doing it for the sake of oneself. For it is not a matter of setting value upon association but rather of maintaining that in which people are associated, associated in a diversity of ways and by doing a diversity of things that are valuable in themselves and have their own standards of performance. In his acquaintance with the traditional standards—his initiation into the difference between the right and the wrong ways of working within his particular craft, the worker becomes conscious of a cultural endowment (though doubtless he would never think of calling it that) to be prized and guarded. Whereas a man who tries to work at a pursuit and is unable to develop a sense of its history and traditions is in the condition of an automaton. His inability to appreciate for himself whatsoever is worthwhile about the work consists in his lack of relation to it as a form of culture. He is—to put it another way—without education in respect to the work, and what he lacks is something common to all education worthy of the name.

I referred therefore to a common understanding, meaning by this an understanding which differs from *expertise* and special knowledge, the kind of understanding all forms of culture demand in common; and the recession of common understanding from the various sectors of life in which it can be exercised is what I take the diminution of life's meaning for a community essentially to be—and it is more or less the same thing as a loss of, or dissociation from, tradition.

Tradition is no less than what makes it possible for us to deal as sentient and thinking beings with our experiences, to cope with our sorrows, to limit and ennoble our joys, to understand what happens to us, to talk to one another, to relate one thing to another, to find the themes which organize experience and give it meaning, to see the relevance of one thing to another. It is of course what makes us human, and what makes us civil. It is typically and decisively the common heritage, that which men do not have to explain to each other; that which in happier days they did explain to their children; that which they can rely on as being present, each in the other's head and heart (Robert Oppenheimer, *American Council of Learned Societies Annual Lecture*, 1959, p. 4).

So far as a man's relation to his work is concerned the most serious and the most intractable problem is not the problem of the distribution of wealth, of the products of labour, but the problem of the distribution of modes of production: where this is to be understood not as a Marxian would regard it, in the sense of machines and material resources, but in the sense of creative activities—the provision and distribution of vocations:

. . . It is not special aptitude, but rather social, political, and customary reasons that determine a man's occupation. At certain times and in certain countries it is caste and heredity; at other times and in other places, the guild or corporation; in later times machinery—in almost all cases necessity; liberty scarcely ever. And the tragedy of it culminates in those occupations, pandering to evil, in which the soul is sacrificed for the sake of the livelihood, in which the workman works with the consciousness, not of the uselessness merely, but of the social perversity of his work, manufacturing the poison that will kill him, the weapon, perchance, with which his children will be murdered. This, and not the question of wages, is the gravest problem (Unamuno, *The Tragic Sense of Life*, 1912, tr. Flitch 1921, p. 271).

There is no solution to be found in canteens, rest rooms, personnel management and community centres, which leave entirely untouched the problem of the work itself: I should mention here also Durkheim's practical remedy against the menace of increasing suicide, which was the setting up of benevolent associations among workers (*Suicide*, pp. 378–83). The gravity of the problem in modern times is connected with the growth of powerful forces which have a considerable history and cannot suddenly be arrested or made innocuous by administrators, who are themselves powerless except in the service of these very forces.

12

The Miraculous

Most people think of a miracle as a violation of natural law; and a good many of those who regard the miraculous in this way incline to the idea that miracles are impossible. I shall argue that the conception of the miraculous as a violation of natural law is an inadequate conception because it is unduly restrictive, though there is also a sense in which it is not restrictive enough. To qualify for being accounted a miracle an occurrence does not have to be characterizable as a violation of natural law. However, though I do not take the conception of miracles as violations of natural law to be an adequate conception of the miraculous, I shall maintain that occurrences are conceivable in respect to which it could be said that some law or laws of nature had been violated—or it could be said equally that there was a contradiction in our experience: and if the surrounding circumstances were appropriate it would be possible for such occurrences to have a kind of human significance and hence intelligible for them to be hailed as miracles. I see no philosophical reason against this.

But consider first the following example. A child riding his toy motor-car strays on to an unguarded railway crossing near his house and a wheel of his car gets stuck down the side of one of the rails. An express train is due to pass with the signals in its favour and a curve in the track makes it impossible for the driver to stop his train in time to avoid any obstruction he might encounter on the crossing. The mother coming out of the house to look for her child sees him on the crossing and hears the train approaching. She runs forward shouting and waving. The little boy remains seated in his car looking downward, engrossed in the task of pedaling it free. The brakes of the train are applied and it comes to rest a few feet from the child. The mother thanks God for the miracle; which she never ceases to think of as such although, as she in due course learns, there was nothing supernatural about the manner in which the brakes of the train came to be applied. The driver had fainted, for a reason that had nothing to do with the presence of the child on the line, and the brakes were applied automatically as his hand ceased to exert pressure on the control lever. He fainted on this particular afternoon because his blood pressure had risen after an exceptionally heavy lunch during which he had quarrelled with a colleague, and the change in blood pressure caused a clot of blood to be dislodged and circulate. He fainted at the time when he did on the afternoon in question because this was the time at which the coagulation in his blood stream reached the brain.

Thus the stopping of the train and the fact that it stopped when it did have a natural explanation. I do not say a *scientific* explanation, for it does not seem to me that the explanation here as a whole is of this kind (in order for something to be unsusceptible of scientific explanation it does not have to be anything so queer and grandiose as a miracle). The form of explanation in the present case, I would say, is *historical*; and the considerations that enter into it are various. They include medical factors, for instance, and had these constituted the whole extent of the matter the explanation could have been called scientific. But as it is, the medical considerations, though obviously important, are only one aspect of a complex story, alongside other considerations of a practical and social kind; and in addition there is a reference to mechanical considerations. All of these enter into the explanation of, or story behind, the stopping of the train. And just as there is an explanatory story behind the train's stopping when and where it did, so there is an explanatory story behind the presence of the child on the line at the time when, and in the place where, he was. But these two explanations or histories are independent of each other. They are about as disconnected as the history of the steam loom is from the history of the Ming dynasty. The spacio-temporal coincidence, I mean the fact that the child was on the line at the time when the train approached and the train stopped a few feet short of the place where he was, is exactly what I have just called it, a coincidence—something which a chronicle of events can merely record, like the fact that the Ming dynasty was in power at the same time as the house of Lancaster.

But unlike the coincidence between the rise of the Ming dynasty and the arrival of the dynasty of Lancaster, the coincidence of the child's presence on the line with the arrival and then the stopping of the train is impressive, significant; not because it is very unusual for trains to be halted in the way this one was, but because the life of a child was imperiled and then, against expectation, preserved. The significance of some coincidences as opposed to others arises from their relation to human needs and hopes and fears, their effects for good or ill upon our lives. So we speak of our luck (fortune, fate, etc.). And the kind of thing that, outside religion, we call luck is in religious parlance the grace of God or a miracle of God. But while the reference here is the same, the meaning is different. The meaning is different in that whatever happens by God's grace or by a miracle is something for which God is thanked or thankable, something which has been or could have been prayed for, something which can be regarded with awe and be taken as a sign or made the subject of a vow (e.g. to go on a pilgrimage), all of which can only take place against the background of a religious tradition. Whereas what happens by a stroke of luck is something in regard to which one just seizes one's opportunity or feels glad about or feels relieved about, something for which one may thank one's lucky stars. To say that one thanks one's lucky stars is simply to express one's relief or to emphasize the intensity of the relief: if it signifies anything more than this it signifies a superstition (cf. touching wood).

But although a coincidence can be taken religiously as a sign and called a miracle and made the subject of a vow, it cannot without confusion be taken as a sign of divine interference with the natural order. If someone protests that it is no part of the natural order that an express train should stop for a child on the line whom the driver cannot see then in *protesting* this he misses the point. What he says has been agreed to be perfectly true in the sense that there is no natural order relating the train's motion to the child which could be either preserved or interfered with. The concept of the miraculous which we have so far been considering is distinct therefore from the concept exemplified in the biblical stories of the turning of water into wine and the feeding of five thousand people on a very few loaves and fishes. Let us call the former the contingency concept and the latter the violation concept.

To establish the contingency concept of the miraculous as a possible concept it seems to me enough to point out (1) that *pace* Spinoza, Leibniz, and others, there are genuine contingencies in the world, and (2) that certain of these contingencies can be, and are in fact, regarded religiously in the manner I have indicated. If you assent to this and still express a doubt—'But are they really miracles?'—then you must now be questioning whether people are right to react to contingencies in this way, questioning whether you ought yourself to go along with them. Why not just stick to talking of luck? When you think this you are somewhat in the position of one who watches others fall in love and as an outsider thinks it unreasonable, hyperbolical, ridiculous (surely friendship should suffice).

To turn now to the concept of the miraculous as a violation of natural law: I am aware of two arguments which, if they were correct, would show that this concept were not a possible concept. The first is in chapter ten of Hume's *Enquiry Concerning Human Understanding*:

Nothing is esteemed a miracle, if it ever happens in the common course of nature. It is no miracle that a man, seemingly in good health, should die on a sudden: because such a kind of death, though more unusual than any other, has yet been frequently observed to happen. But it is a miracle, that a dead man should come to life; because that has never been observed in any age or country. There must, therefore, be a uniform experience against every miraculous event, otherwise the event would not merit that appellation. And as a uniform experience amounts to a proof, there is here a direct and full *proof*, from the nature of the fact, against the existence of any miracle; nor can such a proof be destroyed, or the miracle rendered credible, but by an opposite proof, which is superior.

The plain consequence is (and it is a general maxim worthy of our attention), 'That no testimony is sufficient to establish a miracle, unless the testimony be of such a kind, that its falsehood would be more miraculous, than the fact, which it endeavours to establish; and even in that case there is a mutual destruction of arguments, and the superior only gives us an assurance suitable to that degree of force, which remains, after deducting the inferior.' When anyone tells me, that he saw a dead man restored to life, I immediately consider with myself, whether it be more probable, that this person should either deceive or be deceived, or that the fact, which he relates, should really have happened. I weigh the one miracle against the other; and according to the superiority, which I discover, I pronounce my decision, and always reject the greater miracle. If the falsehood of his testimony would be more miraculous, than the event which he relates; then, and not till then, can he pretend to command my belief or opinion.

Hume's concern in the chapter from which I have just quoted is ostensibly with the problem of assessing the *testimony of others* in regard to the allegedly miraculous. This is not the same problem as that which arises for the man who has to decide whether or not he himself has witnessed a miracle. Hume gives an inadequate account of the considerations which would influence one's decision to accept or reject the insistence of another person that something has happened which one finds it extremely hard to believe could have happened. The character and temperament of the witness, the kind of person he is and the kind of understanding one has of him, the closeness or distance of one's personal relationship with him are obviously important here, whereas Hume suggests that if we give credence to some witnesses rather than others the reason must be simply that we are accustomed to find in their case a conformity between testimony and reality (§ 89). Maybe the weakness of Hume's account of the nature of our trust or lack of trust in witnesses is connected with the fact that in some way he intended his treatment of the problem of witness concerning the miraculous to have a more general application—as if he were trying to cut across the distinction between the case where we are ourselves confronted with a miracle (or something we may be inclined to call one) and the case where other people intervene, and wanting us to consider it all as fundamentally a single problem of evidence, a problem of witness in which it would make no difference whether what were doing the witnessing were a person other than oneself, or oneself in the role of a witness to oneself, or one's senses as witnesses to oneself. This anyway is the view I am going to take of his intention here.

I can imagine it being contended that, while Hume has produced a strong argument against the possibility of our ever having certitude or even very good evidence that a miracle has occurred, his thesis does not amount to an argument against the possibility of miracles as such. But I think this would be a misunderstanding. For if Hume is right, the situation is not just that we do not happen as a matter of fact to have certitude or even good evidence for the occurrence of any miracle, but rather that *nothing can count* as good evidence: the logic of testimony precludes this. And in precluding this it must, so far as I can see, preclude equally our having *poor* evidence for the occurrence of any miracle, since a contrast between good evidence and poor evidence is necessary if there is to be sense in speaking of either. Equally it must follow that there can be no such thing as (because nothing is being allowed to count as) discovering, recognizing, becoming aware, and so on, that a miracle has occurred; and if there be no such thing as finding out or being aware that a miracle has occurred, there can be no such thing as failing to find out or failing to be aware that a miracle has occurred either; no such thing as a discovered or an undiscovered miracle . . . *en fin*, no such thing as a miracle. So Hume's argument is, after all, an argument against the very possibility of miracles. I do not think his argument is cogent either on the interpretation I have just put upon it or on the interpretation according to which it would be an argument merely against the possibility of our having good evidence for a miracle. But before giving my reason I would like first to mention the only other line of argument which I can at present envisage against the conception of the miraculous as a violation of natural law.

Consider the proposition that a criminal is a violator of the laws of the state. With this propostion in mind you will start to wonder, when someone says that a miracle is a violation of the laws of nature, if he is not confusing a law of nature with a judicial law as laid down by some legal authority. A judicial law is obviously something which can be violated. The laws of the state prescribe and their prescriptions can be flouted. But are the laws of nature in any sense prescriptions? Maybe they are in the sense that they prescribe to us what we are to expect, but since *we* formulated the laws this is really a matter of our offering prescriptions or recipes to ourselves. And we can certainly fail to act on these prescriptions. But the occurrences which the laws are about are not prescribed to: they are simply *des*cribed. And if anything should happen of which we are inclined to say that it goes counter to a law of nature, what this must mean is that the description we have framed has been, not flouted or violated, but falsified. We have encountered something that the description does not fit and we must therefore withdraw or modify our description. The law was wrong; we framed it wrongly: or rather what we framed has turned out not to have been a law. The relation between an occurrence and a law of nature is different then from a man's relation to a law of the state, for when the latter is deviated from we do not, save in exceptional circumstances, say that the law is wrong but rather that the man is wrong—he is a criminal. To suggest that an occurrence which has falsified a law of nature is *wrong* would be an absurdity: and it would be just as absurd to suggest that the law has been violated. Nothing can be conceived to be a violation of natural law, and if that is how the miraculous is conceived there can be no such thing as the miraculous. Laws of nature can be formulated or reformulated to cope with any eventuality, and would-be miracles are transformed automatically into natural occurrences the moment science gets on the track of them.

But there is an objection to this line of argument. If we say that a law of nature is a description, what exactly are we taking it to be a description of? A description of what has happened up to now or is actually happening now? Suppose we have a law to the effect that all unsupported bodies fall. From this I can deduce that if the pen now in my hand were unsupported it *would* fall and that when in a moment I withdraw from it the support it now has it *will* fall. But if the law were simply a description of what has happened up to now or is happening now and no more, these deductions would be impossible. So it looks as if the law must somehow describe the future as well as the past and present. 'A description of the future.' But what on earth is that? For until the future ceases to be the future and becomes actual there are no events for the description to describe—over and above those that either have already taken place or are at this moment taking place.

It seems that if we are to continue to maintain that a natural law is nothing but a description then we must say that the description covers not only the actual but also the possible and is every bit as much a description of the one as it is of the other. And this only amounts to a pleonastic way of saying that the law tells us, defines for us, what is and is not *possible* in regard to the behaviour of unsupported bodies. At which point we might just as well drop the talk about describing altogether and admit that the law does not just describe—it stipulates: stipulates that it is impossible for an unsupported body to do anything other than fall. Laws of nature and legal laws, though they may not resemble each other in other respects, are at least alike in this: that they both stipulate something. Moreover the stipulations which we call laws of nature are in many cases so solidly founded and knitted together with other stipulations, other laws, that they come to be something in the nature of a framework through which we look at the world and which to a considerable degree dictates our ways of describing phenomena.

Notice, however, that insofar as we resist in this way the second of the two arguments for the impossibility of the violation concept of the miraculous and insofar as we object to the suggestion that it is possible for our laws of nature to be dropped or reformulated in a sort of *ad hoc* manner to accommodate any would-be miracle, we seem to be making the first argument—the Humean argument against the miraculous —all the stronger. For if we take a law of nature to be more than a generalized description of what has happened up to now, and if at the same time we upgrade the mere probability or belief to which Hume thought we were confined here into certainty and real knowledge, then surely it must seem that our reluctance to throw overboard a whole nexus of well-established, mutually-supporting laws and theories must be so great as to justify us in rejecting out of hand, and not being prepared to assign even a degree of probability to, any testimony to an occurrence which our system of natural law decisively rules out; and surely we shall be justified in classifying as illusory any experience which purports to be the experience of such an occurrence.

The truth is that this position is not at all justified, and we should only be landed in inconsistency if we adopted it. For if it were granted that there can be no certainty in regard to the individual case, if there can be no real knowledge that a particular event has occurred in exactly the way that it has, how could our system of laws have got established in the first place?

On Hume's view, the empirical in general was synonymous with the probable. No law of nature could have more than a degree of probability, and neither for that matter could the occurrence of any particular event. This is what gave point to the idea of a balance of probabilities and hence to his thesis about the impossibility of ever establishing a miracle. But while in the one case, that of the general law, he was prepared (in the passage from which I quoted) to allow that the probability could have the status of a proof, in the other case he was curiously reluctant to allow this.

Now if in the interest of good conceptual sense we upgrade the probability of natural laws into certainty, so as to be able to distinguish a well-established law from a more or less tenable hypothesis, it is equally in the interest of good conceptual sense that we should upgrade in a comparable fashion the probability attaching to particular events and states of affairs, so as to allow that some of these, as opposed to others, can be certain and really known to be what they are. Otherwise a distinction gets blurred which is at least as important as the distinction between a law and a hypothesis—namely the distinction between a hypothesis and a fact. The distinction between a hypothesis and a fact is for instance the distinction between my saying when I come upon an infant who is screaming and writhing and holding his ear 'he's got an abscess' and my making this statement again after looking into the ear, whether by means of an instrument or without, and actually seeing, coming upon, the abscess. Or again it is the difference between the statement 'it is snowing' when made by me now as I sit here and the same statement uttered as I go outside the building into the snow and get snowed on. The second statement, unlike the first, is uttered directly in the face of the circumstance which makes it true. I can be as certain in that situation that it is snowing as I can be of anything. And if there weren't things of this kind of which we can be certain, we wouldn't be able to be uncertain of anything either.

If it were remarked here that our senses are capable of deceiving us, I should reply that it does not follow from this that there are not occasions when we know perfectly well that we are not being deceived. And this is one of them. I submit that nothing would persuade you—or if it would it shouldn't—that you are not at this moment in the familiar surroundings of your university and that in what you see as you look around this room you are subject to an illusion. And

if something very strange were to happen, such as one of us
bursting into flame, you'd soon know it for what it was; and of
course you'd expect the natural cause to be duly discovered
(the smouldering pipe which set fire to the matches or whatever it might be).

But then suppose you failed to discover any cause. Or
suppose that something happened which was truly bizarre,
like my rising slowly and steadily three feet into the air and
staying there. You could *know* that this happened if it did, and
probably you would laugh and presume there must be some
natural explanation: a rod behind, a disguised support beneath,
a thin wire above. Or could it even be done by air pressure in
some way? Or by a tremendously powerful magnet on the
next floor, attracting metal in my clothing? Or if not by
magnetic attraction then by magnetic repulsion? I rise in the air
then, and since it is no magician's demonstration you can and
do search under me, over me, and around me. But suppose
you find nothing, nothing on me and nothing in the room or
above, below, or around it. You cannot think it is the effect of
an anti-gravity device (even if there be sense in that idea)
because there just is no device. And you know that, excluding
phenomena like tornados, it is impossible for a physical body
in free air to behave thus in the absence of a special device. So
does it not come to this: that if I were to rise in the air now, you
could be completely certain of two incompatible things: (1)
that it is impossible, and (2) that it has happened?

Now against what I have just said I envisage two objections.
The first is that my rising three feet into the air in the absence
of some special cause can only be held to be an impossibility by
someone who is ignorant of the statistical basis of modern
physics. For example, the water in a kettle comprises a vast
number of atoms in motion and anything I do to the kettle,
such as tilting it or heating it, will affect the movements of
these atoms. But there is no way of determining what the
effect will be in the case of any single atom. It is no more
within the power of physicists to predict that a particular atom
will change its position in such and such a way, or even at all,

than it is within the power of insurance actuaries to predict that
a certain man will die next week in a road accident, or die at all.
However, reliable statistical statements can be made by
actuaries about the life prospects of large numbers of people
taken together and somewhat similarly, statistical laws are
framed by physicists about the behaviour of atoms in large
numbers. Statistical laws are laws of probability and it gets
argued that, since this is the kind of law on which the
behaviour of water in a heated vessel ultimately rests, there can
be no *certainty* that the kettle on the hob will boil however
fierce the fire, no certainty that it will boil absolutely *every*
time, because there is always the probability—infinitesimally
small admittedly, but still a definite probability—that enough
of the constituent atoms in their molecules will move in a way
that is incompatible with its doing so. Vessels of water and
rubber balls seem to be the most frequently used examples
when this argument is deployed, but the suggestion has been
made to me that it (or some similar argument) could be applied
to the behaviour of an unsupported body near the surface of
the earth, in respect of which it could be maintained that there
is a certain probability, albeit a very low one, in favour of the
body's having its state of rest three feet above the ground.

However, it seems to me that any such argument must rest
on the kind of confusion that Eddington fell into when he said,
mentioning facts about atoms as the reason, that his table was
not solid but consisted largely of empty space. If you add to
this that your table is in a continuous vibratory motion and
that the laws governing its behaviour are laws of probability
only, you are continuing in the same vein. To make the confusion more symmetrical you might perhaps go on to say that
the movements of tables in space are only predictable even
with probability when tables get together in large numbers
(which accounts for the existence of warehouses). Anyway
my point is that, using words in their ordinary senses, it is
about as certain and as much a matter of common understanding that my kettle, when put on a fierce fire, will boil or that I
shall not next moment float three feet in the air as it is certain

and a matter of common understanding that my desk is solid and will continue for some time to be so. The validity of my statement about the desk is not impugned by any assertion about the behaviour of atoms whether single or in the aggregate; neither is the validity of the corresponding statements about the kettle and my inability to float in the air impugned by any assertion about the statistical basis of modern science.

The second objection grants the impossibility of a body's rising three feet into the air in the absence of a special cause and grants my certitude of this. But what I can never be certain of, the objection runs, is that all the special causes and devices that accomplish this are absent. So I am entirely unjustified in asserting the outright impossibility of the phenomenon —especially when I think to do so in the very teeth of its occurrence. My saying that it is impossible could only have the force here of an ejaculation like 'Struth!' *Ab esse ad posse valet consequentia.* Supposing the thing to have occurred, our response as ungullible people should be to maintain confidence in the existence of a natural cause, to persist indefinitely in searching for one and to classify the occurrence in the meantime as an unsolved problem. So runs the second objection.

However, the idea that one cannot establish the absence of a natural cause is not to my mind the unassailable piece of logic it might seem at first to be. Both our common understanding and our scientific understanding include conceptions of the sort of thing that can and cannot happen, and of the sort of thing that has to take place to bring about some other sort of thing. These conceptions are presupposed to our arguing in such patterns as 'A will do such and such unless Y,' or 'if Z happens it can only be because of this, that or the other,' or 'If W cannot be done in this way or that way it cannot be done at all.' An example of the first pattern is 'The horse will die if it gets no food.' My rising steadily three feet in the air is a subject for argument according to the second pattern. The second pattern presents the surface appearance of being more complicated than the first, but logically it is not. Let us turn our attention to the example of the first pattern.

Suppose that a horse, which has been normally born and reared, and is now deprived of all nourishment (we could be completely certain of this)—suppose that, instead of dying, this horse goes on thriving (which again is something we could be completely certain about). A series of thorough examinations reveals no abnormality in the horse's condition: its digestive system is always found to be working and to be at every moment in more or less the state it would have been in if the horse had eaten a meal an hour or two before. This is utterly inconsistent with our whole conception of the needs and capacities of horses; and because it is an impossibility in the light of our prevailing conception, my objector, in the event of its happening, would expect us to abandon the conception—as though we had to have consistency at any price. Whereas the position I advocate is that the price is too high and it would be better to be left with the inconsistency; and that in any event the prevailing conception has a logical status not altogether unlike that of a necessary truth and cannot be simply thrown away as a mistake—not when it rests on the experience of generations, not when all the other horses in the world are continuing to behave as horses have always done, and especially not when one considers the way our conception of the needs and capacities of horses interlocks with conceptions of the needs and capacities of other living things and with a conception of the difference between animate and inanimate behaviour quite generally. These conceptions form part of a common understanding that is well established and with us to stay. Any number of discoveries remains to be made by zoologists and plenty of scope exists for conceptual revision in biological theory, but it is a confusion to think it follows from this that we are less than well enough acquainted with, and might have serious misconceptions about, what is and is not possible in the behaviour under familiar conditions of common objects with which we have a long history of practical dealings. Similarly with the relation between common understanding and physical discoveries, physical theories: what has been said about the self-sustaining horse seems to me applicable *mutatis mutandis* to the levitation example also. Not that my thesis about the miraculous rests on the acceptance of this particular example. The objector who thinks there is a loophole in it for natural explanation strikes me as lacking a sense of the absurd but can keep his opinion for the moment, since he will (I hope) be shown the loophole being closed in a further example with which I shall conclude.

I did not in any case mean to suggest that if I rose in the air now in the absence of any device it would be at all proper for a religious person to hail this as a miracle. Far from it. From a religious point of view it would either signify nothing at all or else be regarded as a sign of devilry; and if the phenomenon persisted I should think that a religious person might well have recourse to exorcism, if that figured among the institutions of his religion. Suppose, however, that by rising into the air I were to avoid an otherwise certain death: then it would (against a religious background) become possible to speak of a miracle, just as it would in what I called the contingency case. Or the phenomenon could be a miracle although nothing at all were achieved by it, provided I were a religiously significant figure, one of whom prophets had spoken, or at least an exceptionally holy man.

My thesis then in regard to the violation concept of the miraculous, by contrast with the contingency concept, which we have seen to be also a possible concept, is that a conflict of certainties is a necessary though not a sufficient condition of the miraculous. In other words a miracle, though it cannot only be this, must at least be something the occurrence of which can be categorized at one and the same time as empirically certain and conceptually impossible. If it were less than conceptually impossible it would reduce merely to a very unusual occurrence such as could be treated (because of the empirical certainty) in the manner of a decisive experiment and result in a modification to the prevailing conception of natural law; while if it were less than empirically certain nothing more would be called for in regard to it than a suspension of judgement. So if there is to be a type of the miraculous other than the contingency kind it must offend against the principle *ab esse ad posse valet consequentia*. And since the violation concept of the miraculous does seem to me to be a possible concept I therefore reject that time-honoured logical principle.

I know that my suggestion that something could be at one and the same time empirically certain and conceptually impossible will sound to many people ridiculous. Must not the actual occurrence of something show that it *was* conceptually possible after all? And if I contend, as I do, that the fact that something has occurred might *not* necessarily show that it was conceptually possible; or to put it the other way round—if I contend, as I do, that the fact that something is conceptually impossible does not necessarily preclude its occurrence, then am I not opening the door to the instantiation of round squares, female fathers, and similar paradigms of senselessness? The answer is that the door is being opened only as far as is appropriate and not to instantiations of the *self*-contradictory. There is more than one kind of conceptual impossibility.

Let me illustrate my meaning by reference to the New Testament story of the turning of water into wine. I am not assuming that this story is true, but I think that it logically could be. Hence if anyone chooses to maintain its truth as a matter of faith I see no philosophical objection to his doing so. A number of people could have been quite sure, could have had the fullest empirical certainty, that a vessel contained water at one moment and wine a moment later—good wine, as St John says—without any device having been applied to it in the intervening time. Not that this last really needs to be added; for that any device should have existed *then* at least is inconceivable, even if it might just be argued to be a conceptual possibility now. The idea that water could conceivably have been turned into wine in the first century A.D. by means of a device is ruled out of court at once by common understanding; and though the verdict is supported by scientific

knowledge, common understanding has no need of this
support.

In the case of my previous example of a man, myself for
instance, rising three feet into the air and remaining there
unsupported, it was difficult to deal with the objection that we
could not be certain there wasn't some special cause operating,
some explanation even though we had searched to the utmost
of our ability and had found none. And I imagined the objector
trying to lay it down as axiomatic that while there is such a
thing as not knowing what the cause or explanation of a
phenomenon might be there can be no such thing as establishing the absence of a cause. The example of water being turned
into wine is stronger, and I would think decisive, here. At one
moment, let us suppose, there was water and at another
moment wine, in the same vessel, although nobody had emptied out the water and poured in the wine. This is something
that could conceivably have been established with certainty.
What is not conceivable is that it could have been done by a
device. Nor is it conceivable that there could have been a
natural cause of it. For this would have had to be the natural
cause of the water's becoming wine. And water's becoming
wine is not the description of any conceivable natural process.
It is conceptually impossible that the wine could have been got
naturally from water, save in the very strained sense that
moisture is needed to nourish the vines from which the grapes
are taken, and this very strained sense is irrelevant here.

'But can we not still escape from the necessity to assert that
one and the same thing is both empirically certain and conceptually impossible? For what has been said to be conceptually
impossible is the turning of water into wine. However, when
allusion is made to the alleged miracle, all the expression *turned
into* can signify is that at one moment there was water and at a
moment later wine. This is what could have been empirically
certain; whereas what is conceptually impossible is that water
should have been turned into wine if one really *means* turned
into. It is not conceptually impossible that at one moment
water should have been found and at another moment wine in

the same vessel, even though nobody had emptied out the water and poured in the wine.' So someone might try to argue. But I cannot see that it does any good. To the suggestion that the thing is conceivable so long as we refrain from saying that the water *turned into* the wine I would reply: either the water turns into the wine or else it disappears and wine springs into existence in its place. But water cannot *conceivably* disappear like that without going anywhere, and wine cannot *conceivably* spring into existence from nowhere. Look at it in terms of transformation, or look at it in terms of 'coming into being and passing away'—or just look at it. Whatever you do, you cannot make sense of it: on all accounts it is inconceivable. So I keep to the position that the New Testament story of the turning of water into wine is the story of something that could have been known empirically to have occurred, and it is also the story of the occurrence of something which is conceptually impossible. It has to be both in order to be the miracle-story which, whether true or false, it is.

That expression 'occurrence of something which is conceptually impossible' was used deliberately just then. And it will be objected, no doubt, that to speak of something which is conceptually impossible is to speak of a nullity. To ask for an example of something that is conceptually impossible is not (I shall be told) like asking for a sample of a substance and you cannot in order to comply with this request produce anything visible or tangible, you cannot point to an occurrence. Indeed you cannot, strictly speaking, offer a description either: you can only utter a form of words. What I have been arguing in effect is that there is a contradiction in St John's 'description' of the water-into-wine episode. But if so, then nothing has really been described; or alternatively something has been—one should not say misdescribed but rather garbled—since a conceptual impossibility is *ex vi termini* one of which sense cannot be made.

I would reply to this that sense can be made of a conceptual impossibility in the respect that one can see often enough that there *is* a conceptual impossibility there and also, often enough, what kind of a conceptual impossibility it is and how it arises. We can see there is an inconsistency; and statements, moreover, are not the only things in which and between which we can see inconsistency. Human actions can be pointed to here quite obviously. And I am maintaining that there is also such a thing as making sense, and failing to make sense, of events. If the objector holds that in the case of events, unlike the case of human actions, the kind of order that makes sense must always be there although one perhaps fails to find it, I ask: how does he know? Why the *must*? It is not part of my case that to regard a sequence of events as scientifically unintelligible, or as having the anomalous intelligibility of the miraculous in it, is to construe it as if it were an arbitrary action, or to see the invisible hand of a super-person at work in it. I have contended that there are circumstances in respect to which the expression 'occurrence of something which is conceptually impossible' would have a natural use, and I have offered examples. The expression 'violation of a law of nature' could also be introduced quite naturally in this connection; or we could speak of a contradiction in our experience.

13

For Ever?

When people are asked what is meant by 'for ever', the explanation they tend to give does not accord with the way the expression is commonly used. The account that seems to them appropriate is of the following kind: 'Some things last a short time and some last a long time, but even so they get destroyed. For a thing to last for ever is for it to go on, not just a long time, but on and on unceasingly so that it exists without end.' This account puts 'for ever' into the family of, and then contrasts it with, temporal adverbs or adverbial phrases which with varying degrees of definiteness specify a length of time. Unlike the contrast between 'for a shorter time' and 'for a longer time' or between 'two hours' and 'four centuries', which are pairs of contrasting relative notions, the contrast between 'a millennium' (say) and 'for ever' is a contrast between a relative conception and an absolute conception. The 'for ever' delineated in the popular explanation is the ideal 'for ever'—Foreverness itself or *auto to aei* as Plato might have called it. As regards the prospect of ordinary employment, this absolute conception is like a labourer in a slump. For a relative sense of 'for ever' and its cognates is autochthonous in daily life, amid the everlasting gas-lighters and permanent creases, where she is for ever blowing bubbles and he is always losing his temper and I bequeath my arboretum to the citizens of West Park in perpetuity. Then there is 'I shall love you for ever', which usually means until the next one comes along.

Daily life can go to hell if that is how it is, someone may say:

and the use of 'I shall love you for ever' which I gave just then was frivolous, to be sure. Used seriously it goes along with 'until death do us part'—which will occur before the year 2090. Concerning its significance as an eternal resolution there is more to be said, and I would in fact count the serious ethical use as an absolute use; but if anyone were to take the 'for ever' here or elsewhere to be a locution signifying the *perpetual duration* of something, I believe he would be either confused or adumbrating something that he could not speculatively comprehend.

The position for which I shall argue could be put by saying that there is for our theoretical understanding no such thing as the absolute or eternal 'for ever' of prolonged existence —despite what may go on in cosmology and in theology as well as in parts of philosophy itself. Impressed by the well established concerns and distinguished minds that have dealt in big F Forevers you may perhaps think that this must be one of the occasions for invoking Wittgenstein's powerful maxim about the attitude which is appropriate when something is part of a game and the game is manifestly played. The game (in cosmology, say) is carried on with this as one of the pieces, and we should accept it as it is: our business cannot be to interfere with it. Hence, if I believe there to be something inherently paradoxical about the unlimited temporal 'for ever', must not the *aporia* be a product of my own myopia—a cramp of the intelligence calling for removal?

I would say on the contrary that to assume this without considering the nature of the *aporia* would be to beg the question. 'The game is played and must therefore be left as it stands' is a line of thought to be rejected in the present context, for the following reason. What goes on in the relevant parts of cosmology, theology and philosophy does not go on independently of what goes on outside, and in particular it is to be noted that these are highly theoretical activities, concept-handling activities, directed towards the task of making sense of things. As such they can only be successful to some relative degree. There will always be that which has not been rendered coherent or which has been clouded in incoherence; and in these practices where the arrangement and rearrangement of concepts goes on, falling into confusion and then subsequently seeing it sometimes, but also sometimes not seeing it, forms part of the business. Although not what is intended, it is nevertheless an aspect of the game.

If a cosmologist therefore, if an applied mathematician believes, on the ground perhaps that a particular kind of model would satisfy certain equations, that an absolutely unending duration is attributable to something physical, then, without being deterred by lack of expertise in his specialism, I am prepared to say, for philosophical reasons which I shall give, that he subscribes to nonsense. I shall not say exactly the same of theologians when they attribute absolute everlastingness to God, for I think they are almost bound to do so. There are traditional prayers which begin 'Almighty and everlasting God . . .'. But I shall maintain that a barrier is brought down against the understanding by this attribution, so that it is not something which theologians can go on to surround with theoretical considerations: for instance, the canvassing of a connection between everlastingness and the kind of substance that the deity might be supposed to have would be a foray into senselessness.

Among those who have accepted the absolute 'for ever' as a genuinely temporal and speculative idea is Martha Kneale, who in her article 'Eternity and Sempiternity' (*PAS*, 1968–9) examines the question 'whether an eternal object can or must be also sempiternal' (p. 223). Mrs Kneale contends that anything which is eternal must also be sempiternal. In the course of her argument she separates off from each other the notions of necessity and timelessness which usually are associated together as the criteria of eternity, so that she is left with necessity as the sole constituent notion of eternity. Her conclusion about the relation between the concepts of timelessness, everlasting duration and necessity is stated as follows (p. 232): 'Timelessness is either identical with sempiternity or they are mutually entailing. Necessity entails sempiternity but not *vice*

versa.' On Mrs Kneale's view, 'timelessness is lack of limitation of existence in time; it is not failure to exist at all times.
Mutatis mutandis this holds of timeless truths' (p. 228). So
according to her it is both meaningful and true to state that two
and two are four today and that they were four yesterday and
that they will be four tomorrow.

I am not inclined to urge that because such statements sound
out of tune (or whatever an Austinian might call it) they
therefore must be meaningless, and Mrs Kneale would be
rightly unimpressed by this suggestion; instead I should want
to enquire what they *might* mean and to test the possibilities.
For instance, if someone says that two and two will be four
tomorrow, or that they will be four for ever, can he be making
a prediction? Can he be intending to assert that they will in fact
be four for ever although it is conceivable that they should not
be? If so, then whatever the 'for ever' might be doing, it is at
least part of his meaning that two and two make four contingently and he will have to be informed that he has misunderstood the nature of the mathematical proposition. So when
Mrs Kneale said with a view to this example that necessity
entails sempiternity, she cannot without confusion have
intended a contingent sempiternity (or a sempiternal contingency: it makes no difference which way round one puts it). If
she had intended this she would have been claiming, at least in
part, that 'is the case necessarily'—this being the only sort of 'is
the case' that we can predicate intelligibly of mathematical
equations—entails 'is the case contingently'; whereas 'is the
case contingently' is precisely what 'is the case necessarily'
excludes. I therefore have to attribute to Mrs Kneale the alternative view that someone may say 'two and two will be four
for ever' and be intending to say that two and two of necessity
must be four—for ever; the 'must' here being not a contingent
but a conceptual 'must'. Well, if they conceptually must be
four, they *must* be four and nothing but mud is contributed by
the 'for ever'!

'Still could not something—not like two and two's being
four, but something else, some factual thing—just happen to

exist or be the case or go on *for ever*?' I would begin my answer
by pointing to a difficulty in the meaning of the question.
There are things which we regard (loosely) as going on for
ever, to the extent that we have no thought concerning their
remote or ultimate future and we do not raise the issue of their
coming to an end: such anticipations form no part of the game.
I have in mind for example our primitive attitude towards the
galaxies or towards whatever elements we might hear of as
being the basic ingredients of which physical objects are composed. These and other more homely features of our environment have for us the status of permanent data, provided that
we are not in some exceptional state of mind. My proviso here
has to do with the problem of meaning presented by the question under consideration. For it is as though it could be raised
by the questioner in anticipation of an affirmative answer so
long as his state of mind were unexceptional, but by his very
raising of the question he shows himself to be in a quite exceptional state of mind: in short he was *capax rogandi nisi rogasset*.
The question he wanted to ask about the possibility of a factual
thing's just happening to exist for ever is rendered unaskable by
the accentuation placed upon the 'for ever', that is to say by the
entry of a metaphysical nuance which so tightens up that
expression as to put it entirely beyond the reach of fact.

   This twist in the question, although it has a shattering effect
upon its meaning, passes unnoticed because the words are so
readily uttered: it is perfectly natural for a person to *think* that
the question has a coherent sense, i.e. to *think* that he knows
what it would amount to for something to go on for ever in the
absolute sense of 'for ever'. However, I am not prepared to
grant that he *can* know and my conviction about this has to do
with the conceptual connections which link together (a) our
understanding of the kind and degree of meaning that is possessed by a speculation, (b) our understanding of what it
would be like for the speculation to have become true so that it
had lost its speculative character and turned into a certainty,
and (c) our understanding of what would be involved in
someone's discovery of its truth.

Once the proposition that something will last absolutely for ever has been accepted as a speculative assertion (in which case, I maintain, the vital mistake will already have been made) the position is that we cannot know what it would be like for the assertion to lose its status as a speculation, because the loss of its speculative character is logically impossible. The reason for this is that no observation capable of settling the issue can in principle be made, not even by a super-Methuselah. Waiting upon the fact is here like waiting for Godot: there is no relevant encounter, no *dénouement*. There appears to be an irreducible or necessary predictiveness about assertions predicating the absolute 'for ever'. But the real significance of this is that they are not predictions at all. What basis is there for applying them to anything? What sort of jumping-off ground could there possibly be for the belief that something will go on for ever?

Imagine a man saying of something that it doesn't look to be the kind of thing that *should*, but maybe by some fluke it *might* go on for ever. He would be fooling. What kind of a fluke, for heaven's sake? And what kind of a thing would look—look *how*?—as if it should go on for ever? Yet there was testimony to a truth embedded in the foolery: I mean in the suggestion that it would become sensible to think of something as destined to go on for ever if we had intimation of its being 'the kind of thing that should'. For when a verdict cannot be founded upon worldly discovery, does it not have to be arrived at (if there is to be any arrival at all) by inference from a concept—by the analysis of a subject's 'essential' nature? You cannot therefore expect to be able to ascribe strict sempiternity of existence to anything unless its sempiternal existence can be regarded as a part of its essence, this being at once the very best and at the same time the only possible foundation you could have for the ascription.

A severe restriction is accordingly imposed upon your choice of subjects. Having begun with the supposition that *some factual thing* might *just happen* to exist for ever, you have to accept that nothing short of a deity is likely to fill your bill. And that is on the assumption that the inclusion of existence within an essence is something you can stomach at all. But it has played a role in proofs or would-be proofs of the existence of God and, whether or not they work in the way that their sponsors wanted them to, the proofs which use this principle make a conceptual point. For when Descartes for instance says in Part IV of his *Discourse on Method* that he has an idea of a perfect Being and on examining it finds it to include the existence of such a Being, it is at least clear that he is wanting to attribute to God a necessary existence. And while this has been made fun of by the suggestion that it means we have only to entertain the idea of a deity and a deity is promptly brought into existence, there is significance in the conceptual admonition it contains to the effect that the God of religion—and what other God is there to be sensibly considered?—cannot be spoken of or thought of as though He might not exist. This is a requirement of good sense. He does not *have to be* referred to of course; one can just shut up on the subject, and that makes good sense too.

But if you wish to bring God in, I would allow that you have found the best possible subject for your predication. At least I do not see how the idealized 'for ever' of existence can sensibly we wedded to anything other than a correspondingly idealized being, a being that is accorded the status of a necessary being. There can be no question here of making a prediction. But then again the trouble is that the role of the 'for ever' appears to be otiose, as Descartes possibly saw, for he did not say that his idea of a perfect Being included existence for ever; he just said that it included existence. After all, if the Being had to exist, then He had to exist, so what could be added by a 'for ever'? Even when sempiternity meets an eligible partner it seems doomed to find nothing to do and it collapses into the idea of necessity as it did in the mathematical case.

However, I am aware that what I have been urging against the notion of sempiternity is exposed to a strong counter-attack and I do not expect my position to emerge as a convincing one until the counter-attack has been examined.

In the case of the alleged sempiternity (when this is conceived to be different from the necessity) of mathematical truths I was able to show, by an appeal to the role played in our life and language by expressions like '2+2=4', that if someone says that two and two will be four for ever he cannot without confusion be regarded as making a prediction. But I was not able to clinch my argument against the conception of a sempiternal *object* in this way. So an opponent of my view may still insist that he can imagine something, for instance a sphere, continuing to exist or continuing to turn for ever. 'There is', he may say, 'nothing to stop me: and anyway I am actually doing it.' He may claim furthermore that if he said it would turn for ever he would quite obviously be uttering a prediction because he would be making an assertion about what would be the case tomorrow and the next day, and the next day . . . and so on.

Leaving the question about prediction on one side for the moment, I want to bring out first the dubiety of the claim that the everlasting existence or perpetual turning of a sphere is something that can be *imagined*. Whether this claim should be allowed to stand will depend on what the imagining is taken to amount to. But in the sense in which it would do any good to the friends of For Ever the claim cannot be substantiated, whereas the sense in which it is admissible affords no jumping-off ground for an inference from 'I can imagine it' to 'it is conceivable'. There is a fallacy in this connection which is important enough to deserve a label, so I shall christen it 'The Fallacy of the Internally Consistent Image or Proposition'—the ICIP fallacy for short. To explain what it is, I shall have to digress a little, taking as my point of departure 'impossible objects' like the endless stairway (see L. S. Rose and R. Penrose, *British Journal of Psychology*, 1958).

R. L. Gregory says of the picture: 'Here incompatible information in the third dimension is given to the eye, and there is no unique solution' (*Eye and Brain*, p. 227). He sounds to be suggesting that the eye, being instructed and counter-instructed, is unable to make anything coherent out of the picture; so that the object depicted cannot be looked at as a single, three-dimensional solid. Yet that is exactly how we *do*

look at it when we say, 'Aha, an endless stairway'. Hunting for
the Snark of Gregory's meaning, I suppose that the extent to
which the stairway would be found *visually* odd or wrong
would be partly a matter of custom and training but would
depend also upon the illustrator's skill (the proportions used,
type of shading, etc.). 'Looks impossible' has a ring of confused meiosis. When the representation is well done, a natural
reaction is 'How clever of the artist to make it look so right'.
For it looks well enough, but we can see it is impossible. The
'it' here is what is represented and the sense of 'see' in which
we see the impossibility is akin to 'comprehend' or 'understand' (some 'impossible figures' cause greater visual unease
than the endless stairway does, but the impossibility of what
they represent as opposed to the offence, if any, that they may
give to the eye is still something for the understanding). What
we understand is shown in what we say of the pictured object
as we relate together the descriptions appropriate to its various
aspects: 'one side has to be both above and below the other
side', 'going downwards all the time, yet coming back to the
same spot' and so on.

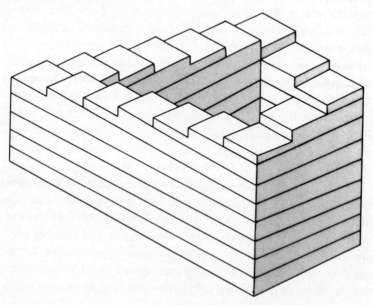

I call the picture of the endless stairway internally incoherent, because in comprehending the incoherence we draw
solely upon material in the picture; so that what the picture
renders for us stands or falls by itself, as it were. The conceptual obstacle to our taking the picture as a picture of a possible
reality arises from within, although of course the ways we
reason about it are ways in which we generally reason and the
words we use are used in other places. Where, on the other
hand, there is no obstacle of an internal kind, there seems to be
nothing to prevent the pictured situation from being a possible
reality. The idea that all internally consistent pictures or
propositions are pictures of, or propositions about, possible
realities is what I am calling the ICIP fallacy and I suspect that
it gets some of its impetus from the slogan that to understand a
proposition is to know what it would be like if it were true. 'If
the description of a picture contains no internal contradiction
then we know that the propositions in the description can be
true and the picture shows us what it would be like for them to
be true.'

It was the summer outing for old ladies and one of them was
heard to remark on the bus, 'My wireless says it will rain
today; what does yours say?'. Just imagine it: twenty-six old
ladies and another thirty on the top deck, all with antennae
sticking out of their transistor radios. I could draw them at a
dozen to the page (five internally consistent and mutually
consistent pictures) with the words of the forecast coming out
of their mouths in balloons according to the convention:
'Mine says windy', 'Mine says no wind', 'Mine says below
zero', 'Mine says 60° Fahrenheit', 'Mine doesn't know any
Fahrenheit' and so on.

Do we then understand what it would be like for the whole
thing to be true? But any inclination to commit the ICIP
fallacy here must surely be stifled by our sense of humour. For
the jest is bound up with the conceptual clash between the old
lady's remark and our understanding of what wireless recep-
tion is, what its relation to a broadcasting service involves, and
what transmitting stations are, and what they in turn entail;

alongside all of which there is the clash with what we understand about the provision of weather forecasts and the kind of thing that is involved in that. Broadcasting and weather forecasting are institutions which have their surroundings and play a particular sort of role in our lives. To imagine them in a radically discrepant role is to represent them incoherently and hence to imagine an impossibility. This is imagining in the fairy tale sense—the sense in which we imagine pots talking to kettles; and we cannot imagine a pot talking to a kettle in anything other than a fairy tale sense.

Now the claim to be able to imagine something substantial in the shape of a sphere continuing to exist or turn for ever rests on two supporting considerations. The first is that the claimant can summon up an image or draw a picture of a spinning sphere; and the second is that the words of the proposition 'This sphere will turn for ever' are not in any internal conflict with each other. I take myself to have shown thus far that these considerations come nowhere near to establishing the conceivability of what he claims to imagine; so that he might only be imagining it in the fairy tale sense. I shall try to show in the next stage of my argument that he cannot imagine it in anything other than the fairy tale sense.

What I now want to stress about images of ever-turning spheres or other fictitious everlasting objects—and they certainly *are* fictitious, for when people say, as they do, that they can easily imagine (for instance) the Tower of London standing up for ever, they know perfectly well that the real Tower of London won't do that—the point I would stress is that while recourse to images of fictitious objects is natural here in view of the absence of real examples from the world, yet these images, although constructed expressly for the purpose and without restriction by the demands of empirical reality, are nevertheless logically incapable of conveying the idea they were summoned up to convey. So that our recourse to them is a flight to enchantment. All we can do with them is stare at them. For instance, how in imagery or out of it is the everlasting Tower of London going to differ from the real Tower of

London? By having harder bricks and stronger mortar? But that would not mark it out as lasting absolutely 'for ever', nor would anything else that we can think of. So we picture the fictitious Tower of London in exactly the way we do the real one and then in order to mark the vital respect in which it is supposed to differ, we inwardly intone our idealized 'for ever' at it. The ever-turning sphere ought to be a more malleable object for our imaginations to handle, since it is not meant to relate to anything real in the way that the fictitiously everlasting Tower of London was. Yet we cannot go further than representing it in some sort of motion, and we only get as far as this because we know of some real spheres in motion. For instance, we may imagine our sphere to have a map on it and then depict it in successive pictures with the continents in different positions. But however we try to elaborate or modify such pictures, we cannot get the modification to represent the idea expressed in the proposition 'This sphere will turn *for ever*' except by stipulating, introducing a convention, that it should: in which case the modification is only a shorthand way of writing out that very proposition.

So in order to get 'for ever' into the picture a proposition is required. Had not the proposition been already in the offing, we could never have begun to take our image as an image of sempiternal motion in the first place: the proposition is the vehicle that bears the whole weight of the imaginative exercise. And this brings me back to the question of predicting. For whatever their verbal dress, propositions containing the idea of the absolute For Ever of duration, the eternity that signifies everlastingness by contrast with the eternity that signifies timeless necessity, have the distinctive feature of being intended predictively. The incessantly turning sphere is one that *will* continue in motion and this predictive element is indispensable to the intended meaning. I am going to argue, however, that assertions involving the absolute For Ever of duration are 'predictions' which cannot be used predictively, so that they are a kind of verbal analogue of the impossible figure—they depict 'predictions' for which there is no logical

space; but whereas impossible figures are internally incoherent, predictions about the absolute For Ever are like the old
lady's conversation about the weather—incoherent without
being internally incoherent.

My previous discussion of predictability was left at the
point where I had established that 'two and two will be four
for ever' cannot, despite what it depicts itself as saying, be a
prediction. But a friend of For Ever was arguing that with
objects it is different and claiming that if he said of a sphere that
it would turn for ever he would obviously be uttering a
prediction because he would be making an assertion about
what would be the case tomorrow and the next day, and the
next day . . . and so on.

An argument against this would be that you cannot sensibly
speak of a prediction for which there is no possibility in
principle of a verification.[1] That something will still be the case
in a thousand years is in principle open to verification. If the
thousand were raised to some suitably gargantuan figure like
the millionth power of a million-to-the-millionth, you would
not have a prediction for which there was any place within a
science and I should feel hesitant on that ground about its
status. But in any case 'for the millionth power of a million-
to-the-millionth years' would be exactly as far distant logically from the idealized 'for ever' as 'until tomorrow' is.

My objector, however, may be ready with the reply that he
does not need to worry about the question of verification since
he has something better, namely the possibility of falsification.
'For while I am predicting that in fact it never will stop,
nevertheless it *could* stop—tomorrow; and if it does, then that

---

[1] To say this is not to invoke the old Verification Principle of the Logical
Positivists. The point is simply that meaning and verification come into a
close connection with each other *in the case of predictions*—closer than they do
in the rest of language. The Logical Positivists both idealized this connection
into an identity and also essentialized it by making predictive propositions
serve as a model for other sorts of informative utterance (assertions of fact in
the present tense being explicitly said by them to be predictions). Verification was thus turned into an 'ism' and made to serve as the foundation of a
theory of meaning in general.

will be the downfall of my prediction.' He may further point out, as Peter Winch did in a discussion from which I benefited, that his proposition that it will go on for ever is a denial of the proposition that it will cease tomorrow. 'And how can a proposition which negates a contingent proposition be itself anything other than contingent?' In short, my objector will maintain that there is little amiss, from what might be called the declarative point of view, with the idea that is expressed by the proposition 'It could stop tomorrow but it never will', whereas what is really peculiar is the idea of necessary existence or necessary movement that comes in on my own interpretation of the 'for ever'.

But now: when you say that you can imagine *an object* continuing to exist or move for ever, I want to know what kind of an object you have in mind. Is it animal, vegetable, mineral or abstract, as they say in the radio game? And I want to know what the surrounding circumstances are supposed to be. You claim that you could *predict* of it that it will go on for ever. But have you ever actually come across anything in regard to which you would be ready to utter this 'prediction' as a thoughtful and fully serious proposition? My submission is that you have not and that this is no accidental matter.

Take the pendulum of the grandfather clock. You would claim that you can imagine it swinging for ever. But you do not, in fact, predict that it will; and supposing you did, would the falsification of your 'prediction' mean that you had just *happened* to be wrong? I say no, because you do not contemplate its going on for ever as a serious possibility. You may say that the pendulum gives you a picture of sempiternal motion—you may attach this phrase to what you see. But that the pendulum of a particular clock might go on swinging for ever is not for you a possible conception in relation to your understanding of the way that clocks and other mechanical contrivances are constructed and driven. You are aware for instance that the weight is moving towards the floor and will soon have reached it, and you know that there is some analogue of this in all machines. You are aware of the friction in the bearings and again you know that there is something comparable in all machines. In order to imagine the *perpetual* swinging of the pendulum your imagining will have to include the abolition of all such considerations. I do not know how you would propose with consistency to abolish them, but to the extent that you managed it you would be constructing the blueprint of a perpetual motion machine. One push and hey presto; only don't tell me that you can conceive it as an actuality.

An ideal mechanism is certainly something you can conceive. But here, the way the parts move will be conceptually dictated. In your original picture you did not idealize the whole mechanism, but you did idealize the pendulum. That is precisely what happens when it is pictured in isolation from the surrounding circumstances so that it is no longer considered to be made of a definite material and to be swinging on a particular sort of pivot, a pivot that from the horologist's standpoint would have its advantages and its disadvantages. To the extent that it was an idealized pendulum that you thought 'might swing for ever' then so far from doing even any imaginary predicting you were uttering a conceptual statement which if it belonged anywhere would belong to theoretical mechanics. Thus the 'for ever' in 'it might swing for ever' turns out on examination to have the sort of significance that we found it to have in the mathematical example 'two and two will be four for ever', where it was a misleading testimony to a conceptual necessity. The word 'might'—for there is no 'might' about the ideal motions of the conceptual pendulum, only the conceptual 'must'—I would call your pineal gland, and in playing this role it is supported by the temporal appearance of the 'for ever'.

How does the point about the negation of a contingent proposition having to be itself contingent look now? The assertion that it will go on for ever conflicts with the assertion that it will stop tomorrow, not in the sense of being a counter-prediction, but in the sense of indicating that the subject under consideration is to be conceived in a different category. When the subject is the empirical behaviour of a material pendulum in a grandfather clock, the prediction that it will stop tomorrow, though it may be an insult to Thomas Tompion, belongs to the appropriate form of understanding, whereas the assertion that it will go on for ever does not. The conflation of the two spheres of discourse, the one empirical and the other conceptual, which generates the idea that the latter assertion could be a straightforward negation of the former, comes out charmingly in the proposition 'It *might* go on for ever'.

There may lurk a suspicion that my objector would have fared better with an example from nature. Then take for instance 'The sun might continue to exist for ever'. I can bring forward considerations in relation to this example which run parallel to the considerations I adduced before. 'The sun will exist for ever' is not a proposition that anyone now could utter as a fully thoughtful prognostication. There is no place for any such 'prediction' within the science of astronomy. The galaxies are something with a history (and this is a conceptual matter: it is as much a conceptual matter as it is for us a conceptual matter that the earth is something with a history). They are evolving; and notwithstanding the largeness of the scale, the permanence of anything that they may contain (say the permanence of the arrangement of the matter which in its present arrangement constitutes a stellar system) is still a relative permanence, as in the example 'I bequeath my arboretum . . .'. The sun is part of a stellar system. Of course if you think away the background of the system, if you think away the conceptual connections by which your idea of the sun is related to your idea of the earth and so on, then you will feel free to entertain any conception you like; for goodness knows what you are then left with—a picture of a shining orb perhaps, which you still call the sun although nothing any longer entitles you to. I shall allow that you can properly call it a sphere because it has a circular shape to it; but apart from that, its nature is now entirely indeterminate, for it is not thought to be composed of anything in particular. It is not thought to have a composition at all in fact, and it is not clear to what logical category anything you said about it would belong. But if all that can strictly be said of it is that it is *round*, then what you have arrived at is an idealization—pure sphericalness or *autos ho kuklos*.

Now provided that the motion envisaged is also ideal, *autos ho kuklos* can move. My argument puts no embargo on the concept of eternal motion so long as this is recognized to be synonymous with 'necessary movement', for which there are perfectly good uses. A rod, for instance, in a lesson on elementary mechanics, is said to be perfectly rigid and of fixed length; fulcrum F is said to be a fixed point.

F

E_1 E_2

Then in relation to the movement of end E_1, the movement in the opposite direction of end E_2 may be said to be necessary movement or conceptually-dictated movement. The rod can for that matter be called a necessary rod—a necessary object, or, if you like, an eternal object. But when eternal (or sempiternal) objects are spoken of outside the context of theoretical mechanics, the effect is if anything to make me want to hoot; and the associated pictures of globes turning continuously with stately ease, which many find impressive, only serve with me to reinforce the hoot-making effect. As though there might be something here that were deep and spiritual: whereas I should not cavil at the idea of there being something deep and spiritual about the science of mechanics.

The conception of an object which is both ideal and unideal (ideal and at the same time actual) is incoherent and therefore something that can only be believed in by a subterfuge; for example, by entertaining pictures of figures in which geometrical or mechanical principles are exemplified and then treating these pictures not only as formal exemplifications but at the same time as pictures of the kind of object (precision-ground perhaps, but unideal) to which the principles are for practical purposes applied.

There is particular need to insist on the distinction between idealization and application in connections where the gap between them may present the appearance of being closed by the hugeness of nature's strengths and constancies. Astrophysicists for instance refer nowadays, not only to the evolution of the galaxies, but also to stars that are approaching or have reached the end of their evolution. Three star-fates are conjectured: the White Dwarf, the Neutron Star or Pulsar, and the Black Hole—all of them the result of contraction and composed of matter at enormously high density, compressed within an area the size of the earth or less. The first two are surmised to have reached a state in which the gravitational pull responsible for contraction is exactly balanced by the 'degeneracy energy' of electrons in very rapid motion (99·99 per cent of the speed of light is a mentioned figure) or by a combination of nucleonic degenerative energy and short-range repulsive forces. These stars have not contracted to the extent envisaged for stellar Black Holes, where the matter is reckoned to be so dense that not even light can escape its gravitational field, but their hardness approaches 10^{22} times that of steel and their stability is such that they are categorized as being at the end of their evolution and expected to continue in their present state for ever. (My summary is based on an account by Malvin A. Ruderman in *The Scientific American*, February 1971.)

I do not quarrel with this account, my point being simply that the 'for ever' here cannot signify an absolute: in other words it must be just the ordinary, non-problematic relative use of 'for ever'. Nothing more is required by science and anything more would be an embarrassment. The attempt to construe the 'for ever' absolutely would have the consequence of making it impossible for a star's continuance for ever in a balanced state to be expected or predicted. However, I do not want to say that confusion can only be avoided by those who construe the expression consciously in a relative sense; for it is used in practice without any special construction being placed on it. When taken as a matter of course it need pose no problem for us, as Wittgenstein observes in his *Remarks on the*

Foundations of Mathematics (IV, 14) where he says that 'we are as
it were excused the labour of thinking of an end'.

Finding no support in genuinely scientific enterprises, the
advocate of For Ever may try the metaphysical: 'Suppose I
take my pictured sphere to represent the Universe. Surely I can
wonder whether the world as a whole will last for ever or
whether it will go out of existence one day.'

You can wonder at the world's existence all right. However,
I do not think you are doing that here, or not seriously at any
rate, because you speak as though it were a toss-up between a
pair of rival speculations. Speculations can have their overtones. When we get to Usk will the big pike be in the river, will
the old barn still be there? With this there goes a sigh or a
fluttering in the stomach. Maybe then your question has its
aesthetic overtones. But apart from that, I do not know what it
could mean to frame a speculative hypothesis about the destiny of the world as a whole. We can speak intelligibly of
lasting or not lasting when the thing in question is one among
others. Something can sensibly be said to cease to exist *within
the world*, where something else goes on. The meaning of what
we are asserting here is shaped by the contribution to it which
comes from the sense there is in asking what happens to it and
how, where it goes or what the consequences of its destruction
are, what difference its cessation makes. And the sense of these
questions in turn is linked with that of a further range of
questions, where cessation is not at issue, like 'Where did it
come from?', 'What is it like?', 'What does it do?', 'What is it
made of?' and so on. Our grasp of what it means for something to endure or fail to endure—exist lastingly, exist ephem-
erally or just exist—is bound up with comparisons and dependent on connections that are no longer available to us once we
start speaking of the world as a whole. When questions about
the duration of stars give place to questions about the duration
of the world as a whole, the words 'last' and 'exist', or whatever equivalents of them the speaker may be using, undergo a
change of sense. Now there is no reason in principle why a
shift to some new sense (if such can be found) should hinder

rather than help with the problem of finding employment for the absolute For Ever. But all that has happened thus far is that the old sense has gone; and because a new one has yet to be established we run into confusion or at best into vacuity—with a sense-place in our discourse waiting to be filled and no notion how to fill it. But whatever we do we must set our faces against the idea that the world as a whole might be said, for instance, to last as long as the longest lasting thing in it. This suggestion, like every other of its type, tries to skate over the trouble by treating the world as just another thing and creating thereby the illusion of our having preserved the kind of comparison and connection that permits the sense of 'lasts' and 'exists' to remain unchanged and undiminished.

'Then it begins to look as if the only kind of existence one could sensibly predicate of the world as a whole would be necessary existence.' There is much to be said for this proposal, but it is not what I am suggesting. 'The world could come to an end tomorrow' is an utterance that I should not call senseless if it were surrounded by thoughts about the dependence of all things for their reality upon the Creator, about the superabundance of God's goodness and the sinfulness of mankind. But in that case it would have nothing to do with alternative speculative pictures of suns or rotating spheres and nothing to do with anyone's claim about what he can imagine to be the case in respect of such pictures. The suggestion I did want to make as to what was pointed to by the shift in the sense of 'lasts' and 'exists' which occurs when we try to apply these predicates to the world as a whole could be expressed as follows: that it is impossible to make any theoretical statement whatever about the world as a whole.

And if we now bring in the idea of God the Creator as well? This is in fact the advocate of For Ever's sole remaining resource and a characteristic question for him to ask about the relation between God and the world would be why anything once created should be destroyed—not in expectation of an answer, but as though the very raising of the question somehow compelled one to 'think the absolute For Ever'. Yet for whom is this 'question' supposed to be a question? It concerns Creation and must therefore be a question about God's will. But what kind of a question about God's will? It is not like asking whether it be God's will that I should do such and such. Where *that* question is asked, the preoccupation that gives rise to it is ethical and practical. How does it come to be thought that quite another kind of question, a theoretical question, can be asked about God's will? The way in which room is found for this other kind of question is by thinking of the Creator as a Leibnizian deity. However, the deity of the rationalist metaphysician is nothing other than a deified Rationalist—a deity who, being supposed to have made cosmic dispositions for the most refined of reasons, thereby serves as a super-Explainer; a deity who (to put it shortly) thinks in idealizations. To invoke such a deity is to invoke a zetetic counterpart to the *deus ex machina* of Euripidean tragedy. It is to go through the motions of a further theoretical move beyond the stage at which a limit for the understanding has been reached. When a question about constitution and destruction, or coming-into-being and passing-away, is posed in that ultimate metaphysical way which conjures up the idealized For Ever, the illusion is created of an application's having been established although in reality nothing has been established at all.

'But a sempiternal existence for God at least can scarcely be denied.' I agree, it cannot be denied. Nor if put forward as a theoretical proposition can it be intelligibly asserted. However, there may here be scope at last for a non-relative 'for ever' other than the bogusly speculative; hence my leaving open from the start the possibility of an ethico-religious employment and what I would call the adumbration of a mystery. The assertion of God's sempiternal existence might be put forward as a paradox in Kierkegaard's sense. That would leave it still a pretty lifeless proposition apart from the vehemence with which I should expect it to be voiced, and the sort of vehemence I mean is something that would not be there but for the speaker's sense of his creaturely dependence: it would not be there but for the connection with worship. So as not to put too fine a point on the matter, the attribution of sempiternity to the deity has force to the extent that it expresses the religious idea of God *qua* object of worship. I would suggest therefore that it could do with being couched in worthier language: for example, 'Who liveth and reigneth for ever'. Divine Praise calls for words and forms and music of noble quality—expressions that look back to the past and come from the life of a people, and communicate real awe and exaltation, not some gawping scientistical copy of it.

The theoretician against whom I have been arguing may only feel at home perhaps with spheres and the Tower of London—a topic on which he is welcome to a final expostulation: 'I can imagine the Tower of London standing for as long as I like'. Quite so: has anyone denied it?

14

'The Link Between Cause and Effect'

The fat man heaved a sigh. Down in the forest something stirred.

P. G. WODEHOUSE

Although there have been protesting voices, the philosophy of causation remains so much under the influence of Hume that we still find it hard to make an entry into the problem except from his position, whether we think of it in its original version or as modified by the kind of development which it received from the Logical Positivists and other Neo-Humeian Analysts a generation or so ago. As it has been bequeathed to us, the problem of the nature of causation takes the form of a search for 'the link between cause and effect' conducted on the understanding that it is not going to be found in the place where one is inclined to look for it. The quotation marks I have put around my title are intended as a fog warning: this search for 'the link between cause and effect' has been the pursuit of an idealization.

Hume distinguishes three claims about causality: first that whatever begins to exist must have a cause of existence, secondly that particular causes must necessarily have particular effects and thirdly that some pairs of objects are necessarily connected together (*Treatise*, Bk. I, Pt. III, Sections III and XIV, pp. 78 and 155 in the Selby-Bigge edition). The idea that there is some kind of necessity involved in causation is expressed in all three claims and is taken by Hume to be fundamentally the same idea in each case. His central contention is that this idea of a causal *necessity*, although it is in everyone's mind, turns out on examination to have no objective foundation. 'We have no other notion of cause and effect, but that of certain objects, which have been *always conjoin'd* together, and which in all past instances have been found inseparable' (Section VI—it is to be noted that he says 'have been' and 'past instances'). And: 'Upon the whole, necessity is something, that exists in the mind, not in objects; nor is it possible for us to form the most distant idea of it, considered as a quality in bodies' (Section XIV).

Hume now finds himself with the task of explaining how the idea of causal necessity got into our minds, and in order to do this he has to depart from one of his basic epistemological principles. For it was laid down early in the *Treatise* that, aside from a complication over compounds, ideas are derivable only from impressions which they 'exactly represent'. However, the only object of awareness he can find bearing 'any relation to the present business' is a 'propensity' or 'determination of the mind' to make associations. The difficulty about this from the standpoint of his own epistemology is that, as the impression of something within the mind (an 'impression of reflection' technically speaking), it is hardly represented with exactitude by the idea of a necessity in the world outside. Nevertheless he styles this impression 'the essence of necessity' (Section XIV) and he summarizes his account in two well known definitions of a cause, the first of which makes no mention of the 'essence of necessity' and the second of which does:

(A cause is) an object precedent and contiguous to another, and where all the objects resembling the former are placed in like relations of precedence and contiguity to those objects, that resemble the latter.

A cause is an object precedent and contiguous to another, and so united with it, that the idea of the one determines the mind to form the idea of the other, and the impression of the one to form a more lively idea of the other.

In the first definition, the words 'all the objects . . . are placed' must be taken, in the light of the passage I quoted from Section VI, to apply only to the class of objects available for inspection up to now. What Hume gives us in his two definitions is a reductionist account followed by one that embodies a reconstruction.

The word 'determines' in the second definition is a synonym of 'causes' and the circularity has often been pointed out. If we try to get rid of it by making use of the other definition or—which amounts to the same thing—by applying what is said about the causal relation in the first part of the same definition, we get the peculiar result that an object is a cause provided that it has a constant concomitant and provided also that this concomitance has in turn another constant concomitant, namely a movement of 'the mind': as though there could be no causal transactions other than those that had unremittingly impinged on us.

Something of importance could be salvaged from Hume's psychologizing of the causal relation if it were reinterpreted as an allusion to one of the big facts about human life which underlie our language games. Thus it is a fact that there are agreements in response among human beings, for instance in our perceptual discriminations and recognitions. Also it is a fact that in certain situations the shared reaction is of a particular kind, as Wittgenstein points out in his discussion of belief in the uniformity of nature (Investigations §472 ff). I am thinking especially of his remark at §480: 'And if you are surprised at our playing such a game I refer you to the *effect* of a past experience (to the fact that a burnt child fears the fire).' But of course to one who is asking what exactly it is for one thing to be the effect of another, that remark of Wittgenstein is no more helpful than Hume's allusion to a determination of the mind.

The philosophers I am calling Neo-Humeian, for example Schlick, believed that in dropping Hume's allusion to a determination of the mind they were simply being more consistently and commendably anti-necessitarian than their mentor. Hume, while operating an epistemology that broke everything up into loose and separate items, had kept in reserve a pot of 'natural' mental glue. Schlick makes the comment that the philosopher wants to go on after the scientist has stopped: 'So he invents a kind of glue and assures us that in reality it is only his glue that holds the events together at all. But we can never find the glue; there is no room for it, as the world is already completely filled by events which leave no chinks between them' (*Causality in Life and Science*, reprinted in *Readings in Philosophical Analysis*, ed. Feigl and Sellars, p. 522).

Although Schlick talks about glue like a teetotaller at a brewers' congress there is something, another form of the same stuff, from which he cannot abstain. For his deflation of Hume's psychological constructivism—the side of Hume's account on which tribute was being paid to the necessity of a connection—has to be offset by a compensatory inflation of Hume's destructive side, so as to enable this instead to harbour some necessity or quasi-necessity. The destructive aspect of Hume's account was his reduction of the link between cause and effect to *de facto* concomitance or constant conjunction up to now. Schlick at first tells us that 'the word cause . . . implies *nothing but* regularity of sequence' (p. 516). But then he goes on to assert that the necessity which we attribute to laws of nature signifies that 'there is *no exception* to the laws, that they hold in *all* cases' (p. 523, his italics). And in speaking of regularity he brings in the word 'always': 'the regularity may at first be hidden, but it must be discoverable, if we are not to fall into the snares of conventionalism; that is, we must be able to find a C^1 such that C and C^1 together will always be followed by an E. . . .' (p. 519). It is an 'unfortunate always' (*sic*) because of the unverifiability of the propositions in which it occurs. 'Verification', Schlick says, 'would be possible only if a finite number is substituted for "always", but no finite number is satisfactory, because it does not exclude the possibility of exceptions' (p. 518).

The alleged unverifiability has for Schlick the consequence that 'we simply have no clear concept of causality' (p. 518). Nevertheless he goes on discussing it in a way that shows he is in no difficulty at all with the handling of the concept. For instance he has a passage about the effect of a drug on a patient (p. 521):

The drug, e.g., is injected into the veins, we know it comes into immediate contact with the blood particles, we know that these will then undergo a certain chemical change, they will travel through the body, they will come into contact with a certain organ, this organ will be changed in a particular way, and so on.

Maybe there is trouble about verification in other contexts but it is conspicuous by its absence *here*.

On a reductionist view, the incoherence of Schlick's account of causality will be seen to arise, like the incoherence in Hume's account two centuries before, at the point where he feels obliged to introduce something that corresponds to the element of necessity which had been seen by Spinoza for instance as a kind of entailing power in the cause itself. The supposedly superfluous glue comes back in the form of that 'always' which, because it is inherently exception-free, is actually an idealized and theoretical always, or at least it is that when looked at consistently; but because its character as an idealization is not understood it straddles the distinction between theory and application in such a way as to present itself as a holder-together of the basic elements of reality, a link which passes all material forces by and hence cannot possibly be disrupted by them. Causal necessity is in this way reinstated.

How then should we look at the piece of philosophical history that I have just been outlining? In the opinion of Professor Anscombe the association between causation and necessity is a dogmatic slumber which runs like river Lethe through the whole of our intellectual history and we are still snoring our way along it at the present time. Regarding Hume's part in the affair, she remarks (in her Inaugural Lecture, *Causality and Determination*, Cambridge 1971, pp. 3–4) that though he dismissed forcibly the view that the connection between cause and effect is a necessary connection in the logical sense, Hume's thinking nevertheless did nothing against the equation of causality with necessitation but curiously reinforced it. The consideration she has in mind is that, by the stress which he placed upon constant conjunction, Hume gave to a whole topic a 'twist' which 'suggested a connection of the notion of causality with that of deterministic laws—i.e. laws such that always, given initial conditions and the laws, a unique result is determined.'

There is no doubt about the twist or that there has been a serious neglect of the category of non-necessitating causes, but I do not see the history in the same light as Professor Anscombe. For I believe that the idea of necessity, which she underplays, enters indispensibly into our understanding of causation (to believe this is not to assent to the confused extrapolations of determinists). The history of misunderstanding which we find in the philosophy of causation does not therefore result in my view from the fact that the philosophers concerned entertained the notion of a necessary or necessitating connection: it results from something else, namely the fact that they idealized both the necessity and the connection. As for the effect of Hume's discussion, I think that what Miss Anscombe says, although important, is no more than a half of the truth and that Hume sent things wrong in a more original and devastating way than she suggests.

The concept of necessity, as it is connected with causation, is elucidated by Professor Anscombe in the following definition: 'A cause C is a necessitating cause of an effect E *when* (I mean: on the occasion when) if C occurs E is certain to occur unless something prevents it.'[1] The example she gives to illustrate this is rabies, which she says is a necessitating cause of death because it is not possible for one who has rabies to survive without treatment.

[1] She adds that 'C and E are to be understood as general expressions, not singular terms. If "certainty" should seem too epistemological a notion: a necessitating cause C of a given kind of effect E is such that it *is* not possible (on the occasion) that C should occur and neither should an E occur, nor should there be anything that prevents an E from occurring' (p. 23).

Now this example is of a type of case which I think should be regarded as secondary in relation to what I want to call the primary examples of causal necessitation, the primary cases being those where it is certain *simpliciter* that something is going to happen. For instance a fragile object is about to be smashed, and we may say without qualification that it is bound to happen; nothing can be done about it and no other outcome is possible. Such cases are not appropriately represented by a definition like Miss Anscombe's which has an 'unless' clause permanently written into it. There are people who fall into the habit of adding a *D.V.* after nearly everything, like the student who at long last undertook to produce a routine exercise 'God willing'. But generally when we introduce 'unless' clauses into our talk about what will happen we do so against the background of an appreciation of the difference between cases where such a qualification has significance and cases where it has not. For instance there is no *D.V.* or 'unless' about the lettuce's getting wet when you wash it or the butter knife's going through the butter. The suggestion that (for instance) 'if the temperature were below freezing it mightn't, because the butter would be frozen' is hardly more to the point than the observation that at 1,000° centigrade neither butter nor knife would be there: the number of *otiose* qualifications that are appendable to causal statements is indefinite.

When Professor Anscombe writes 'unless something prevents it' into her explanation of what causal necessity is in general, it seems to me as though she were adding a *D.V.* And this gives a distorted picture of the role played by causal necessities in our lives. The man who falls into a vat of molten metal or is run over by a steamroller meets with a horrible death and no two ways about it. If he is given a massive dose of cyanide, stabbed several times through the heart and thoroughly strangled, his death is not just determined but overdetermined. Necessitating causes such as these are no more apt for qualification by an 'unless' than are the logical necessities with which they are equipollent. They are equipollent in the sense that for us there is no more mutability, no more scope for avoidance, in the one case than in the other. Our certainty of the outcome involves in some instances both a certainty concerning the efficacy of the cause and also the certainty that, at least on the occasion we are considering, nothing can impede the result—though maybe we can conceive of something that might do so on some other occasion. But in other instances there is only the efficacy to be considered and it is frequently of the kind that I would call superabundant, for instance the superabundant efficacy of sledgehammers among walnuts. Or take the superabundant impossibility of curbstones floating on water. There is no question here of 'the particular case we are considering'. All of this I think belongs to common understanding.

Our grasp of causal necessity is not by any means the same thing as precision of knowledge. The heavy door that slams on somebody's finger may or may not sever it or break the bone, but will certainly do injury to the finger. However, precision can come in, and in many technical enterprises, as also in scientific experimentation, there will have been careful planning in which rigorous and recherché steps will have been taken to ensure that a causal process takes place in a controlled way, and the operation is insulated from whatever may be going on around it. That the world we live in is of such a sort that this can be done is one of the big facts of human existence which condition our lives.

That our environment is also the locus of accidents and contingencies is another big fact of existence. The world is not like Bishop Butler's watch, a single system with one main spring, but includes many sources of energy, many independent centres of activity and growth, many forms of material, many forces of differing degrees and types which in some cases continuously and in other cases intermittently interact with and limit each other. This is the aspect of reality on which Professor Anscombe's 'unless something prevents it' has a bearing. In opposition to Butler's model or to the model of the solar system which determinists have been gripped by, she speaks of 'the hurlyburly of many crossing contingencies' (p. 22).

I have no idea how one might set about to weigh the proportion or summarize the blending between necessity and chance as this stands over the world as a whole, but I suppose that the question of their balance must derive any sense and interest that it may have from its bearing upon *our* activities and sufferings and aspirations. The world affords the sort of balance between the stable and the unstable, between the fixed and the variable, that a human life requires. And as a model for the whole, the model of an uproar or the jostling of a vociferous crowd, which is what a hurlyburly is, makes no more sense than the solar system does. We can use the model of the hurlyburly most profitably when thinking about aspects of natural and human history. But the haphazards of historical development, the growth and decline of species and of peoples, the turning points where things might go one way or they might go the other have still to be seen against a background of necessity—of the necessary limitations upon what men can do, the inevitability of the direct effects of particular material changes, the realities of physical force and the inescapability of the results of particular short-range devices. Our knowledge of causes and their effects is rooted in the cases where there is immediacy, where there is not enough of a gap in space or time for the insertion of a wedge that says 'unless'; it is rooted in our familiarity with the more obvious causal properties of common substances like water, wood, wrought-iron and stone and in our use of simple but effective instruments like the crowbars and hammers with which we prise things apart or knock them together; it is rooted in the causal transactions whose unsusceptibility to upset is always and everywhere taken completely for granted by us and relied upon without question as part of the permanent background of our lives; in short it is more than anything else a knowledge of causal necessity. As an example of a non-necessitating cause, Professor Anscombe (p. 24) mentions a bomb which is 'connected with a Geiger counter, so that it will go off if the

Geiger counter registers a certain reading; whether it will or not is not determined, for it is so placed near some radioactive material that it may or may not register that reading.' What is particularly noticeable about this example I think is the extent to which it draws upon our understanding of causal necessities.

Returning to Hume's investigation of what has seemed ever since his time to be the mystery of the causal tie, my contention is then that he did not err in supposing it was causal necessities that he ought primarily to be considering. Any enquirer into this 'mystery' would be stacking the cards against himself were he to concentrate on flukes, outcomes that hang in the balance, complex and non-repeatable historical developments or any other instances of what might naturally be categorized as non-necessitating causation. Nor did Hume err in supposing that the billiard table afforded endless examples of necessitating causes: when the red is firmly struck by the cue ball it cannot but move. He might have chosen an easier type of case to start on. Still the reason why he ran into confusion was not because he had the thought of necessity: it was because he idealized the necessity, as his Rationalist predecessors had done. He did it in a different way from them under the promptings of an epistemology which atomized everything into impressions: so that instead of the sustained observation of material things and their repercussions on each other there could only be successive glimpses of events. Hume still alludes to objects in his two definitions of a cause, but the allusion is to one object's being followed by another. And it is evidently not the sort of following that can be spoken of in the continuous present, as with the dog upon its master's lead or the white ball's following the red into a pocket. In fact the objects of which Hume speaks are such as his epistemology requires. They 'put in their appearances' so to speak without being anything over and above the appearances that they put in. The 'following' is the sequences of these appearances, which are in themselves inert as Berkeley had noted; so that all we are really 'given' is a cinematographic parade of events.

Events become henceforward the *relata* between which the link between cause and effect has to be postulated and the terminology of events is used, as we saw, by Schlick.

This is the development I meant when I spoke of the more original, more devastating way in which Hume sent things wrong. And today the idealization of the causal connection into a relation between events is a commonplace among philosophers who on the whole have dropped their subscriptions to a Humeian or sense-datum epistemology.

As they have gained an immunity against the enticement to turn things into events so long as they are dealing with the philosophy of perception, it is—or it ought to be seen as—remarkable that when they turn to the philosophy of causation they should still hang on to Hume's *Nachlass* concerning the *relata* of causal relations. One of the factors at work has been the tradition of running together the problem of the nature of causation with that of induction and running the latter in turn together with the theory of probability. To the extent that there can be theories of it, that is to say by the exclusion of probabilities which are not idealizable, probability or 'probability and induction' becomes a province of logic. And approaches to the problem of the causal relation from the side of logic have a tendency to make it look to be the sort of relation that *could* directly hold between events.

Then in addition to the tendencies which have conspired to make the problem of the cause-effect relation seem to belong to one of the technical branches of philosophy, there is the habit of concentrating attention upon the words 'cause' and 'effect' themselves and citing examples in which one or both of these words occur rather than examples in which the causal relation is expressed in some other more definite way, by the use of specific causal concepts chosen from the vast and variegated host available.

It is not—and this is one of the points that Professor Anscombe brings out in her Inaugural Lecture—it is not in our use of the terms 'cause' and 'effect' that our primary knowledge of causality is expressed. 'The word "cause" can be added to a

language in which are already represented many causal concepts . . . But if we care to imagine languages in which no
special causal concepts are represented, then no description of
the use of a word in such languages will be able to present it as
meaning *cause*' (p. 9). 'The word "cause" itself,' she says, 'is
highly general.' What is further worth noting is something she
does not go into, namely the kind of generality that it has.
Verbs signifying specific causal concepts, like *melt*, *cut*, *stain*,
catch, *bite* and *drop* are mostly what one might call 'doing-to'
verbs: something affects another thing in one way or another;
maybe it alters it, maybe it makes it do something, maybe it
stops it from doing something, maybe the two join with each
other in some mutual process of interaction. These are surely
to be regarded as the central sorts of *causing*; yet there is a
certain awkwardness about this way of putting it. For the verb
cause hardly functions as a 'doing-to' verb; or at least it does
not do so in the way that the specific causal verbs do. *Cause*
does not range as a variable over *melt*, *cut*, *stain* and the rest in
such a way that they are substitutable for it as individuals and
in such a way that it in turn can immediately replace them as
their umbrella-term. The sun melted the snow. But if you do
not happen to know the particular word for what it was that
the sun did to the snow you cannot say that the sun caused the
snow: caused it to melt, yes, but this at once puts something
episodic on the end of the relation—the melting of the snow,
which is an event. (The terms 'cause' and 'effect' are in fact
mainly at home in cases where there is ignorance of where we
are deliberately being unspecific or where we are looking for
an explanation—not so much in the giving of one—or where
we are speaking, perhaps as historians, about the origins of
large and complex developments.) When the sun melts the
snow then, it is the melting of the snow and not the snow that
is caused and is the effect. And this effect *qua* event becomes
henceforward the anchoring point, the 'real' second term of
the relation—into which the snow itself disappears, having
been melted away by grammatical sleight of hand so to speak
before the sun actually melts it. As for the cause, this can still be

said to be the sun, but if after so putting it we reflect on the grammar of our statement, it is apt to present itself now as something of a mixture; and so our tidying-up instinct prompts us to tighten the grammar of the part which signifies the cause so as to make it symmetrical with the effect-part. Until we do this we feel that the logical character of the first term of the relation is not so clearly and accurately represented as the logical character of the second term has been. So we tell ourselves that 'properly speaking' it is the shining of the sun, the sun's casting its rays upon the snow, that causes the melting of the snow. As something that happens, the action of the sun belongs in the same category as the melting of the snow and our desire to have both terms of a relation standing on the same logical level is therefore satisfied. If now the question is asked (still on the assumption that the causal relation is that relation for which 'causing' is the general name), 'To what logical category do the terms of this relation belong?', the answer that is clearly indicated is 'Events'—this being the category into which the terms of the relation have been put by the way of talking about causality which is taken to have the greatest consistency as well as having, as it certainly does have, the widest applicability.

Professor Davidson calls the idea that 'causes are individual events and causal relations hold between events' a 'basic *aperçu*', remarking rightly enough that 'much of what philosophers have said of cause and causal relations is intelligible only on [this] assumption' (*Causal Relations, Journal of Philosophy* 1967, p. 702). He says this in the course of an enquiry into what he calls 'the logical form of singular causal statements', an enquiry which he distinguishes from the investigation of the nature of the causal relation itself. However, the account he gives of the logical form turns out to be no more than a re-expression, in standard logicians' jargon, of the popular metaphysical assumption that it is at bottom a relation between events. For example 'the flood caused the famine' would be formulated by Davidson as: 'There exist events e and e' such that e is a flood and e' is a famine and e caused e''

(*cf.* p. 696; a modified version is available to bring out the singularity of the references).

Now it might be urged on behalf of this account that so far from being the expression of a metaphysical assumption it is simply the embodiment of what we know to be the case on the basis of common understanding. Surely nothing could be more obvious than that, when there is any causing, something first has to happen whereupon something else happens in causal connection with it. However Davidson is not entitled to write this into the form of the propositions concerned unless it is not just the case generally but universally. And that it is not universally the case is shown by two considerations. One is that in some examples there is only a single event to be considered: when the knife cuts the paper, the paper's being cut by the knife is not an additional event over and above the knife's cutting of the paper. (Possibly someone will object that really it is the movement of the knife that causes the paper to be cut and that the movement of the knife is shown to be a different event from the paper's being cut, i.e. coming apart, by the fact that the knife, even when it is in contact with the paper, can move without cutting the paper, either because the paper is too hard or the knife too blunt. In reply, I would ask the objector to stick to the example cited, in which the paper *is* cut by the knife: whatever may be the case elsewhere, the movement of the knife here is its movement through, or cutting of, the paper. Whereas the knife and paper stand as irreducibly separate items here as elsewhere, the duality of events can only enter the picture *here* as a product of verbal manoeuvring). The second consideration is that there are examples of causal relationships in which nothing happens at all and the flood's causing the famine (which is one of Davidson's own examples—p. 691) can be included among these cases on one perfectly natural interpretation. Thus the mention of the flood could be taken as a reference to the static presence of standing water on the fields of a community which prevents them from growing their food, so that they starve—a causal relation in which there are no events; nothing is happening. ('Still the water had to get there.' Yes, heavy rains caused the flood, but this changes the example.) Or take examples like 'The veneer is sticking to the underlying wood', 'The bricks hold up the beam', 'Soot is blocking the pipe' and so on. In these cases of causality without change, there are no events for any proposed analysis to find a place for, though a place is needed for substances, and there had to be substances in the non-static cases too.

So the thesis that causal relations hold between events can be seen to rest *inter alia* on the idealizing move from 'most' to 'all' which is characteristic of metaphysical theories in general. Moreover, when considered only in relation to the cases which it fits, the merit that it may seem on the surface to have of highlighting changes, of putting in the forefront the role of happenings by making these as it were the 'stuff' of the causal relationship—this apparent merit evaporates on closer examination, because although the analysis focuses our attention on the events, on the changes, it does not do this in a way that furthers our understanding of them. For there has to be in the first place non-metaphorical, i.e. material, stuff. The 'behaviour of events-as-such' is not a possible subject of study. Aside from our awareness of the properties and relations of different materials and aside from our handling of variously shaped and sized pieces of them we should have no understanding of modifications and transformations, of construction, destruction, obstruction or generation. But on the 'event' analysis all the material detail of the doings and undergoings, all the actual processes which go on when modifications, transformations and other forms of causal transaction take place, are frozen into lifelessness by being packed into one or other of the terms that are related by 'the causal relation'. They are shared between the two nominalizations, each of which is now supposed to designate a single event. And along with this absorption of all force and movement into the terms of the relation goes the emptying of all content from the connection which relates them. The second event—the one which is caused—is not represented as standing in any one out of a host of possible relations to the first event. The verb 'causes' does not function as a variable of the kind that is appropriate for this; and the result would be utterly peculiar if it did. Nothing can be done with the idea of events standing in a whole variety of causal relations to other events: there is only the one relation of simply and absolutely *causing*, that is to say *metaphysically causing*. The wonderfully diaphanous relationship that this turns out to be is a consequence of the style of the analysis and is really only what was to be expected of a relationship whose terms are, and can only be, events. Since events lack all such properties as hardness, springiness, liquidity, porosity, causticity and tensile strength, there is nothing they can do but stand in ideally regular, universal-law-fulfilling relationships.

An advocate of the type of analysis I am criticizing may still protest that where there are transactions, modifications and so on there must be events and that these events must be related. And he may tax me with an example like 'The spark caused an explosion' where the classification of the *relata* as events is natural if not unavoidable.

I am not concerned to legislate about ways of speaking. Say if you wish, here or elsewhere, that events are related. It does not follow, save in a word-spinning sense, that what they are related by is a relation between events. In the case of the explosion, bear in mind that it was the explosion of a gas, i.e. of something material, and that something else, for example a small fiery particle, had to make contact in one way or another with that material. It is in such material contacts or quasi-contacts that 'the causal link' is mainly to be found. If you think of it as a 'link between events' you only land yourself in a typical metaphysical quandary as to its nature: 'Surely it must consist in something more than a history of repeated concomitances; yet however hard we look, nothing else can be discovered.'

Hume I suggested was right, in general as well as in respect of the example he was considering, to think at the outset in terms of necessity; and a comparison with other cases might have helped him to understand the sort of necessity it was.

Not, however, the comparison with other past cases on the billiard table, which could only nourish the notion of a pure concomitance while affording no further insight into the nature of the material connection. The examples for comparison that might have helped are those which bear a certain likeness yet stand at a certain distance from the example he was considering; so that there is a gap for the understanding to bridge but one that is not too difficult for it to bridge—a gap that can be closed by the finding or invention of intermediaries.

Admittedly it is fanciful to speak of what might have helped Hume because his epistemology of impressions put him beyond reach of help, but for anyone who is not committed to impressionism a suitable collection of examples is furnished by the shunting yard, where a light railway engine, its driving wheels coupled by connecting rods, may be seen pulling and pushing trucks. Through the connecting rods, the wheels on the axle to which power is applied turn the wheels on the other axle—an example of causal necessitation that is as clear and obvious as any: the wheels on the unpowered axle cannot but turn. This is not the idealized 'cannot but' of the mechanical theory of the matter, but from the standpoint of what we can rely on it is no distance from it. For while nothing on the engine is ideally strong, these particular parts have been forged, milled and tested to specifications that permit them to withstand forces vastly greater than those encountered in use.

Between the engine and the truck that it is pulling is a link in the root sense of the word. It ties something to something else: not a cause/event to an effect/event, but a hook on the engine to another hook on the truck. And the truck moves because of this link—to the metaphysical dissatisfaction of the Humeian bystander who says to the foreman shunter: 'Yes, I see you have a metal link between the engine and the truck; but what I am looking for is the *causal* link, the one between the cause and its effect!'

With Hume's example of the billard balls the trouble was the apparent absence, under close scrutiny, of any link. We

have only to make the scrutiny less ideally close and at once
something is noticeable—a contact. Not only do we see it but
we hear the click. There was not just a click but a clang when
the engine ran up to the truck which it is pushing. The first
contact was momentary and on the impact the truck ran ahead
of the engine, but then the contact became continuous. And by
a steady push with the cue, billiard balls can be kept in continuous contact as they roll down the table. Linkages are
devices for ensuring continuous contact. Diseases are caught
from contacts, and a disease causes (for instance) paralysis
when the disease-germs have been in long enough contact
with part of a nerve to eat it away—the nerve itself being also a
connecting or contacting link.

Our understanding then of 'the link between cause and
effect' is basically an understanding of physical contacts in all
their various kinds—carrying, pulling, jolting, pushing, ob-
structing, gashing, rubbing, gnawing, scooping, severing,
grappling, getting entangled with, absorbing, falling on top
of, crushing, mixing and so on. It is to be noticed that our
words for the various sorts of contact usually indicate a pattern
of motion and a degree of force or power. 'Motion', 'force' and
'contact' are in fact a non-accidentally associated trio of concepts which a full-scale philosophy of causation would have to
examine and make sense of together along with the concept of
substance. My particular concern in this discussion has been
with what it is for a cause to be related to its effect—with the
problem of the relation in virtue of which something that is
endowed with, or has become the vehicle of, an appropriate
power can operate as a cause or in other words do something
to something else. An exemplification as homely as any of
what it is for something to be endowed with power can be
found in the muscular strength of human beings and animals;
and by an appropriate power I mean for instance the power of
a horse to pull a cart, or, to bring in something unmentioned
by Hume when he referred to the causal transactions on the
billiard table, the power of the man with the cue. Even if
Hume had admitted to having, in the manner of Berkeley,

some *notion* of that power, his epistemology would still have precluded cognizance of the mode of its transmission, the manner in which it was brought to bear. The primary instances of the bringing to bear of power are, as I have said, cases of physical contact. Not that physical contact is either sufficient or necessary for there to be a causal transaction. It is not sufficient since a contact with less than a certain degree of force may have no effect and it is not necessary in the case of gravitational effects. That contact is neither necessary nor sufficient, however, is not a reason for denying that the idea of it enters into our primary concept of causation. The idea of contact is a readily extendable idea. I spoke at one point earlier of 'material contacts or quasi-contacts' and the phenomena I had in mind were those of radiation. A young person's understanding, as it grows, of what it is for something to be burned, charred, scorched, heated or just warmed, is held together in a unity. This unity moreover comprises recognition of both necessitating and non-necessitating causes; but there could be no understanding of the latter in the absence of an understanding of the former and no understanding of field effects in the absence of an understanding of effects brought about by contact.

15

On the Form of 'The Problem of Evil'

Is the evil in the world compatible with the existence of an omnipotent, omniscient and completely good deity? I am concerned with the kind of discussion that is possible of this question for the diminishing number of those to whom it can mean anything, and it seems to me that the primary philosophical task as usual is to put a stop to what generally goes on.

Until fairly recently the situation was that while some producers and followers of the literature were interested only in technicalities, there were plenty for whom an outcome that they could regard as established would have meant a great deal. These were the theists and atheists who saw themselves as solution proposers and solution critics respectively. The critical point of view would harden into the position that consistency could only be achieved by abolishing belief in, or as it would more likely be called the hypothesis of, the deity. The solution proposer's capacity for religious belief on the other hand bred confidence in him that the makings of a harmonization were available, but whenever he tried to work one out his lines of thought would snap on obstacles he could not get around.

Over the last dozen years the picture has changed on the surface in a way that has flattered the theists. They have not progressed with their solution proposing but take themselves to have benefited from the emergence of a new critical position according to which the possibility of a solution to the problem cannot be ruled out. The new critical position in other words purports to establish the existence of a solution-space without putting anything in it. I have the impression that this result is widely thought to represent 'the present state of the art' so far as English-speaking treatments of the problem are concerned: if so, I think it is a compliment to Nelson Pike (Hume on Evil, *Philosophical Review* 1963).

Despite the gulf between the new critic with his ironical support for the theist and the older critic with his propensity to urge that the problem was insoluble, and despite the gulf between either of them and the classical solution proposer, I hold the resemblance between all these positions to be vastly greater than the differences. For when there is consensus about the way an explainer would have to set about explaining something, when there is agreement as to what would be needed in order to account for it although there may be dispute over whether the necessary item is available, those concerned are making sense of the business in the same way. If the parties to a controversy in the field of value agree as regards what ought to be but not as regards what is, there is an altogether greater kinship between them than there would be if they agreed about what is but not what ought to be (indeed if one is speaking from the standpoint of value, what I have just said is analytic).

The relation between the positions of the solution-critic and solution-proposer in their dispute over 'the problem of evil' is that what the one thinks evil ought to do but does not, the other thinks it ought to do and does. The problem presents itself to each as what I call 'the problem of evil' in inverted commas, the form of which is the same as that of the family of its would-be solutions. The solution-space envisaged for it is of a certain shape and when attempted solutions are condemned as unsatisfactory they are dismissed for not being self-consistent fillers of a space of that shape. Again, when it is emphasized that the problem has not been shown to be unsusceptible of solution, the possibility held to be unexcludable is the possibility of a solution which if it existed would be of the form taken by those already proposed.

For the purpose of supporting my contention I shall now use, in a way the author did not envisage, a justly admired article on 'the problem of evil' by J. L. Mackie called Evil and Omnipotence (*Mind* 1955, reprinted in *The Philosophy of Religion*, ed. Mitchell, Oxford 1971). Mackie divided the available solutions into two categories, the adequate and the fallacious. He did not spend time on the former and neither shall I because 'adequate' solutions on his definition deny one or more of the propositions constituting the problem and I agree with him that the problem cannot be dismantled in that way. So the only solutions in the running are of the kind he classed as fallacious and it is this class of solutions I had in mind when I said the form of 'the problem of evil' was that of its solutions. In considering his account of them I shall not be interested in any particular fallacies he says they commit, for it would make no difference to my position if none existed. From Mackie's point of view the fallacies have to be there because the 'fallacious' solutions which assert all the propositions constitutive of the problem (along with some further thesis that is supposed to show how they are mutually compatible) attempt something that cannot with consistency be done. There are various haverings by which he says they present the appearance of doing it without actually doing it and he offers an account of the way this happens in a range of cases. However this may be, it is to be noticed that the role of a solution to 'the problem of evil' is that of providing an extra thesis which, when tacked on to the set of propositions constituting the problem, will allow them to be seen as consistent.

The range of extra theses that offer prospect of helping is not unlimited. Mackie lists four without claiming his survey to be exhaustive but with the sentiment: if anyone can think of another then let him produce it (and I echo that sentiment). The four theses are: (1) 'Good cannot exist without evil' or 'Evil is a necessary counterpart to good'; (2) 'Evil is necessary as a means to good'; (3) 'The universe is better with some evil in it than it could be if there were no evil'; (4) 'Evil is due to human free will' (pp. 95, 97 and 100). Mackie gives various reasons for rejecting these theses. The significant fact about them for me is that they all have something in common—a shared theme which can be identified quite readily in the case of the first three. It is that evil is to be explained as being in one way or another required to exist for the sake of good. The first thesis represents evil as a logical requirement of good and holds this requirement to have an ontological implication: however, without assistance from one of the other theses it cannot withstand the objection that the amount of evil in existence is greater than the amount if any that would logically be required. Thesis 1 then is hardly more than a prelude to the development of the solution theme in theses 2, 3 and 4; and thesis 4 involves thesis 3 since, as Mackie puts it, 'To explain why a wholly good God gave men free will although it would lead to some important evils, it must be argued that it is better on the whole that men should act freely, and sometimes err, than that they should be innocent automata, acting rightly in a wholly determined way' (p. 100).

The general character of the solution theme to 'the problem of evil' may be further brought about by asking what the good that evil is necessary *for* is supposed on this conception to be the good *of*. The answer that in one way or another is being given or implied is: the good of the world. I would say too that the world is being considered from the standpoint of a rational assessor who is passing judgement on it as something which either does or does not come up to scratch as an intelligently designed place, bearing in mind that it is to be lived in by beings who *are* something—bearers of value, members of a Kingdom of Ends. The idea of Heaven may be brought into the calculation, but when it is, there is no change of perspective. The world *qua* obstacle course is judged to be a good world on the ground that with its evil it provides the training needed for the development of souls. In all of its versions then the solution theme for 'the problem of evil' says or implies that the evil in the world makes a necessary contribution to the good of the world.

Although this idea about the role of evil in the economics of goodness does not entail the idea that everything is for the best in the best of all possible worlds, the two ideas hang closely together: they invoke the same deity—the one I have called the deified rationalist (p. 208)—and the solution theme for 'the problem of evil' is either an application of Leibniz's principle of optimism or else a relative version of it which I would call the principle of meliorism. The principle of optimism affirms that the world is the best of all possible worlds and in that light explains why everything within the world is the way it is. The solution theme for 'the problem of evil' picks out, from the class of all things so to say, the class of evils and explains why they in particular are as they are, by saying that without them in all their existing quality and quantity the world would be neither as good as it is nor as good as it could be. If it is thought in addition that the world *is* as good as a world could be, the principle of optimism is being applied: if it is allowed that the world could be bettered by some other world or if that question is left open, the principle applied is the principle of meliorism. The difference is not in my opinion important. Either way the goodness of the world is viewed as a kind of general good or good mix from which evil could not without detriment be subtracted, and either way the same kind of perspective is attributed to the world-designer. It is a Utilitarian style of thinking—like that of the Chairman of the Praesidium who conceives his country's wellbeing as something for the sake of which those he is shooting ought to be profoundly glad to be shot.

Offering an explanation of evil in which the Creator is represented as a contriver and credited with the thought-style of a President of the Immortals is rather like tackling Bubonic plague by breeding rats. For the response which was anticipated when the problem was posed, and which might have been expected to be given its quietus by the solution, is called for more obviously by the solution than by the problem. I mean: it is when you are told that evil, and terrible evil too, has been brought into being on purpose for the sake of achieving some good, that you are as clearly justified as you ever could be in protesting—not about the price being too high, as though the ratio between entry fee and pay-off were the trouble. It would then be a question of compensation and someone for whom this were the issue could be assuaged by the promise of infinite comfort in a realm unseen. No, I am thinking of the protest you could make simply by pointing to a signal case of suffering, such as a child's dying of meningitis (Somerset Maugham's example). You would ask only that it be looked at, that attention be directed to the nature of the affliction. Good cannot possibly be purchased by a plan that brings such things in its train and would not be by any decent human being. I shall recur to the spirit of this protest and would ask you to note that I claim on its behalf no less and no more than that if it were appropriate anywhere it would be as clearly appropriate as it could be here, that is, in relation to the form of the solutions to 'the problem of evil': I am not considering it as a response to the problem of evil and *a fortiori* have not advocated that it should enter into our dealings with that.

The accepted or rejected solutions to 'the problem of evil' have, as I said, the function of supplying an extra thesis which when conjoined with the propositions constituting the problem would effect a reconciliation and allow them to be seen as consistent with each other. Yet the original propositions, 'God is omnipotent and omniscient', 'God is completely good' and 'Evil exists' were not inconsistent in the first place—which is as well, since if there really had been an inconsistency between them when taken by themselves it would have been out of the question logically to try to remove it by adding something. But then in that case, how did it come to be thought that there was a task of reconciliation for the solution theme to perform? By *havering*. That was Mackie's term for what goes on later in the minds of the would-be solvers of the problem, and no doubt it does, but only after the crucial piece of havering has already taken place. The havering I am now concerned to expose occurs in a trice at the stage when the problem is being presented and is of first importance because it introduces a twist in what the problem is taken to be. So that the problem is said to be one thing (the problem of evil) but treated as another ('the problem of evil'): it is supposed to be the problem of whether a certain small group G of propositions can be entertained together, but is dealt with as though the difficulty were that of asserting together without contradiction another group consisting of G + 1. Although Mackie's exposition of the problem does not escape my charge of havering it is the most revealing that I know: he does his havering with the lights on.

Mackie repudiated the automatic assumption that there was an inconsistency between the original propositions mentioned in the last paragraph. He pointed out that in order to generate a contradiction, some further proposition must be found and added. He added one. But at the same time he spoke as if the contradiction were somehow latent in the original propositions—'the contradiction does not arise immediately . . .' (p. 93). The proposition he introduced was that 'a good, omnipotent thing eliminates evil completely'. Having made the addition, he did not examine what he had added but proceeded to argue that the contradiction thus generated could not be eliminated and that any 'solutions' which tried to get round it, by adding something yet again, were fallacious.

Such is the logic of 'the problem of evil'. Starting with a consistent set of propositions—the familiar triad which although consistent poses the problem of evil—someone adds a thesis which in conjunction with them creates a contradiction, thereby producing what I call 'the problem of evil' (in inverted commas). He then finds, as well he might if he has done the job properly, that the problem is insoluble. He still takes the problem to be that of maintaining the original set of propositions, notwithstanding the fact that he enlarged the set with an importation. And a striking feature of his treatment is the readiness with which he attributes to the imported proposition a well-foundedness which makes it more immune against denial than any of the original propositions. In this way the problem is found to be insoluble. Unless . . .

A visitor from outer space might suppose that the only way of carrying the discussion further would be to blow down the house of cards; if so he would be wrong, for it is possible to build another storey on top. Here we come to the development which 'the problem of evil' received at the hands of Pike and which has been turned into an industry by Plantinga. Pike like Mackie sees that unless some further thesis is introduced the original propositions can be maintained without a contradiction's being involved, indeed he emphasizes the point; but again like Mackie, he has his eye on an additional proposition which presents itself to him as an indispensible component of the problem. The proposition which in Pike's treatment turns the problem of evil into 'the problem of evil' is that 'an omnipotent, omniscient being could have no morally sufficient reason for allowing instances of suffering' (p. 183). The respect in which Pike goes beyond Mackie lies in his willingness to countenance the possibility that the additional proposition may not be true. In fact he offers a demonstration that it is the sort of proposition that cannot be known to be true, so his conclusion is that the problem cannot be shown to be insoluble.

But was this not already the situation at the start? I mean: in so far as the problem of evil is taken to be the question whether anyone who wishes to assert the original triad of propositions can do so without inconsistency of belief, all he has to do is to go ahead with the assertion and decline to add anything. He is not then open to a charge of inconsistency. He does not have to wait to see what some other person might do with an additional thesis that has not been demonstrated to follow from what is on the table. Nor is there any logic by which the proposer of the thesis can think it might be demonstrated to follow. Rather, the extra thesis presents itself to him as what is called 'intuitively obvious'.

There is more than one thing that comes in that category so far as Pike is concerned. For he also says (p. 193): 'a theologian who accepts the existence of God' (which I find an interesting way of putting it) '. . . must conclude either that there is some morally sufficient reason for God's allowing suffering in the world, or that there are no instances of suffering in the world. He will of course choose the first alternative.' So the theologian must deny the imported proposition if he can —that too is a *datum* and more of a *datum* than the imported proposition itself was, because it turns out that Pike thinks the theologian *can* deny it. But let no one ask in stupefaction why the imported proposition had to come in, for the immediate answer is obvious. (There is a further explanation to be given when I come to the connection between Pike's importation and Mackie's.)

The imported proposition, that an omnipotent, omniscient being could have no morally sufficient reason for allowing instances of suffering, has to come in because the theologian must deny it. And the theologian must deny it in order to be—when judged from Pike's perspective—a rational and moral theologian.

But suppose there were a theologian who would not deny it: not because he wanted to assert it, but because he would neither assert nor deny it. As I said before, anyone wishing to assert the original propositions constitutive of the problem of evil can go ahead with his assertion and decline to add anything, and in particular he need have no truck with a proposition that refers to God's having or not having a morally sufficient reason for anything. I shall now go further and offer an argument for rejecting Pike's importations as nonsense.

It makes sense for *us* to have or fail to have moral reasons for our doings and refrainings because as human beings we are members of a moral community. We have been born and brought up into a shared form of life in which there are, as there would be in any other form of human life, customs and traditions; ideas, more than one set of them perhaps, about what it is for instance to keep or break faith with another, what ways of behaving incur ignominy, what it is to treat someone well or badly, what justice and injustice are. And we have a sense of what does and what does not raise these issues: some members of the community have it more strongly than others. But it can only be there for us at all insofar as we are able to use words in their meanings, that is to say in the meanings which they have within and for the community. I am thinking especially of expressions like 'deceive', 'cruel', 'a disgrace' or expressions which signify analogous ideas. Reasons for acting or for refraining from acting are given and received, and have their natural stopping places, in connection with *inter alia* ideas of the kind just mentioned; and without this connection they could not exist as reasons of the type which *in* this connection they are—that is, moral reasons. So I assert that having or failing to have a moral reason presupposes membership of a moral community.

But God is not a member of a moral community or of any community. To be sure there are small 'g' gods who have been conceived in that way, like those of the ancient Greeks: such gods are like fairies. To credit the one true God with having a moral reason for doing anything is to conceive Him in the manner of Greek popular religion as a being among beings instead of the absolute being who is the Creator of the world. When 'God' is conceived as a one among many he becomes subjectable to moral judgement; and within a moral community of course it would make perfectly good sense for the one by whom, or let us say the chief one by whom we are judged, to be submitted to our moral judgement. When conversely someone speaks in a way that is tantamount to subjecting God to moral judgement—and it belongs to the grammar of 'the problem of evil' that you will not find any treatment of it in which this does not happen in one way or another—then he is regarding God as a being within a community of beings and moreover as belonging to the same community as himself. There is a tone of voice which often goes along with this. Listen to Professor Swinburne: 'For myself I can say that I would not be too happy to worship a creator who expected too little of his creatures'. (*Reason and Religion*, Ed. S. C. Brown, Cornell U.P. 1977, pp. 101–2.) It seems to me that

Swinburne there is invoking a moral fairy and that the creator he *would* be happy to worship would be another fairy out of the same pack—one who set a more commendable standard.

In Pike's discussion of 'the problem of evil' the moral reason which God cannot be shown not to have is represented as one which a theologian must think God does not merely happen to have but must have. So in arguing that God cannot have one I have been offering to any theologian who, like Plantinga, has drawn sustenance from Pike's argument a proof that God does not exist. Other theologians need not be downhearted: it is only God's Pikean or Plantingarian existence I am disproving. In order to do that moreover it is not necessary to go as far as I have gone. An argument that God *need not* have a moral reason when He acts or refrains from acting in relation to evil will suffice if successful. And there is one that can be given independently of the consideration I have put forward about God's not being a member of a moral community. Thus: God need not have a moral reason whether sufficient or insufficient because He need not have any reason. So far from its being the case that *God* in acting or refraining from acting in relation to evil must have a reason, it is not even true of human beings that they must. On the contrary it is characteristic of the highest actions we know and particularly of the highest exercises of restraint that the person should not just be unable to give but that there should not be any reason for his attitude. Suppose that when subjected to a buffeting he does not hit back but turns the other cheek. What reason could he have for meeting the evil in that way? If it were said that he had a reason for it, the implication would be that his response were a semblance of something else.

Suppose he has been hounded for years by a persecutor who has made repeated attempts on his life. He has escaped by much exertion and knows his strength is failing. At last he finds himself with the tormentor in his power. He has a reason, a moral justification, for eliminating him but instead for no reason he spares him, sets him free to fight another day at yet more cost. The imported proposition by which Mackie converted the problem of evil into 'the problem of evil' was that 'good is opposed to evil in such a way that a good thing always eliminates evil so far as it can'. Always? Mackie's proposition is not even true of our cat.

The two imported propositions I am considering, Mackie's and Pike's, differ in surface appearance, but when the 'unless' clauses by which each is governed are taken into account and it is noted that what the one proposition states the other implies and *vice versa*, it can be seen that in effect they are interchangeable and the fundamental idea is explicit in Mackie's. The 'unless' clause allowed for by Mackie makes his proposition say that a good thing eliminates evil unless the evil is needed for the production of good, in which case the evil's being of such service constitutes the reason for its not being eliminated, and this reason is of the kind Pike calls 'morally sufficient'. Pike's proposition that an omnipotent, omniscient being could have no morally sufficient reason for allowing instances of suffering implies that if the being is good it will not allow but will eliminate suffering. And again there is an 'unless' clause, since Pike envisages the possibility of a morally sufficient reason's being furnished after all, in which case the proposition would have to be negated. But when he concludes that his proposition is in a permanent state of negatability he nevertheless cannot drop it. It must remain on view in the state in which he had first formulated it (that is as a necessary proposition) for the sake of the essential idea it contains about the non-allowance of suffering. Expressed in Mackie's terms, the first principle by which the goodness of Pike's omnipotent being is tested is that such a being would want to eliminate evil (suffering) completely. Without this idea, neither of these writers can take a step. Yet Mackie only states it as an aside and Pike never states it explicitly at all. What I would like you to see as astonishing is the disparity between the perfunctoriness with which the essential idea is imported and the momentousness of the question to which it offers an answer.

When Mackie intimates that good and evil are opposed, and that the way in which they are opposed is that the first eliminates the second, you are to take what he says not as an observation about just any kind of goodness but as expressing the relation in which supreme goodness stands towards evil. Now it seems to me that whatever anyone tried to say about that—about the disposition of a, or as it should rather be, *the* supremely good spirit towards evil and suffering—would have to be uttered *de bas en haut*. If it were not, this would show that the speaker did not take the idea of supreme goodness seriously and were not mindful of his own position in relation to it. If he did not think he were addressing himself to an awesome wonder, the likely alternative would be that he would theorize as though supreme goodness could be relied upon to do something commonplace.

The man who accepted the evil that came to him when he showed mercy to his adversary did something not commonplace but nevertheless intelligible. He could have been guided by a familiar conception, that of the sporting chance. He was dealing with another human being; one whose enmity he could understand (at any rate up to a point—'war is war', 'that is how men are').

The difficulty presented to theodicy by the evil human beings suffer at the hands of their fellow creatures is invariably (I do not say rightly) held to be nowhere near so great as that presented by the evil which comes to them of necessity in their sufferings from natural causes. The former is, a matter of the cruelty of man to man and if more needs to be said there can be recourse to the Christian doctrine of The Fall or to what is called in the literature of 'the problem of evil' The Free Will Defence. The latter is not susceptible to such treatment. If it is not God's cruelty to man, what is it?

It is not impossible for it to be seen as God's love. I offer this neither as *the* answer nor as *my* answer to the question but cite it as a perspective: one which is not accessible to many but one from which it is possible for suffering to be seen, possible because it has been seen that way, by Julian of Norwich for instance: 'But freely our Lord giveth when he will; and suffer us in woe sometime. And both is one love'. I was quoting then from her *Revelations of Divine Love*, of which she said, 'These Revelations were shewed to a simple creature that could no letter the year of our Lord 1373, the eighth day of May. Which creature desired afore three gifts of God. The First was mind of his Passion; the Second was bodily sickness in youth, at thirty years of age; the Third was to have of God's gift three wounds'.

Someone who did not find this incoherent might still wonder how far it touched the most difficult aspect of the problem. An attitude possible for an exceptional person in suffering is not necessarily adoptable towards the suffering of another. Could Julian have wished that the serious illness which was to come to her should go to someone else? Obviously not. But she used the plural in the passage about the one love—'and suffer us in woe sometime'. And it may have been that she could see more clearly in the suffering of another the Passion of Christ which she prayed her own suffering might in some way resemble.

When I turn from her position and look again at the other, where the speech is of God's cruelty to man, of handing in one's ticket and so on, there seems to be an element of rhetoric in it which I do not find in Mother Julian. That the speeches of protest can express something strongly felt I do not question. The speaker has compassion, otherwise he would not be driven to fulminate as he does. Yet his words do not exactly express compassion but rather something else—a further and different element in his perspective which apparently is more central to it than the other, since it is what he mainly expressed. My name for it is the ethics of indignation; and with this I come to my final point though it is not my least about the form of 'the problem of evil'.

The literature of 'the problem of evil' presents a theodicy extrapolated from the ethics of indignation. There is nothing out of the way about this ethics: on the contrary it is the most captivating form of the ethics of praise and blame which current orthodoxy in moral philosophy dresses into a theory. Pike is among the subscribers to this orthodoxy. In connection with his claim about the theologian's having to conclude that God has a morally sufficient reason for allowing suffering, he tells us what it is for someone to have a morally sufficient reason for his action: 'To say that there is a morally sufficient reason for his action is simply to say that there is a circumstance or condition which, when known, renders *blame* (though, of course, not responsibility) for the action inappropriate' (p. 183). So the God who cannot be shown not to have a morally sufficient reason for whatever he does or sanctions is a God whom you cannot confidently blame—you cannot wax indignant about him without jumping the gun. The type of solution for which 'the problem of evil' allows space is thus calculated to preserve your proclivity to indignation to feeding a sop to it. Theologians whose theodicy is a branch of prescriptivism find this comforting.

INDEX